Asa Oscar Tait

Heralds of the Morning, the Meaning of the Social and Political Problems of To-day and the Significance of the Great Phenomena in Nature

Vol. 3

Asa Oscar Tait

Heralds of the Morning, the Meaning of the Social and Political Problems of To-day and the Significance of the Great Phenomena in Nature
Vol. 3

ISBN/EAN: 9783337715304

Printed in Europe, USA, Canada, Australia, Japan

Cover: Foto ©Suzi / pixelio.de

More available books at **www.hansebooks.com**

HERALDS
OF THE MORNING

The Meaning of the
Social and Political Problems of To-day
and the Significance of the Great
Phenomena in Nature

"Watchman, what of the night? Watchman, what of the night? The watchman said, The morning cometh, and also the night; if ye will inquire, inquire ye; turn ye, come."—*Isaiah.*

ASA OSCAR TAIT

OAKLAND, CAL.
PACIFIC PRESS PUBLISHING COMPANY
SAN FRANCISCO   PORTLAND   KANSAS CITY

Entered according to act of Congress, in the year 1899, by
A. O. TAIT,
In the office of the Librarian of Congress, at Washington.

CONTENTS.

CHAPTER.		PAGE.
	Foreword.	9
I.	"Watchman, What of the Night?"	13
II.	He Will Come Again	21
III.	"This Same Jesus"	33
IV.	"Shall So Come in Like Manner"	39
V.	We May Not Know the Hour	45
VI.	"Know That He Is Near"	49
VII.	"Watch Ye Therefore"	54
VIII.	Great Deceptions	60
IX.	Prophetic Outlines	70
X.	The Good News of the Kingdom to All the World	74
XI.	A Remarkable Century	78
XII.	The Bible among the People	96
XIII.	The Gospel's Progress	107
XIV.	What Many People Shall Say	117
XV.	The Prevalence of Crime—A Sign of Our Times	128
XVI.	Judgment Is Turned Away Backward	134
XVII.	The Earth Is Filled with Violence	151
XVIII.	"The Social Vice"	159
XIX.	Maintaining the Form but Denying the Power	171
XX.	"Lovers of Pleasure"	183
XXI.	Ye Have Heaped Treasure for the Last Days	190
XXII.	And the Nations Were Angry	214
XXIII.	Divine Restraint of the Spirit of War	258
XXIV.	The Voice of the Elements	264
XXV.	The Testimony of the Earth	282
XXVI.	"When Ye Shall See All These Things"	292
XXVII.	And There Shall Be a Time of Trouble	297
XXVIII.	The Earth Was Lightened by His Glory	307
XXIX.	A Refuge in This Time of Distress	315
XXX.	The Seven Last Plagues	322
XXXI.	Our Refuge and Fortress	330
XXXII.	The Triumphant Victory and Everlasting Reward	336
XXXIII.	In This Generation	348

LIST OF ILLUSTRATIONS.

	PAGE.
The morning cometh	Frontispiece.
"Watchman, what of the night?" (chapter heading)	13
Society banded into factions	14
The dove of peace lies wounded and dying	15
What will be the end of all these threatening dangers?	16
The long roll sounding	17
The Omnipotent Power that balances the world in space	18
Earthquakes and tidal waves	19
He will come again (chapter heading)	21
"All that are in the graves shall hear His voice"	22
Drifting toward the vortex	24
Heralds trumpeting the morning	25
The Consoler	27
Shoals and rocks along the farther shore	31
"This same Jesus" (chapter heading)	33
"Behold how He loved him"	34
"At the pool of Siloam"	35
Shall so come in like manner	39
"And He shall send His angels"	40
"Shall so come in like manner"	41
We may not know the hour (chapter heading)	45
"The swelling of the buds in the spring-time"	46
"As a thief in the night"	47
Know that He is near (chapter heading)	49
Watch ye therefore (chapter heading)	54
The magicians in Moses' time	57
Great deceptions (chapter heading)	60
A charmer	65
The Shepherd	69
Prophetic outlines (chapter heading)	70
The good news of the kingdom sent to all the world (chapter heading)	74
A remarkable century (chapter heading)	78
Overland in the '40's	80
Overland to-day	81
The Brooklyn Bridge	83
The "Lucania"	84
The ship of yesterday	85
Ocean liner leaving dock	86
A great railway station	87
The old "Franklin hand-press"	88
"Imagine Franklin's surprise"	89
Robert Fulton	90
Samuel F. B. Morse	90
Peter Cooper	90
Charles Goodyear	91
Sir Henry Bessemer	91
C. H. M'Cormick	91
James Watt	92
Thomas Edison	92
Cyrus W. Field	93

LIST OF ILLUSTRATIONS. V

Laying the Atlantic cable 93
Combined harvester and thresher 94
The Bible among the people (chapter heading) 96
Grain was cut with the cradle-scythe 97
The steam hammer at work 98
"Hammer, anvil, and forge" 99
"Boots and shoes were slowly made by hand" 99
The knitting machine 100
"Were knit by hand" 100
"To-day she has a machine" 101
"The simple needle and thimble were the implements" 101
The carpenter did everything by hand 102
The dim light of the candle 102
"Our writing was done with a pen" 103
To-day the typewriter does it more rapidly 103
"Let the floods clap their hands" 105
The Gospel's progress (chapter heading) 107
Bible house, New York 108
British and Foreign Bible Society's building, London 111
Corner in Bible storeroom 112
Bible Society, Shanghai, China 113
Bible cart, Japan 114
Bible boat, Siam 116
"What many people shall say" (chapter heading) 117
The prevalence of crime a sign of our times (chapter heading) .. 128
"Lot went out of Sodom" 129
"As it was in the days of Noah" 130
"Judgment is turned away backward" (chapter heading) 134
The earth is filled with violence (chapter heading) 151
"The social vice" (chapter heading) 159
"He that is without sin among you" 167
Maintaining the form but denying the power (chapter heading) . 171
"Lovers of pleasure" (chapter heading) 183
Ye have heaped treasure for the last days (chapter heading) 190
An alley of poverty, Chicago 194
Lodging-house for the poor 195
"Misery exists in these sweat-shops" 206
And the nations were angry (chapter heading) 214
Evolution of the battle-ship 217
The British navy 219
War-ships of the world 220
Battle-ship *Iowa* 222
Cross-section of revolving turret 223
Washington gun factory 224
Interior of gun shop 225
Big cannon on specially constructed steel car 226
Battle of Manila 227
Marine gun 229
Maxim automatic machine gun 230
Nine-pounder machine gun 231
French quick-fire field gun 231
Range finder 232
Mortar elevated for firing 233
Section of mortar battery in action 233
Actual penetration of trial shot from big gun 234
Effect of modern cannon on steel plate 234
Results of armor plate tests 235
Dudley pneumatic dynamite gun 236

LIST OF ILLUSTRATIONS.

The 15-inch pneumatic dynamite gun 237
Grains of slow-burning powder 238
Blowing up of the *Maine* 240
Battle-ship *Maine* after the explosion 241
Ten-inch gun being fired from disappearing carriage 242
Gun on disappearing carriage, lowered, ready for aiming 243
On a Chinese war-ship 246
Japanese sailors working rapid-fire gun 247
Battle of Santiago 251
Divine restraint of the spirit of war (chapter heading) 258
The voice of the elements (chapter heading) 264
"Fire and pillars of smoke" 266
"All the birds of the heavens fled" 267
"The foundations of the earth do shake" 268
"The land shall be utterly emptied" 269
"The whole land shall be desolate" 272
"The cyclone, whirling with terrific fury" 273
"Storms of hail" 274
'And the waters shall overflow" 275
"The Lord turneth it upside down" 276
The testimony of the earth (chapter heading) 282
"When ye shall see all these things" (chapter heading) 292
"When the Son of Man shall come in His glory" 295
And there shall be a time of trouble (chapter heading) 297
The earth was lightened with his glory (chapter heading) 307
I saw another angel having great power 309
A refuge in this time of distress (chapter heading) 315
The seven last plagues (chapter heading) 322
The first angel poured out his vial on the earth 324
"The second angel poured out his vial upon the sea" 325
"The third angel poured out his vial upon the rivers and fountains of waters" . 326
"The fourth angel poured out his vial upon the sun" 327
"The fifth angel poured out his vial upon the seat of the beast" 328
'The sixth angel poured out his vial upon the great river Euphrates" . . . 328
"The seventh angel poured out his vial into the air' 329
"Our refuge and fortress" (chapter heading) 330
He brought His people out of that dark land 333
The triumphant victory and everlasting reward (chapter heading) 336
In this generation (chapter heading) 348
The navigators locating their vessel 350
Measuring the movements of the heavenly bodies 351
Receiving the book of prophecy 353

HERALDS OF THE MORNING.

"Henceforth I call you not servants; for the servant knoweth not what his lord doeth; but I have called you friends; *for all things that I have heard of My Father I have made known unto you.*

"Ye have not chosen Me, but I have chosen you, and ordained you, that ye should go and bring forth fruit, and that your fruit should remain; that whatsoever ye shall ask of the Father in My name, He may give it you."—*The Apostle John.*

FOREWORD

Among the most expressive and beautiful words of the English language, is the noble, tender term, "Home." Among the sweetest songs ever sung by loving lips, is "Home, Sweet Home," given to a needy world by one who never had a home, yet whose heart ever cried out for what the world never gave him. His very homelessness voiced sweeter and deeper the longing of every true human heart.

Among the blessed occurrences that surround the home, "be it ever so humble," is the "home-coming" of loved ones. This is especially true when a loving father has been long gone and is about to return. What thought and action it arouses and inspires. How it quickens heart and eye and tongue and foot. How often and anxious the inquiries of the mother as to when he is coming. What preparations are begun to welcome him. How short the days seem to do the work which ought to be done. How long the days seem when the separation is brought to mind. How slowly roll Time's chariot wheels. Over and over say the children: "Father is coming, the best, the strongest, the wisest friend on earth. He is bringing back for each one of us some beautiful and appropriate gift. He has sent various gifts during his absence, he will bring better ones this home-coming, and bestow them with his own hands; and, best of all, he himself will come. We shall look into the eyes that have so many years looked upon us in love. We shall be clasped by the hand that helped and sheltered and shielded us in trouble and danger. He will call us by name, fold us in his arms, and kiss us glad greeting. And then, too, he will take us to a better home for a while till this home is made far more beautiful than we have ever dreamed it could be made."

Thus the thoughts of the loving children run on, and the glad mother recounts the nobleness of character in times ante dating the children. At last preparation is over, the last touch is given, and mother and children lovingly, impatiently, wait. Surely there is no event in that home like the home-coming of the one who is to all the others chiefest in the household.

We all know it to be at least ideally true; yet it is but a faint picture of a greater, more far-reaching, more blessed, spiritual fact, around which cluster all the greater glorious events of the Christian life.

"The earth is the Lord's and the fulness thereof." He made it to be a glorious home forever for the family of man. But sin entered, and the home was marred, and the trail of the serpent may be traced over the fairest of earth's domain. With the entrance of sin came death, and the earth, designed as the abode of the living, would have become a vast charnel-house had it not been for the constant, abundant blessings of grace poured out upon it from the inexhaustible storehouse on high.

"When the fulness of time came," the Son of God, with all-glorious divinity veiled in humanity, truly God and truly man, came unto His own, but "His own received Him not." The vast majority would not receive Him as the only Saviour. But earnest souls did receive Him, and found Him to be the Son of God, the Saviour, Friend, and Brother of men.

Before He went away He told them He would come again,— that His going away would be like that of a nobleman who "went into a far country to receive for himself a kingdom, and to return." As priest on the Father's throne, Jesus Christ, through angelic and human ministers, has been gathering out subjects for His everlasting kingdom—this earth made new by God's creative power. That work is about completed; the long roll of the ages is nearly finished; the characters inscribed "before the foundation of the world" "in the Lamb's book of life" are nearly all wrought out; the tested and polished stones for the eternal, spiritual temple of God are nearing the end of their numbering; the gifts of His Spirit, brought anew into exercise in His church, will soon perfect that church, that He may present her to Himself, a beautiful church, "not having spot or wrinkle or any such thing," but "holy and without blemish," clad in the robes of His own glory. And then comes the Homecoming of the Master, the triumphant, glorious finale of all earth's sorrow and travail. The Master of the house comes to remove for a time to the heavenly mansions His loved ones, while the marred and blasted earth passes through its last stage of disintegration prior to its re-creation as the eternal home of the souls saved by grace. "The bondservant [of sin, Satan and his own] abideth not in the house forever; the Son [Christ and His own] abideth forever." And Christ is coming to complete the great and all-absorbing work of the universe, the vindication of the character of God and the salvation of every trusting, faithful soul.

And, reader, this unworthy foreword only serves as an introduction to the pages following, written by my friend and brother, Asa Oscar Tait. In them are arrayed some of the many evidences of God's Word which show that the great Home-coming of our Lord and Master is nigh. In plainest, clearest language, by illustration and quotation, are the evidences rehearsed, fortified and demonstrated. "Christ is coming" is the fitting close to every chapter. The whole work is vibrant with the intensity of the times through which we are passing. Read its pages, ponder its sublime and awful facts, receive its truth, and then when the great drama shall have closed, you will be among those who shall, with glad hearts filled with heavenly melody, welcome the Home-coming of the King.

MILTON C. WILCOX

Editorial Rooms
"Signs of the Times,"
Oakland, Cal.

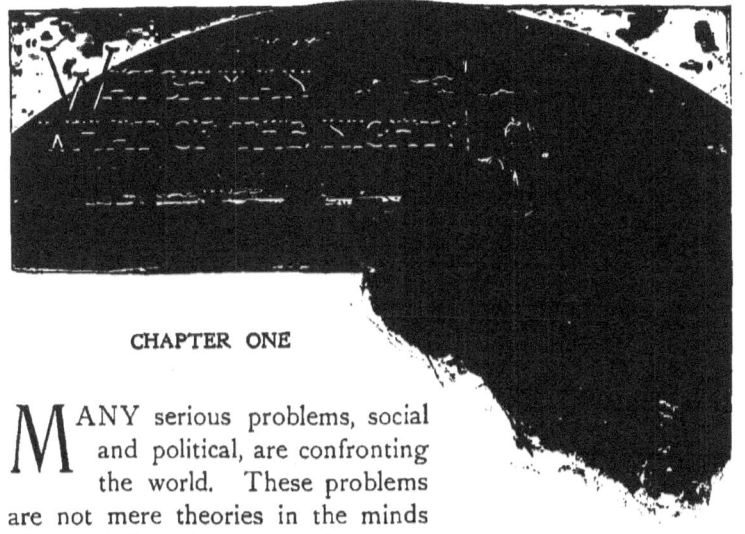

CHAPTER ONE

MANY serious problems, social and political, are confronting the world. These problems are not mere theories in the minds of fanatical enthusiasts, neither are they confined within the narrow limits of one or two nations, but thoughtful men everywhere see the dangers that are threatening the whole world, and are in dread before the alarming conditions of our time. As we meet persons on the street, in the shop, on board the train,—anywhere and everywhere, in this nation and in that,—we find them earnestly and seriously discussing the portents of danger that thicken as the days pass by.

The great amassing of wealth by a few men in each of the various nations of earth is without a parallel in history. The consequent murmurings of the discontented classes strikingly remind one of the turbulent conditions in France on the eve of her great Revolution and Reign of Terror.

On every one of the three hundred and sixty-five days of the year, the newspapers come to us laden with their recital of crime. Murder is of daily occurrence. Highway robbery,

HERALDS OF THE MORNING

Society has banded itself into factions and organizations, each struggling to gain the mastery.

bold and arrogant, as well as petty thievery, is a source of continual annoyance, and to many persons it is a cause of dread and fear. Embezzlers, defaulters, bribers, and bribe-takers have become alarmingly numerous. Millions of dollars are every year fraudulently taken by these, the basest of all methods.

Our large cities in particular, and most of the smaller places in general, are filled with immorality and vice. Drunkenness is every year hurling a vast multitude to the lowest depths of debauching degradation. Public houses of prostitution disgrace our streets, and to this open shame must be added the daily records of broken marriage vows along with all the rest of this unspeakable torrent of pollution.

These various social cancers have so completely polluted the very fountains of society that many conclude that honesty and straightforward integrity are only the ideals of dreamers. The money-god is so supreme in the mind that it is confidently asserted that "every man has his price." "Only approach him in the right way, and offer him the proper bribe," it is affirmed, "and he will yield." Everywhere is heard the mocking jeer at the thought of any one possessing absolute virtue and purity.

Reformers, filled with noble impulses, have sought for the

cause of all this evil that is coming in like a deluge. They have attempted to drive out the houses of shame and to abolish the dens of vice and crime. But on the very threshold of their efforts they are met with the appalling fact that the officers of the law are to an alarming extent in league with this vile and criminal class. Hence the detection and arrest of the criminal is becoming more and more difficult. And even if he is arrested, technicalities and quibbles, prolonged through one court after another, defeat the purpose of the law, and make "courts of justice" a mockery. In consequence of this condition of things, mobs are becoming very common and violent, and lynchings are rapidly increasing; and, incredible though it may seem, men occupying high stations in life are upholding "this lynch form of executing justice."

It passes without contradiction that politics has become a sort of disreputable business, at which men work for the "boodle" there is in it. From the lowest offices in the village or township on up to many of the highest positions of the state and nation, bribery and fraud are freely used to elect the candidate who will be the most lavish in dividing the "spoils of office" among his political friends. Yet instead of this condition of things exciting a healthful and wide-spread sense of indignation and protest, it is altogether too generally treated with jesting and indifference.

We have been promised that the field of politics would produce statesmen—diplomats, who, by their powers of arbitration rather than by the sword, would keep the nations of earth in the highway of peace. Indeed, it has been a dearly-cherished thought—and all should applaud such kindly, humane sentiments—that

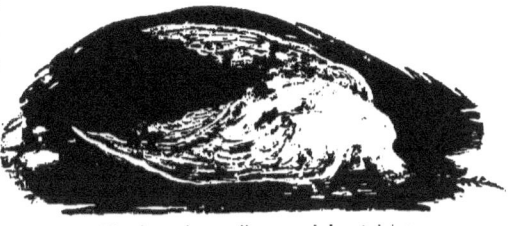

The dove of peace lies wounded and dying

the civilization of the morning of the twentieth century would form an impregnable fortification, beyond which the barbarities of war would never go. But instead of the realization of these exalted hopes, we hear the long roll sounding; the greatest armies that the world has ever known are falling into line and the most formidable navies known to history are patrolling the seas. The weapons of modern warfare are sufficient, it would seem, to inspire terror in the bravest breast; but notwithstanding the destructiveness of the present war implements, there is no lack of men—and women too, for that matter—who are impatiently eager to exchange the pursuits of peace for the camp and battle-field.

There is to-day a general quarreling among the nations, and they are straining every resource to increase their fortifications, armies, and navies. Settling like a heavy cloud over the minds of men, there is a deepening conviction that a universal war can not be averted. The suddenness with which the nations of the whole

What is the world coming to? What will be the end of all these threatening dangers?

world are inflamed to the point of the war-fever gives evidence of the pent-up volcanoes of strife; and the fearful carnage and final results, should this international war spirit develop such a conflict, are a source of much uneasiness and deep concern.

When computing the perplexities of open warfare among the nations, account must also be taken of the various internal factions that threaten the national life of every kingdom, empire, and republic. Society has banded itself into factions and organizations, each struggling to gain the mastery, and this struggle is marked by a notably growing intensity and a manifestly increasing belligerant determination. All the world powers are contending with their discontented revolutionary elements at home, yet anxiously struggling to keep them united for the still greater contest in the field of international strife.

While these topics of the social and political world are presenting so many strange and perplexing features, "old mother earth" herself has laid aside her usually quiet habits, and is participating in the general unrest. Cyclones and hurricanes, earthquakes and tidal waves, and strikingly fearful volcanic action are no longer among the unusual things, neither are they confined to a few localities. But storm-swept land, bursting mountain, and lashing ocean tell us in unmistakable language that the days of earth's tranquility are at an end.

These things, together with others that will suggest themselves to the reader, are leading many anxious minds to inquire: "What is the world coming to? What will be the end of all these threatening dangers?" Book after book, discussing the various phases of the situation, is

We hear the long roll sounding, and the greatest armies that the world has ever known are falling into line.

The omnipotent power that balances the great systems of worlds in space, can alone stay the mind.

published; magazines and papers devoted entirely to the subject of remedying the social and political evils of our time are constantly sent out; and there is scarcely a speaker or writer, no matter what his field of research or labor, but is frequently drawn aside to give words of caution, admonition, or suggestion concerning the common danger.

But despite all these discussions, and the exposures of criminality that are made, the difficulties continue to increase. As one editor of a leading daily suggests, crime is exposed, and the criminals are pointed out, but all to no purpose. They are still permitted to continue in their evil career, apparently without shame and beyond remorse. Many thoughtful and highly-educated men are seriously saying that unless this deluge of crime, turbulence, and discontent can be allayed, the whole world will surely plunge into a revolution that will render insignificant the most fearfully bloody scenes that history records.

The foregoing is not a statement of theory, but a presentation of existing facts. The densest darkness of the night of sin and crime is surely enshrouding the world.

The scientist seeks for the cause of the frequently recurring volcanic activity, earthquake, cyclone, and storm, but his wisest solutions afford no shelter. In the presence of nature's sublime and awful convulsions the hand and mind of man shrink to the infinity of nothingness. The omnipotent Power that balances the great systems of worlds in space can alone stay the mind and keep alive the spark of courage in the heart when the most substantial structures of men are tossed about as grains of sand, and the mountains themselves are trembling because of the forces that are loosened within. The tremblings of earth amid the commotions of the elements and the unsettled condition of society, force the conviction, despite ourselves, that here we have no secure abiding place.

There is no denying the fact that these conditions, which are so apparent in all the world to-day, form a very dark picture, and we may seek to close the avenues to the mind so that we will not see it; but shutting the eyes while drifting toward the vortex, induces only a delirious *dream* of security, which renders our destruction doubly sure.

The dark picture that the actual facts disclose needs to be seen with a clear and unfaltering eye so that we may turn from it to behold, appreciate, and possess, another, whose landscape is the blossoming bowers of the indescribable Eden, and whose

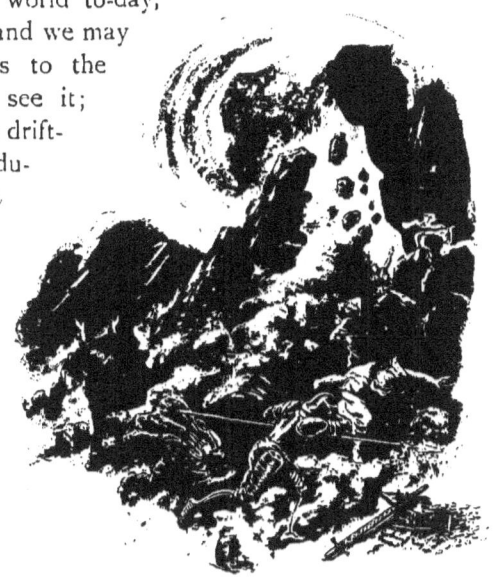

"Earthquakes and tidal waves are no longer unusual things."

halo of glory is brilliantly reflecting the saphires and emeralds, the jaspers and crysolites, of the eternal city of God.

Despite every foreboding outlook, there is an approaching day. There are heralds that are unmistakably trumpeting the dawn of a morning into which every dazzling orb of the universe will flash some splendid rays. He who is the "Root and Offspring of David" is also the "bright and morning Star," and He has promised to come in person to put an end eternally to this perplexity, distress and evil. No one who trusts himself to the care of the Omnipotent will be involved in the impending ruin.

To know this great truth of the Lord's second coming really and fully, and to have the bright picture of the second advent become a soul-satisfying reality, lightens every dark cloud and dissipates every terrorizing danger of this turbulent world. These dark clouds and threatening dangers will then appear as mere atoms that can never reach even the horizon of our divinely bequeathed haven of security and power.

What a consolation it is to know that we have such a faithful Friend! What an indiscribable peace and rest floods the soul as we cast our anchor in the secure haven of Him who is the Almighty!

An examination of the sure and living promises of His Word will disclose the fact that they are life, and joy, and peace to us, and especially so in this time of strife and storm.

CHAPTER TWO

LOOKING at the distressing conditions prevalent in the world to-day, and seeing these things alone, the mind is filled with dark forebodings. But we should not look upon these dark things alone. They should be viewed through the prophecies and promises of the Word of God. As we turn to that Word, we find that the second coming of Christ has been set forth as the cheering banner of hope. The Word abounds in promises of that event. To all who may be led to trust Him the Master sends the joyful proclamation: "Let not your heart be troubled; ye believe in God, believe also in Me. In My Father's house are many mansions; if it were not so, I would have told you. I go to prepare a place for you. And if I go and prepare a place for you, I will come again, and receive you unto Myself; that where I am, there ye may be also." John 14:1-3.

By studying the latter part of the thirteenth chapter of John it will be seen that the Lord, while sitting with His disciples at that memorable "last supper," on the very night when He was betrayed to be crucified, had been telling them that He was to be taken away from them for a time. This statement filled their hearts with sadness. But the Master does not leave them in despair. He at once gives, not only to them but to us also, that most precious promise, "I will come again, and receive you unto Myself."

Again, after the Crucifixion, and at the time of His ascension, while the disciples were yet intently looking into the heavens, whither He was going, angels of God were commissioned to say to them: "Ye men of Galilee, why stand ye gazing up into heaven? This same Jesus, which is taken up from you into heaven, shall so come in like manner as ye have seen Him go into heaven." Acts 1:11. Note the promise, It is *"this same Jesus."*

The disciples had found in Jesus the "Desire of all nations." Their hungry souls had feasted on the words of life that He uttered, and they were resting in the inexpressible joy experienced by those who are conscious of pardoned sin and the invigorating powers of a renewed life. Naturally they desired to have Him remain with them. But, although they had tasted the bliss of a Christian's happy experience, they had not as yet grown into that fulness of faith and knowledge that would enable them to comprehend all that the Master had been seeking to instil into their minds. They did not understand the

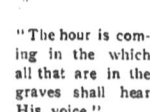

"The hour is coming in the which all that are in the graves shall hear His voice."

great truth, although it had been so plainly stated by the Saviour, "It is expedient for you that I go away: for if I go not away, the Comforter will not come unto you; but if I depart, I will send Him unto you." John 16:7.

The Lord states His truth in plain language; but it takes time for it to be assimilated by the human mind. And when that truth has to uproot prejudices and errors of long standing, the task is a most difficult one. The idea that at His first advent the Messiah was to establish a temporal kingdom, and by force of arms overthrow the Romans, thus relieving the Jews from a foreign yoke, though a false hope, was dearly cherished and firmly fixed. So deeply entrenched was the thought that Christ was to be a temporal king and reign in Judea, that all His teaching to the contrary had not fully driven this delusion from the minds of even the disciples themselves. For in His last conversation with them (a conversation which took place after His crucifixion and resurrection), and on the very occasion when He made His ascension to His Father's throne, it is stated that "they asked of Him, saying, Lord, wilt Thou at this time restore again the kingdom to Israel?" Acts 1:6.

The Master had taken particular pains to make it plain to all that His first advent was to be a time of hardship and suffering, finally culminating in His death on the cross. He had pointed to His resurrection, and expounded the prophecies that foretell the subsequent long night of darkness through which the church would have to pass; and finally He had dwelt upon the great event of His second coming, to put an end to sorrow, suffering, and sin.

But the disciples had not understood nor realized the significance of the words of their Lord. Their minds were still engrossed with the idea of a temporal kingdom to be established then and there, in which the Lord would be King and they would act a prominent part. It seemed impossible to

But shutting their eyes while drifting toward the vortex, only induces a delirious dream of security.

draw their minds away from this cherished error to the exalted sphere of the divine plan. God's ways and plans are always best; but how hard it is for fallen humanity to surrender the false and accept the true! So the Father permitted the disciples with their natural eyes to behold their Saviour as He made His ascension to the heavenly throne. Thus He forever cut off all possible hope of a temporal reign of the Messiah over the Jewish nation in Palestine.

Then while their minds were the most impressible, while they were yet with amazement watching their ascending Lord, the angels were bidden to remind them that "this same Jesus which is taken up from you into heaven, shall so come in like manner as ye have seen Him go into heaven." Acts 1:11. What a lesson of tender solicitude for the needs of His children is here given! And how impressive is the thought that God will exhaust every means to elevate our minds from the bewitching entanglements of error to a knowledge and full enjoyment of His exalted truth!

From this scene of their Lord's ascension the privileged disciples retired to engage in careful meditation and earnest prayer. They tarried in their private lodgings at Jerusalem until the words of truth so carefully planted in their minds

HE WILL COME AGAIN

by the Master had prepared their hearts for the baptism of the Holy Spirit. Then error was driven out; and truth, enthroned within, was permitted to occupy its rightful place. Then they could proclaim with power a crucified and risen Saviour; they could present with confidence the sinner's never-failing hope, telling to all that the chains of sin and death were forever broken. Yes; and they knew the promise, too, that "this same Jesus" will "come again."

This glorious hope of the second coming of Christ is a theme that has called out the most sublime utterances of the inspired writers in all the ages. Of one of the prophets who walked with God, it is said:—

"Enoch also, the seventh from Adam, prophesied of these, saying, Behold, the Lord cometh with ten thousands of His saints." Jude 14.

There are heralds that are unmistakably trumpeting the dawn of a morning.

This is a part of one of the sweet songs of the psalmist: "Sing unto the Lord with the harp; with the harp, and the voice of a psalm. With trumpets and sound of cornet make a joyful noise before the Lord, the King. Let the sea roar, and the fulness thereof; the world, and they that dwell therein. Let the floods clap their hands; let the hills be joyful together before the Lord; for He cometh to judge the earth; with righteousness shall He judge the world, and the people with equity." Ps. 98:5-9.

The "Gospel prophet" declares: "And it shall be said in that day, Lo, this is our God; we have waited for Him, and He will save us; this is the Lord; we have waited for Him, we will be glad and rejoice in His salvation." Isa. 25:9.

Our Master Himself assures us: "The hour is coming, in the which all that are in the graves shall hear His voice, and shall come forth; they that have done good, unto the resurrection of life; and they that have done evil, unto the resurrection of damnation." John 5:28, 29.

The great apostle to the Gentiles avers: "For the Lord Himself shall descend from heaven with a shout, with the voice of the Archangel, and with the trump of God; and the dead in Christ shall rise first; then we which are alive and remain shall be caught up together with them in the clouds, to meet the Lord in the air; and so shall we ever be with the Lord. Wherefore comfort one another with these words." 1 Thess. 4:16-18.

And thus proclaims the beloved disciple from rock-bound Patmos: "Behold, He cometh with clouds; and every eye shall see Him, and they also which pierced Him; and all kindreds of the earth shall wail because of Him." Rev. 1.7.

"And the heaven departed as a scroll when it is rolled together; and every mountain and island were moved out of their places. And the kings of the earth, and the great men, and the rich men, and the chief captains, and the mighty men,

THE CONSOLER

and every bondman, and every freeman, hid themselves in the dens and in the rocks of the mountains; and said to the mountains and rocks, Fall on us, and hide us from the face of Him that sitteth on the throne, and from the wrath of the Lamb; for the great day of His wrath is come; and who shall be able to stand?" Rev. 6:14-17.

"And, behold, I come quickly; and My reward is with Me, to give every man according as his work shall be." "He which testifieth these things saith, Surely I come quickly. Amen. Even so, come, Lord Jesus." Rev. 22:12, 20.

Could promise and positive statement be made in more forcible or explicit language than is used in the foregoing scriptures? Study each one of these texts closely and observe just what they say. When a scripture is so very plain as are these promises of the second coming of the Lord, comment is unnecessary. Have it to say that you see the cheering truth of the Saviour's glorious advent in the promises of His own Word, rather than in the comments that some one may have made upon that Word. Not only is Jesus coming again, but He is coming as the Saviour of all who have not persistently rejected the sinner's Friend. For "Christ was once offered to bear the sins of many; and unto them that look for Him shall He appear the second time without sin unto salvation." Heb. 9:28.

The One who has inspired all the foregoing promises is no less a personage than He who created the universe. He possesses in Himself all the power that holds in place the vast world on which we live, guiding it in harmony with the countless number of vaster worlds which He is also sustaining and directing in space. In considering a statement or promise it is also proper to consider the power and ability of the one who makes it. Surely the One who has made this wealth of promises that Jesus the Lord will come again, has a towering abundance of power to sustain Him in making good His Word.

Therefore even though the world be filled with distress and wo, so that brave-hearted men tremble before the threatening evil, yet are there heralds of the coming morning. The Master has promised to return, and all who know Him are longing for the time to come.

Hence we may expect to find as we study the prophecies that accompany these promises of His coming, that all the disasters and dangers we see threatening the world are nothing more than the shoals and rocks that lie along the farther shore of time. They are not to be dreaded since we have taken the Master Pilot on board. They are only the visible and evident tokens that we have sighted the land of our eternal Eden home. What a joy is this knowledge! What an anchor of rest to the soul!

"All the disasters and dangers we see threatening the world are nothing more than the shoals and rocks that lie along the farther shore of time. They are not to be dreaded since we have taken the Master Pilot on board."

CHAPTER THREE

SAID the angel, "This same Jesus, . . . shall so come in like manner as ye have seen Him go into heaven. Acts 1:11.

It is the "same Jesus" who was here in person, that is coming again in person. All that He was when He was here He will be when He comes again, only He will come in the manifestation of His glory, rather than in the manifestation of His meekness and lowliness.

It is the privilege of every one to look forward to His coming with a perfect joy, for does not the Word of God proclaim to all the world that Christ is the sinner's Friend? Every act of His self-sacrificing life was a living expression of the great truth that He loves us. As we read the Gospel story, we are touched by the deep compassion of the Saviour, and the tenderness with which He devoted Himself to fallen man. He came so close to us, and became so fully identified with us, that He is "touched with the feeling of our infirmities." Heb. 4:15. And when we are overwhelmed with sin and grief and pain, and know that there is no human friend that can understand us and give us sympathy and help, and even though words may fail us in expressing our distressed and perplexing condition, yet we may come with confidence to our Redeemer, and tell Him that we know He understands us fully. We can say to Him that He "feels" our "infirmities," and that He knows from a personal experience how to apply

'Behold how He loved him. John 11:36."

the healing balm to our aching hearts. Oh, what a sympathizing Saviour! See Him at Bethesda, seeking for the lonely sufferer who said, "I have no man, when the water is troubled, to put me into the pool; but while I am coming, another steppeth down before me." The active, throbbing power of life was in the words that the great Physician spoke to this afflicted and friendless man; and he found complete healing for every ailment in the command of the Master, "Rise, take up thy bed, and walk." John 5:7, 8. Why did the Lord pass by all others, and seek out this friendless and helpless one? Oh, it is because He has so closely united Himself with humanity that He *feels* our weakness and distress! How gracious! how considerate! how tender!

On another occasion we find Him at the tomb of Lazarus. About Him are the sorrowing sisters and friends of the dead. He *feels* the grief that rends their sad hearts, and not only *their* affliction, but pressing upon His soul of love is all the sadness to be wrought by sin and death adown the ages. The record says, "Jesus wept." John 11:35. What a universe of meaning to us now, as well as to them, is summed up in these two short words! In His tender, all-comprehending love the heart of the Creator is touched, and His sympathetic grief commingles with that of His creatures. Is it any wonder that the Jews standing by said, "Behold how He loved Him"? And yet it was not alone love for Lazarus or his sisters which moved the heart of Jesus, but love for the mourning, suffering, and afflicted out of all the ages. And well may we all join the apostle in saying that "God commendeth His love toward us, in that, while we were yet sinners, Christ died for us." Rom. 5:8.

Thus we may follow the Master all through His devoted life, and always do we find Him mingling with the people, sharing their joys and their sorrows, relieving their distress, and healing their sick. He gave Himself without any reserve to humanity—the great object of His love. This love was not quenched even when cruel hands and sin-hardened hearts were mercilessly torturing Him on the cross. Even there He poured out the prayer, "Father, forgive them; for they know

"At Bethesda, seeking for the lonely sufferer."

not what they do." Then with what a thrill of joy must the words come to us, "This same Jesus, which is taken up from you into heaven, shall so come in like manner as ye have seen Him go into heaven." Acts 1:11. He is the *same Jesus;* the same compassionate and tender Saviour; the same One who "hath borne our griefs, and carried our sorrows;" He who was "wounded for our transgressions," and "bruised for our iniquities," and with whose "stripes we are healed." How this good news should cause our hearts to overflow with joy!

He is to "*come in like manner* as ye have seen Him go." Yes, "in *like manner.*" When they saw Him go, he was the personal, literal Jesus that they had associated with and loved and adored both as their dearest companion and Saviour, and "*in like manner*" He returns: He comes as the same literal, personal friend for all who will receive Him.

The apostle Paul says that "the Lord Himself shall descend from heaven with a shout, with the voice of the Archangel, and with the trump of God; and the dead in Christ shall rise first." 1 Thess. 4:16. Then, standing not at the tomb of Lazarus only, but in the presence of all the chambers of death in which His people are awaiting His summons, the voice of the great Victor is heard, and "the dead in Christ" arise. Such is a part of the Lord's own description of His coming, and we know that He is the same desirable Friend.

There are many persons who look back with longing desire to the time when Jesus was on earth. They would have been overjoyed at the privilege of having been with Him then, listening to Him speaking as never man had spoken, and feeling the rejuvenating touch of his healing power. But these same persons are terrified at the thought that the second coming of the Lord may take place in their day. Perhaps they recognize the fact that His second coming ushers in the great judgment day, and that the execution of the decisions of that majestic tribunal will destroy every sinner out of all the fair universe of God. It is well to seek to grasp the magnitude of the whole truth. It is well to know that the doom of every unrepentant sinner will be eternally fixed at the second coming of Christ; but we should not make our calculations on being among the sinner-class in that great day. We should come to Jesus the "sinner's Friend," and have Him cleanse us wholly from every taint of sin, so that we may enter into the indescribable *joy* of His second coming.

The gentleness, the kindness, the sympathy, and all the rest of the tender virtues that were so divinely blended in the life of Christ our Lord were thus manifested in order that men might behold the goodness of God and so be led to love, espouse, and enjoy the right. There is no true joy except in the way of righteousness; and it is only when we are clinging to our sins and rejecting the repentance, cleansing, and righteousness that our Heavenly Father proffers, that we are terrified at the thought of meeting face to face the glorified and returning world's Redeemer.

"And, behold, they brought to him a man sick of the palsy, lying on a bed; and Jesus seeing their faith said unto the sick of the palsy; Son, be of good cheer; thy sins be forgiven thee. And, behold, certain of the scribes said within themselves, This Man blasphemeth. And Jesus knowing their thoughts said, Wherefore think ye evil in your hearts? For whether is easier, to say, Thy sins be forgiven thee; or to say, Arise, and walk? But that ye may know that the Son of Man hath power on earth to forgive sins, (then saith He to the sick of the palsy), Arise, take up thy bed, and go unto thine house. And he arose, and departed to his house. And when the multitude saw it, they marveled, and glorified God, which hath given such power unto men." Matt. 9:2-8.

"This same Jesus" is seeking to draw you to Him to-day so that He may implant in your heart the living faith that was in the "man sick of the palsy," and also in the hearts of them who brought him to Jesus; and just as soon as we open the heart for that faith to enter we shall hear from the Word of the Lord, "Son, be of good cheer; thy sins be forgiven thee." When this faith comes into the soul we "know that the Son of Man hath power on earth to forgive sins." Not only do we know the experience of this forgiving power, but we will join in ascribing glory to God who has "given such power unto men."

Then when the cleansing power of the life-blood of Jesus has washed away every defilement and stain of sin; when the power of God, the Creator of our new life, floods our souls with a realizing sense of the fact that we are actually in possession of the heavenly gift of righteousness; when we rise into the strength and the raptures of this new life of freedom from guilt,—then truly do we joy and rejoice in the fact that "this same Jesus" is coming again.

The knowledge that Jesus is coming again, and that He is coming soon, is an anchor that holds. With this great hope filling the soul, there are no dark forebodings because of the evil that is rising like a tidal-wave all over the world; for when the dark clouds are hanging so heavily that it would seem that all the world must soon be swept with a hurricane of destruction, then will the Son of God, with all His host of shining angels appear, and every waiting, hoping, trusting one will be immortalized, to join in swelling the triumphant shout of deliverance.

O, glorious hope! O, glorious day! O, glorious fact that the time is near! Speed onward, ye lagging moments, and bear to us quickly the glad day when "this same Jesus" shall come again.

CHAPTER FOUR

WE have already found that the Scriptures make it perfectly plain that the "same Jesus" is coming again. They are equally clear in telling us that "this Jesus, who was received up from you into heaven, shall so come in *like manner* as ye beheld Him going into heaven." Acts 1:11, R. V.

The Master was fulfilling His word by ascending to His Father's throne; and right while this was taking place the angels present themselves to the disciples to tell them that He "shall *so* come," and in "*like* manner."

The manner in which He went away is stated in language that is easily understood. "And when He had said these things, as they were looking, He was taken up; and a cloud received Him out of their sight." Acts 1:9, R. V. It was while "they were looking" that the Master departed. He had their attention fixed upon Him, for the next verse adds, "And while they were looking *steadfastly* into heaven as He went, behold, two men stood by them in white apparel; who also said, Ye men of Galilee, why stand ye looking into heaven? this Jesus, who was received up from you into heaven, shall so come in like manner as ye beheld Him going into heaven." Acts 1:10, 11. R. V.

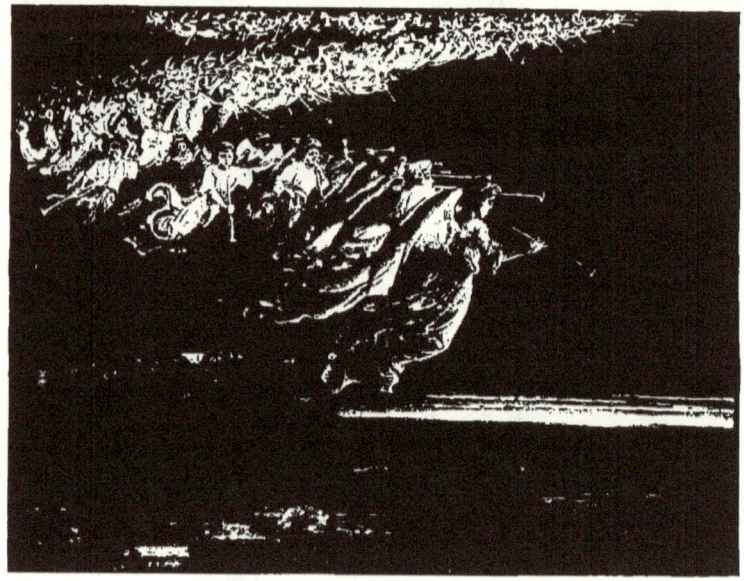

"And He shall send His angels with a great sound of a trumpet."

The disciples were not only "looking," but they were looking *"steadfastly"* at the Lord Jesus as He went away. They must soon be called upon to describe His departing, and also to tell of His returning. They must be able to explain what they mean by saying He "shall *so* come in *like* manner."

They tell us that "He was taken up, and a cloud received Him out of their sight." Acts 1:9. Issues of eternal moment center in the second coming of Christ, and hence that event must not be left to conjecture or speculation. The most definite, positive, clear knowledge must be given in regard to it; for the great adversary will seek to bewilder the minds of men concerning the manner in which the Lord will return. Hence everything is made perfectly clear and obvious.

"A cloud received Him out of their sight" as He went

away. Not only does this text in Acts declare that He will "so come in like manner," but other scriptures besides tell us that the clouds will attend Him again when He comes. "Behold, He cometh with clouds; and every eye shall see Him, and they also which pierced Him; and all kindreds of the earth shall wail because of Him." Rev. 1:7. "And then shall appear the sign of the Son of Man in heaven; and then shall all the tribes of the earth mourn, and they shall see the Son of Man coming in the clouds of heaven with power and great glory." Matt. 24:30. "And then shall they see the Son of Man coming in the couds with great power and glory;" Mark 13:26.

These scriptures tell a plain truth in such very definite language that there is no need of a mistake. The Lord wants us to know just what to look for in His second coming, and we need not be imposed upon by the sophistries of any deception if we are only careful to give heed to what is revealed in the inspired Book.

The Word of God goes further and tells us that when the Redeemer comes the second time, the brightest glory will attend Him; "for the Son of Man shall come in the glory of His Father with His angels; and then He shall reward every man according to his works." Matt. 16:27. And again: "When the Son of Man shall come in

"This same Jesus . . . shall so come in like manner."

His glory, and all the holy angels with Him, then shall He sit upon the throne of His glory." Matt. 25:31. Mark the description of His coming: "The Son of Man shall come *in the glory of His Father;*" and, "the Son of Man shall come *in His glory.*" Thus in this event, as in everything else, the glory of both the Father and the Son is blended into one effulgent harmony.

And observe that He is not coming alone. For with Him, in the shining brightness which God has given to each one of them, are "*all* the holy angels." Speaking of the number of the angels, it is said: "I beheld, and I heard the voice of many angels around about the throne and the beasts and the elders, and the number of them was ten thousand times ten thousand; and thousands of thousands." Rev. 5:11. "Ten thousand times ten thousand" is a hundred million. But this is only a part of the vast throng; for the prophet immediately adds, "And thousands of thousands."

What a glorious event the second coming of the Lord will be! What majestic power and floods of dazzling light will shine forth from this mighty host when the Lamb of God returns in triumph for the trophies of His grace and love! "As the lightning cometh out of the east, and shineth even unto the west; so shall also the coming of the Son of Man be." Matt. 24:27.

He who is the Creator of every shining luminary in all the infinite expanse of space, He who holds in His person the power that produces every ray of light that floods the systems of the universe, when He comes in person to rescue the redeemed from this revolted planet, He will shine with a glory to befit that event as well as befitting to the majesty of His person. The mind should be aroused to its highest capabilities when contemplating the splendor of that soul-rejoicing day of the Lord's second coming. Even then our limited, finite powers will enable us to grasp but dimly the brilliancy of the glory of the King of kings and Lord of lords in this supreme event.

But the great deceiver does not want us to have a proper sense of what the second coming of Christ means to this sinful world, and therefore he seeks to becloud the minds of men in regard to both the nearness of the Master's coming and what the event really is. The Saviour tells us, "Many shall come in My name, saying, I am Christ; and shall deceive many." Matt. 24 : 5. But no pretender can ever present to the world a literal fulfilment of all the inspired specifications that are to mark the coming of the glorified Son of God. Still it is said of these "false christs and false prophets" that they "shall show great signs and wonders; insomuch that, if it were possible, they shall deceive the very elect." Matt. 24 : 24.

The Word of God not only gives a faithful description of the manner and appearance of the second coming of the Lord, but it also unmasks the deceptions by which the enemy would ensnare and ruin us. Hence we should be faithful students of the Book of books. The ordinary reading of the Bible is not sufficient to barricade the heart against the deceptions prepared by the evil one for the last days. We must literally feed on the divine Word. We must commune with God through that Word and by prayer. In this way we may become so fully assimilated into His life and character, grow into such an intimate friendship with Him, and be made so sensible of the power of His coming, that we shall not be deceived. We shall know the voice of the true Shepherd, and no impostor, be he never so cunning, can possibly lead us astray; for when the true Shepherd "putteth forth His own sheep, He goeth before them, and the sheep follow Him; for they know His voice. And a stranger will they not follow, but will flee from him; for they know not the voice of strangers." John 10 : 4, 5.

We know only "this same Jesus;" only Him with the perfect character; only Him whose life was so unselfishly sacrificed for lost mankind. Only the Son of God, who loved me, and gave Himself for me, can ever fill the place that He has won in the Christian's heart. A cunning enemy may present deceptions, and, among his "great signs and wonders," may even show a brilliant spectacle that will cause some to think that Christ has already come; but only those will be deceived thereby who have rejected or failed to heed the warnings of the Word of God.

Then through faith in His Word receive the Redeemer as your personal Saviour. He says, "Behold, I stand at the door, and knock; if any man hear My voice, and open the door, I will come in to him, and will sup with him, and he with Me." Rev. 3:20. And if you court the presence of His Holy Spirit and thus allow Him to draw you into this intimate association, you will learn to know Him as a personal Friend. You will become actually acquainted with the real Son of God. And the individual who really knows the Friend of sinners, earnestly longs for the day of His coming. He carefully observes every herald of the approaching morn; and however this world may be filled with terrors, and however dark it may be to others, to him it is all lighted up by the sure promises that the eternal day is at hand. His heart is throbbing for the time, and his eyes are longing to behold "this same Jesus," the one object of his joy and love.

CHAPTER FIVE

ALTHOUGH the Word of God abounds in promises of the second coming of Christ, yet we are told, "Of that day and hour knoweth no man, no, not the angels of heaven, but My Father only." Matt. 24:36.

This scripture is so very plain that the truly loyal Christian will readily see that it is no part of his work to figure out a definite date on which the Lord is to come. The "day and hour" of that great event the Father has not seen fit to reveal. And we may rest assured that whatever is not made known is withheld because of a wise and good purpose. Then we should be content to leave all such matters in the hands of God, without troubling our minds over them in the least.

But though the Word of God is very explicit in telling us that the "day and hour" of the Saviour's coming have not been made known, we shall find that it clearly shows that we may know when the event is near. The disciples asked Jesus, "What shall be the sign of Thy coming, and of the end of the world?" Matt. 24:3. The Saviour proceeded to give a definite answer to this direct question, and concluded by saying: "And then shall appear the sign of the Son of Man in heaven: and then shall all the tribes of the earth mourn, and they shall see the Son of Man coming on the clouds of heaven with power and great glory. And He shall send forth His angels with a great sound of a trumpet, and they shall gather together His elect from the four winds, from one end of heaven to the other.

Now from the fig tree learn her parable: when her branch is now become tender, and putteth forth its leaves, ye know that the summer is nigh; even so ye also, when ye see all these things, know ye that He is nigh, even at the doors." Matt. 24:30-33, R. V.

Luke, in the twenty-first chapter of his Gospel, records this same conversation between the disciples and Christ concerning His second coming. Speaking of the signs that are to precede His advent, the Lord says, "When these things *begin* to come to pass, then look up, and lift up your heads; for your redemption draweth nigh." Verse 28.

"The swelling of the buds in the spring-time."

Thus the Lord foretells certain signs that are to betoken His coming. He first points us to the signs, and then He declares that when these *begin* to come to pass, we may know for a certainty that our redemption is near, and that He is "even at the door." The swelling of the buds in the spring-time is a never-failing evidence that summer is nigh; and upon the Master's own word, the tokens of His coming are to be relied upon with the same certainty.

The language of the apostle Paul is equally clear upon this subject: "But of the times and the seasons, brethren, ye have no need that I write unto you. For yourselves know perfectly that the day of the Lord so cometh as a thief in the night. For when they shall say, Peace and safety; then sudden destruction cometh upon them, as travail upon a woman with child; and they shall not escape. But ye, brethren, are not in darkness, that that day should overtake you as a thief. Ye are all the children of light, and the children of the day; we are not of the night, nor of darkness." 1 Thess. 5 : 1–5.

From this scripture we readily see that those who stand in the light will know "the times and the seasons" of "the day of the Lord." Speaking to his "brethren," the apostle says, "Yourselves know perfectly that the day of the Lord so cometh as a thief in the night." Verse 2. But that great day does not thus come upon all; for he says further, "Ye, brethren, are not in darkness, that that day should overtake you as a thief." Verse 4. The "brethren" stand in the light, and so know "the times and the seasons" of "the day of the Lord."

Then there will be a class who will say, "Peace and safety," and upon whom "sudden destruction cometh;" and another class who "are not in darkness," and hence that day does not

"As a thief in the night."

"overtake them as a thief." This destruction comes upon the one class because they have chosen to hide away from the light, while the others are delivered because they have accepted "the true Light, which lighteth every man that cometh into the world." John 1:9. For "light is come into the world, and men loved darkness rather than light, because their deeds were evil. For every one that doeth evil hateth the light, neither cometh to the light, lest his deeds should be reproved. But he that doeth truth cometh to the light, that his deeds may be made manifest, that they are wrought in God." John 3:19-21.

Those here spoken of who "loved darkness rather than light," will very naturally say, "Peace and safety," even though in the immediate presence of "sudden destruction;" and while they remain in that blinding darkness, they can not see the evidence showing that "He is near even at the doors." But the psalmist says, "Thy Word is a lamp unto my feet, and a light unto my path." Ps. 119:105. The reverent student who will open the heart and mind to the reception of that Word, will thereby stand among those who discern the signs of the times.

Our heavenly Father has seen fit to reserve to Himself the knowledge of the exact "day and hour" when the Saviour will come. But by every sign that foretells that event He who is the "Friend of sinners" is now inviting us to prepare for His glorious coming, and thus be ready to receive Him with joy when He shall "appear the second time without sin unto salvation." Heb. 9:28.

He is coming soon to gather all His people from this world of sin. All are entreated to be ready against that time. The invitation is, "Whosoever will, let him take the water of life freely." How can any one refuse this great salvation,—salvation from our personal sins now, salvation from the evils of this age; and then, at His coming, salvation and eternal bliss in the realities of immortal life?

CHAPTER SIX

THE scripture quoted at the beginning of the preceding chapter is very clear in saying that we may not know the hour when the Lord will come. It is equally as plain in commanding us to know when He is near. The fact should be repeated and emphasized that the Lord Himself tells us to know of the time of this great event. We are altogether too prone to treat the statements of the Bible as mere matters of speculation.

Greek and Roman literature has been very closely studied all through the Christian era; and the habit of those ancient philosophers in speculating upon matters of religion has been altogether too strongly imbibed by the teachers and adherents in general of the Christian faith. We can excuse those men who had no light but their speculative philosophies to guide them, for making their religion a subject for fanciful dreaming and speculative discourse. But the Christian can not be excused in taking any such course. We have for the basis of our Christian faith the Word of God. He who is the Source and Creator of all true wisdom and knowledge, has given us an infallible guide, and commanded us to *know* and *understand*.

There are many among the professors of the Christian

religion who seem to think that it is almost presumption for them to claim to *know* anything about their faith; hence it seems expedient to devote this short chapter to the work of emphasizing the thought that we should *"know"* the facts of our faith with the same definiteness that we know the facts and principles of our mathematics. We speak of mathematics as one of the exact sciences. We have tested the accuracy of figures until we understand the definite knowledge of this great field of fact; but the same God who is the Author of the valuable and accurate and certain science of mathematics, is also the Author of the Bible. He is not only the Author of its soul-uplifting spirituality and infinitely broad and high morality, but He is also the Author of its complete, clear, definite, and altogether accurate prophecy. Throned in omnipotence and omniscience, His eyes sweep the eternity of the future as well as of the past; and with the accuracy that belongs only to unerring perfection, He gives us the evidences by which we may *"know"* what is the meaning of the unfolding of the events and phenomena that are causing so much concern in the world to-day.

We know that the problems and evils among the men of this time, as well as the unsteady course of the elements so violently voiced in volcano, earthquake, tidal wave, and hurricane, are filling men with a dread for the developments of the immediate future. We know this not only because we may meet men everywhere who are discussing it, but we have also the infallible Word, which says: "And there shall be signs in the sun, and in the moon, and in the stars; and upon the earth distress of nations, with perplexity; the sea and the waves roaring; men's hearts failing them for fear, and for looking after those things which are coming on the earth; for the powers of heaven shall be shaken. And then shall they see the Son of Man coming in a cloud with power and great glory." Luke 21:25-27.

"Men's hearts" are "failing them for fear" because they see the things that are coming on the earth. They see the "distress of nations, with perplexity;" they hear the "sea and the waves roaring," and they are uncertain as to what it means. They are unnerved because of the thought of the possibly disastrous outcome of it all. But to every one who can be reached with God's Word, to every one who will allow the seeds of faith to be implanted in his mind and heart, there is the cheering message, "When these things begin to come to pass, then look up, and lift up your heads; for your redemption draweth nigh." Luke 21:28. The individual who knows what should be known by every one in this day is not downcast because of the issues of this time and the possibilities of a general cataclysm next week or next month. No indeed! The individual who "*knows*," is the one who is "looking up," and he is filled with rejoicing because he "*knows*" that his redemption is right at hand.

Everything in all God's great universe shows the precision of His accuracy. No science that can justly claim Him as its Author is a field for vain and mystic speculation. We enter its domain to study for definite truth that can be made practically beneficial. Then why should we enter the inviting portals of God's great temple of spiritual truth, especially in the realm of prophecy, with any other intention than actually to *know* and understand?

We not only have the prophecy of God's Word plainly telling us the meaning of the things that are coming on the world, so that we may be able to look up and lift up our heads because of our redemption drawing nigh, but we have also the assurance of the fact that His Spirit will be our ever-present teacher, so that there may be no possibility of mistake. Hear the words of the Master upon this point: "Howbeit when He, the Spirit of Truth, is come, He will guide you into all truth: for He shall not speak of Himself; but whatsoever He shall hear, that shall He speak; and He will show you things to come." John 16:13. How definite and accurate is the promise in these words: "He will guide you into all truth," and He can guide us into nothing else but truth; for does not the text say He is "the Spirit of Truth"? But let it be ever remembered that the light with which He guides us is the Word of God. "And [take] the Sword of the Spirit, which is the Word of God." Eph. 6:17. We must take our stand upon the plain words of the Bible, and with the definite "Thus saith the Lord" for our eyepiece, we can then call upon the Spirit of God and know that "He will" indeed "guide you into all truth."

The verses immediately following the foregoing beautiful and assuring promise from the book of John, read: "He shall glorify Me; for He shall receive of Mine, and shall show it unto you. All things that the Father hath are Mine; therefore said I, that He shall take of Mine, and shall show it unto you." John 16:14, 15. The same divine Spirit of Truth that the Master promises shall "guide you into all truth" will also take of the things of God and show them unto us. This is the statement of God's own Word in the presentation of a great spiritual truth. And this spiritual truth is as perfectly scientific in its operations as is electricity in its field of action. The same God who created the laws that make the flow of the electric current possible, and who gave to man the enlightenment that enabled him to discover these laws, is also the One who has given to mankind His Spirit to guide him into a knowledge of all the spiritual truth that is spoken in His Word. We can not see the electric current, but we may study to know the law that it operates upon, and the work it will do when allowed properly to operate. And so, while we can not see the Spirit of God, yet the Word of God forms the wire over which this Spirit comes to us, serving also as the motor through which the Spirit performs its definite work.

With these promises of being guided into all truth, and with the command of the Master to *"know"* when He is near, thus placed before us in His Word, we should not have any vague understanding of the future. For when He commands us to *know*, He also makes it possible for us to know. This definite knowledge is in His Word. Let us seek till we find it, and let us *know* that we KNOW it; it is a thing of too much value to be neglected or lightly esteemed.

CHAPTER SEVEN

AFTER stating to His disciples that "of that day and that hour knoweth no man," the Lord said: "Watch ye therefore; for ye know not when the Master of the house cometh, at even, or at midnight, or at the cockcrowing, or in the morning; lest coming suddenly He find you sleeping. And what I say unto you I say unto all, Watch." Mark 13:35-37.

Satan is continually waging an active warfare against every soul. He is determined that no one shall accept Christ if he can possibly prevent it. Says the Scripture, "Wo to the inhabiters of the earth and of the sea! for the devil is come down unto you, having great wrath, because he knoweth that he hath but a short time." Rev. 12:12. As the Lord's coming draws nearer and nearer, Satan's time for working becomes shorter and shorter. And when "He knoweth that he hath but a short time," his "great wrath" is manifested by increased and cunning deceptions, in order that he may bind as many as possible for the "sudden destruction" that awaits the wicked world. By his delusive arts Satan seeks so fully to engross the mind in the things of this life that the evidence of our Lord's coming will not be seen, even though that evidence stands out before the world as an unobscured and blazing light. But we are put on our guard against the deceptions of the great adversary by the ringing words, "Watch," "lest coming suddenly He find you sleeping."

The great necessity of watching when the closing days of time are reached, is repeated and emphasized in the Word of God. Only by constantly reading and giving heed to these warnings can we preserve a realizing sense of their importance. By the apostle Paul we are told that "then shall that Wicked be revealed, whom the Lord shall consume with the spirit of His mouth, and shall destroy with the brightness of His coming; even Him, whose coming is after ["according to," R. V.] the working of Satan with all power and signs and lying wonders, and with all deceivableness of unrighteousness in them that perish; because they received not the love of the truth, that they might be saved. And for this cause God shall send them strong delusion, that they should believe a lie; that they all might be damned who believe not the truth, but had pleasure in unrighteousness." 2 Thess. 2 : 8-12.

Observe with care the warnings in the foregoing scripture. "The brightness of His coming," it is stated, "shall destroy" "that Wicked." And His "coming is *after* [or "according to"] the working of Satan *with all power* and *signs* and *lying wonders*, and with *all deceivableness of unrighteousness* in them that perish." The Lord's coming, then, we should be particular to observe, is "*after*" ("according to") this deceptive working of Satan with such "power" and "deceivableness of unrighteousness." In other words, when Satan's workings of evil become so bad that sure destruction to every living thing must soon result, then the Master will appear to end it. Thus is the

Lord's coming "according to" the working of Satan. It is in and through "them that perish" that Satan works; and it is all in consequence of the fact that *"they received not the love of the truth, that they might be saved."*

So, then, Satan works with power, but he masks himself by "deceivableness of unrighteousness;" and this working of the enemy becomes fiercer and stronger as we near the end. While Satan is working so powerfully, the Father in heaven is also sending out His great Gospel truth to save people from these deceptions and the consequent destruction; but some, as stated in this scripture, receive not "the *love* of the truth." The truth is presented to them; they hear it, and are convicted by it; but they do not "love" this Heaven-sent message. They prefer to cling to their sinful lusts, and so they doom themselves to perish; and in doing this they become a channel through which Satan works his masterly deceptions.

In this connection note the facts set forth in another scripture: "This know also, that in the last days perilous times shall come. For men shall be lovers of their own selves, covetous, boasters, proud, blasphemers, disobedient to parents, unthankful, unholy, without natural affection, truce-breakers, false accusers, incontinent, fierce, despisers of those that are good, traitors, heady, high-minded, lovers of pleasures more than lovers of God; having a form of godliness, but denying the power thereof; from such turn away. For of this sort are they which creep into houses, and lead captive silly women laden with sins, led away with divers lusts, ever learning, and never able to come to the knowledge of the truth.

"Now as Jannes and Jambres withstood Moses, so do these also resist the truth; men of corrupt minds, reprobate concerning the faith. But they shall proceed no further; for their folly shall be manifest unto all men, as theirs also was." 2 Tim. 3 : 1–9.

We are not left in darkness as to the time when the foregoing scripture applies. It is plainly stated that it is "in the *last days*," and in verses 2-5 are recorded the sins that are the occasion of these "last-day" "perils." In verse 8 we are told that "as Jannes and Jambres withstood Moses, so do these also resist the truth; men of corrupt minds, reprobate concerning the faith."

The ancient records of the Jews, as well as the history and traditions of many of the Eastern countries, preserve the names of Jannes and Jambres. They were two of the leading magicians, who, prompted by the spirit of Satan, were able to counterfeit for a time the miracles that by the power of God Moses wrought before Pharaoh. Then let it again be observed that the text says: "Now as Jannes and Jambres withstood Moses, *so* [*i. e.*, in like manner] do these also resist the truth " How clear the

" The . . . power of the magicians in Moses' time was . . . great."

prophecy that just as Moses was withstood by the magicians in his day, so will the "truth" be resisted by "men of corrupt minds," amid the "perilous times" of the "last days"! In view of this, how full of importance is the Saviour's admonition to watch!

The deceptive working and power of the magicians in Moses' time was so great, and they were able to produce such marvelous counterfeit miracles, that the carnally-minded Pharaoh persuaded himself that their work was equal to that which was wrought by the Spirit of the living God. And in answering the question, "What shall be the sign of Thy coming, and of the end of the world?" Jesus makes prominent mention of the fact that "there shall arise false Christs, and false prophets, and shall show great signs and wonders; insomuch that, if it were possible, they shall deceive the very elect." Matt. 24:3, 24.

Thus the never-failing Word of God places before us warning after warning against the deceptive, wonder-working power of the "false Christs and false prophets" that Satan will use in the "last days" to lure men into eternal ruin. How carefully, then, should we cherish the warning: "Take heed that no man deceive you. For many shall come in My name, saying, I am Christ; and shall deceive many." Matt. 24:4, 5. We can not be too careful or too guarded; for that fallen angel, who has given all his great powers for the whole six thousand years of this earth's history to the one work of deceiving mankind and leading them away from God, is making his last and most persistent effort to delude and destroy.

God's Word faithfully unmasks all these delusions, so that we may recognize them as just what they are as fast as they appear; and by giving heed to the utterances of the divine Book, we may rest secure in the promises of our heavenly Father, and so escape every one of the snares of the enemy. To be ready to meet the Master at His coming should be our one great aim; for He loves us with an everlasting love, and His coming is for the purpose of destroying sin, with all the consequent curse, and taking all who receive Him to the perfect and eternal home.

Since He has so fully manifested His love toward us, how can we slight His warnings against the great delusions of our time, and, turning away from the study of His Word and an abiding faith in what it says, be forever lost? The Word of God, the blessed Bible, should be our trusted teacher and guide. "The law of his God is in his heart; none of his steps shall slide." Ps. 37:31 "Thy Word have I hid in mine heart, that I might not sin against Thee." "Thy Word is a lamp unto my feet, and a light unto my path." Ps. 119:11, 105. "Thou wilt keep him in perfect peace, whose mind is stayed on Thee; because he trusteth in Thee. Trust ye in the Lord forever; for in the Lord Jehovah is everlasting strength." Isa. 26:3, 4.

God's Word is filled with these "exceeding great and precious promises." Seek them out and feed upon them; for by so doing every peril may be seen and avoided. Careful study of the Word of God must, in the very nature of things, form the basis of our giving intelligent heed to the Saviour's command to "watch" "lest coming suddenly He find you sleeping."

GREAT DECEPTIONS

CHAPTER EIGHT

HAVING in a general way called attention in the preceding chapter to the delusions and wonder-working power of Satan that will be manifested so marvelously in the "last days," it may be well to notice more particularly two or three of the deceptions against which we are especially warned in the Word of God.

The following scripture will help us to understand what one of these delusions is: "And I saw three unclean spirits like frogs come out of the mouth of the dragon, and out of the mouth of the beast, and out of the mouth of the false prophet. For they are the spirits of devils, working miracles, which go forth unto the kings of the earth and of the whole world, to gather them to the battle of that great day of God Almighty." Rev. 16:13, 14. Then when "that great day" is imminent, the "spirits of devils" will be "working miracles." Nothing could be plainer than the statement of this important fact.

It is worthy of note that these "spirits of devils" go to the "*kings* of the earth," thus showing that they will seek to captivate the leading influential men of the world; and, to accomplish their design, they will have to present deceptive miracles, such as will arrest the attention of the most intelligent and best-educated classes. All such artfully devised deceptions are in perfect harmony with the character of the wily foe. "And no marvel; for Satan himself is transformed into an angel of light." 2 Cor. 11:14. Satan would be at once rejected if he came in any other garb than that of "an angel of light." He is a deceiver, and the real character of his iniquitous plans must be so skilfully hidden that his snare will not be detected till his victim is hopelessly, even though unconsciously, entangled in his net.

Very forcible and clear concerning this great latter-day deception of Satan are the words of the apostle Paul: "Now the Spirit speaketh expressly, that in the latter times some shall depart from the faith, giving heed to seducing spirits, and doctrines of devils." 1 Tim. 4:1. Here is an expression from the Lord that is given with emphasis. "The Spirit speaketh expressly;" and we should pay careful attention to the divine message "so expressly" given.

To "depart from the faith" is to disbelieve or reject the plain words of the Bible; for "*faith* cometh by hearing, and *hearing* by the *Word* of God." It is the "Word" of God, then, that we are to hear; and it is by hearing this Word that *faith* comes. Hence he who departs from the faith must first either neglect or reject the Word of God. It is not necessary openly to express infidelity in order effectually to reject God's divine Book. If by human interpretations, explanations, and mystifications that Book is allowed to be so completely covered up that it is no longer the direct voice of God to the soul, the Bible is as verily driven from the mind as if one were an out-and-out infidel. Explanations or criticisms that cast doubt upon the Word of God, and that lead men to believe that it does not mean what it clearly says, inevitably cause them to depart from the faith, and the way is thereby opened for the next step, which is the "giving heed to seducing spirits, and doctrines of devils."

But no interpretations, explanations, or mystifying teachings of the Bible can compare, in their evil results, with the neglect individually to study the sacred Book. With the mass of professing Christians the Bible is seldom opened from one year's end to the other. These people, while professing to believe the Bible, know scarcely anything of what it really contains. They have not delved into its mines of promises, instructions, and warnings, and so may be led to give heed to these "seducing spirits," even while thinking to follow the guidance of the Lord. God has placed these warnings in His Word against "seducing spirits" so that every individual may read and understand. To fail to study the Bible is to turn from the light that discloses the pitfalls of the deceiver.

Concerning this departing from the faith, it is left to the reader to answer the question for himself if either the pulpit or religious press (with but few exceptions) is to-day teaching the pure Word of God in the "demonstration of the Spirit and of power," as was once the case. The Word predicts a departing from the faith in the "latter times." It is the boast of men to-day that "this age has outgrown many of the things taught in the Bible," and they call it an indication of great intellectual advancement. But, instead, it is one among the sure signs that we are in the time when "some shall depart from the faith,"— one of the positive evidences that the "latter times" are reached. Every true believer in the Word of God will know this now, and all others will be forced to acknowledge it soon.

It should also be carefully observed that this departing from the faith is followed by "giving heed to seducing spirits, and doctrines of devils." It could not be otherwise; for when men fail to heed the Bible, which exposes all the deceptions of Satan, of course he will then drive them headlong into his snares. The great extent to which these wonder-working deceptions will be carried may best be expressed in the words of the prophet: "And he doeth great wonders, so that he maketh fire come down from heaven on the earth in the sight of men, and deceiveth them that dwell on the earth by the means of those miracles which he had power to do in the sight of the beast; saying to them that dwell on the earth, that they should make an image to the beast, which had the wound by a sword, and did live." Rev. 13:13, 14.

Reader, what think you? If you should see a power working such a miracle as making "fire come down from heaven," would it not be quite convincing to you? But be on your guard. God, in the clearest and most direct language, is warning you against these "spirits of devils" that "go forth unto the kings of the earth and of the whole world," exhibiting their miracle-working power. How needful for us, then, in these times of peril, to cling close to the mighty Rock, so that no masterpiece of the enemy's deceptions may overthrow us!

Of course the miraculous power that makes this great display, even causing fire to "come down from heaven," has not yet been reached. But the "consulter with familiar spirits," who, as we shall presently see, is acting directly contrary to the Word of God, is to be found everywhere, and is seeking to convince all that there are "great wonders" wrapped up in Modern Spiritualism. "Only honestly investigate," say they, "and you must be convinced." A representative statement upon this point may be quoted from a leading minister in Boston, who recounts his experience with Spiritualism. After telling, through the columns of a leading magazine, what he had seen the mediums do, he says: "Here are most *wonderful* facts. How shall they be accounted for?" The prophet's prediction is that he "doeth great wonders." How literally is it fulfilled in the "wonders" presented by the modern spirit medium, and in the belief among highly educated men that the claims of Spiritualism are *"wonderful facts"!*

The "leading thinkers" at first regarded Spiritualism as nothing more than artful trickery. The "rappings," "table-tippings," etc., of fifty years ago were done with lights turned down, and there was much room for the assertion that it was all a slight of hand performance; but now this same thing is done in open day, or under the glare of the evening lamp. All minds, however, are not alike, and hence every person can not be convinced by this one kind of spiritualistic manifestation. Telepathy and hypnotism and mind-reading seem more "scientific," and some of the educated are attracted to Spiritualism through these channels. A still larger class is attracted to the mediums because of the assurance that through them they can hold communion with their dead friends. So we might go through the list of the many ways that this many-sided Spiritualism has for attracting men into its bewitching, entrancing net.

Satan is very cunning in his deceptions, and does not bring forward at first his greatest marvels; but by degrees, and with numerous devices, he advances. The illiterate and superstitious, and even some who are well educated, are easily ensnared by "rappings" and the like. Others have to be taken in a more subtle snare; but in one way and another he is advancing, producing greater and still greater "wonders," and myriads in all the walks of life are being drawn into his various nets. In this way Spiritualism is stealthily gaining influence, preparatory to the master deception of Satan, when he "maketh fire come down from heaven on the earth in the sight of men." Rev. 13:13.

Satan "knoweth that he hath but a short time." He also knows the prophecies that tell so vividly of that splendid scene when the Son of Man shall appear in such dazzling glory; and hence deceptions are prepared to represent flaming fire in the heavens, and this "fire" comes down "on the earth in the sight of men." Thus he will seek to beguile the very ones who are following the Bible the most closely, and who are looking for the coming of their Saviour in glory. Who can withstand this great culminating deception, unless securely fortified against it by the Word of God and a daily experience in following the leadings of the Light of the world? But we have the never-failing promise of our heavenly Father that none can be deceived who rely in faith upon the sure foundation.

The prophet Isaiah, speaking in regard to those who have familiar spirits, says: "And when they shall say unto you, Seek unto them that have familiar spirits, and unto wizards that peep and that mutter; should not a people seek unto their God? for the living to the dead? To the law and to the testimony; if they speak not according to this word, it is because there is no light in them." Isa. 8:19, 20. Every one knows that there is scarcely a corner of the whole world in which may not be found the individual who has "familiar spirits" hovering about him. The "spirit medium" is now in nearly every neighborhood; and thousands of individuals who a few years ago scoffed at Spiritualism, considering it a superstition of the most ignorant, are embracing it to-day as a "wonderful" truth. More than twenty millions are claimed as believers in, and consulters with, these "familiar spirits;" and if the exact statistics could be obtained, doubtless it would be disclosed that a much greater number are in the toils of this delusion.

"A charmer,
. . . a wizard,
or a necromancer."

There is nothing that the Word of God more forcibly condemns than resorting to "them that have familiar spirits." "Regard not them that have *familiar spirits*, neither seek after wizards, to be defiled by them; I am the Lord your God." Lev. 19:31. "There shall not be found among you any one that maketh his son or his daughter to pass through the fire, or that useth divination, or an observer of times, or an enchanter, or a witch, or a charmer, or a *consulter with familiar spirits*, or a wizard, or a necromancer. For all that do these things are an abomination unto the Lord." Deut. 18: 10–12. While millions are being deluded by these "familiar spirits," God has so arranged it that no one can ever be perfectly satisfied with what they have to offer. There is a vague mysticism about it all, and a fog of superstitions hovers over it. It does not set the mind free, even though it may give it at times some degree of rest. The only thing that can perfectly satisfy, and render us perfectly sure both of the present and the future, is the truth which comes from God Himself. He employs no mediums except His Word and His definitely specified operations of His Spirit. These are always plain, having no taint whatever of mysticism, and they fill the recipient with satisfaction and perfect peace and rest.

No additional evidence need be given to show that Spiritualism — which is "seeking unto familiar spirits" — is forbidden by the Word of God, and is a deception of the evil one. Little do men in general realize what Satan is doing, as in every corner of the world he is so busily entangling the feet of such vast multitudes in the enticing net of Modern Spiritualism. Reader, review again, and again, and again, the warnings that God has given against the delusions of the enemy, prepared under his deceptive hand for these last days; and do not forget that the Master has said that His coming is "after ["according to"] the working of Satan with all power and signs and lying wonders," and that His earnest admonition is, "What I say unto you I say unto all, Watch."

THE CRY OF PEACE AND SAFETY

Next to this crowning delusion of Spiritualism prepared by Satan for these last days, perhaps there is no worse deception than the soothing doctrine of "peace and safety," that in our day is proclaimed by so many pens and voices.

The Word of God says, "All that will live godly in Christ Jesus shall suffer persecution." 2 Tim. 3:12. This statement is direct, and no one who regards it will be found preaching "peace and safety" to the Christian so long as he remains in this present world of sin. For it is said that "*all*," not a part merely, but "*all* that will live godly in Christ Jesus shall suffer persecution." Another text says, "In the world ye shall have tribulation." It is only "in Me," the Master assures us, that we shall have "peace." John 16:33.

The fact confronts us that the Christian church has ceased almost entirely to suffer persecution. Nor does it follow that this lack of persecution is wholly due to the general enlightenment of the age. Should we open our eyes fully to the situation, we would see that it is largely due to the fact that godliness "in Christ Jesus" has very greatly died out from the hearts of the professed Christians of to-day. All will agree that the Bible plainly teaches that there should be a clear-cut distinction between the church and the world; but does not observation impress each one's inner consciousness with the thought that our churches to-day are courting, and in turn being courted by, the devotees of this sinful life?

Read further from the Word of God: "This know also, that in the last days perilous times shall come." And again: "Evil men and seducers shall wax worse and worse, deceiving, and being deceived." 2 Tim. 3:1, 13. In that startling contrast to the words of "peace and safety," so commonly heard, do these Scripture texts strike the ear! The great mass of teachers to-day are saying that the world is getting better and better, and that good times are ahead; but the infallible Word says exactly the opposite. In no uncertain language are we told that "evil men and seducers shall wax worse and worse;" that "in the last days" not good but "perilous times shall come."

The Word further states upon this point that "as the days of Noah were, so shall also the coming of the Son of Man be." Matt. 24:37. What the condition of things was in "the days of Noah" is made very plain in the Bible. It says, "God saw that the wickedness of man was great in the earth, and that every imagination of the thoughts of his heart was only evil continually." Gen. 6:5. All who, under the spell of the enemy are being captivated by the belief that the world is rapidly getting better, should ponder these texts well. Our God reads the future, and He has given us a faithful portrayal of the true condition of things in the last days. The enchantments of a cunning foe may cause us to seem to see what does not exist, but we should believe the Word of God, no matter how dazzling may be the presentations to the contrary.

He with whom it is impossible to err has plainly told us that in the days when we are to be looking for the coming of the Son of Man, as in the days of Noah, "the wickedness of man" shall be "great in the earth, and that every imagination of the thoughts of his heart" shall be "only evil continually." Since God has so directly spoken, who can assume to set aside His declaration by teaching the "peace-and-safety" fable that the world is growing better instead of "worse and worse," as the Word declares?

How can we fail to see that Satan has already so completely soothed the world with his lullaby of "peace and safety" that it is well-nigh asleep? And while the sensibilities of many are being stupefied by this false doctrine, so that they will refuse to hear the ringing words of divine truth, the net of Spiritualism is being subtilely spread to complete the ruin of the drowsy world.

Reader, will you not heed the earnest and faithful warnings of the Lord's Word? The Heavenly Father has laid the deceptions of the enemy so bare that we can not stumble into Satan's pitfalls while guided by Him who is the "Light of life."

GREAT DECEPTIONS

"Behold, I stand at the door, and knock; if any man hear My voice, and open the door, I will come in to him, and will sup with him, and he with Me." Rev. 3:20.

"My sheep hear My voice, and I know them, and they follow Me; and I give unto them eternal life; and they shall never perish, *neither shall any man pluck them out of My hand.* My Father, which gave them Me, is greater than all; and no man is able to pluck them out of My Father's hand." John 10:27-29.

PROPHETIC OUTLINES

CHAPTER NINE

THE preceding chapters are devoted to a review of some of the promises of the second advent of our Saviour, together with the scripture warnings of the deceptions of Satan, with no attempt to present the evidence that the great day of the Lord's coming is near at hand. We have seen as the Scriptures were reviewed that many promises are left on record telling us that the Master will return in person, and no promise in all the Bible is made more prominent than the ones that assure us that Jesus will come "in the clouds of heaven," attended by "all the holy angels." The words of the Master are familiar, telling us that we should "know that He is near, even at the door," and His apostle declares that "ye, brethren, are not in darkness, that that day should overtake you as a thief."

In view of these scriptures the evidences pointing to the tokens of His coming are abundant and clear.

Some of the evidence that God has given by which we may discern the approach of the end of time, is in the form of connected chains of prophecy. These record in advance the rise, decline, and overthrow of kingdoms and empires, giving a general view of the social and political scenery along the highway of time, ever keeping before us the coming of the Lord when the reign of sin, sorrow, and distress will be ended forever, and the Christ of God will reign supreme. To understand these great chains of prophecy a general knowledge of history is required; but all do not become historians, and therefore those who may be deprived of this historical knowledge may not be able to understand such prophecies; but other evidence that all must see, and that every one may understand, is given by our Heavenly Father.

These chains of prophecy all point to the closing days of time. They tell us how we may know when the last days of earth's history are at hand. But the evidences in addition to these connected lines of prophecy have to do with the last generation of men, the generation that will be living on the earth when the Lord comes. In order that all who are living in that time may have the indisputable evidence that will cause them to "*know*" that He is near," there is given a minute description of the conditions that will prevail in those days. The evidence of the Master's coming must stand above mere conjecture. Those who are without a knowledge of books, as well as the most learned, must be stirred by the unusual things about them and anxious to know their meaning. What the Lord has to offer in the second coming of Christ is of too great value for Him to allow that event to come to the children of men without giving every one a vivid and clear view of the light that heralds its approach.

Leaving to others the work of presenting the chains of prophecy which involve a knowledge of history, these pages will be confined to a consideration of those evidences of His coming which may be seen in the world to-day, even by those deprived of special education or large mental training.*

As this evidence is examined it will be seen that the Scrip-

---

*Thoughts on "Daniel and the Revelation" by the late Prof. Uriah Smith is one of the best books on these chains of prophecy. Professor Smith holds before his readers both the history and the prophecy, and it is a constant delight to observe how perfectly the great hand of Omnipotence has woven them together.

tures foretell a wonderful outpouring of the Spirit of God in the last days, an outpouring which will lead men to proclaim the Gospel of peace and pardon, and the news of the Master's coming, to the ends of the earth. It will be seen that remarkable preparations have been made that this work may be accompished completely and minutely in an incredibly short time. What many persons will be actually saying in the last days is foretold. The prevalence of crime, violence, and vice, and the lack of judgment and justice come under the view of the prophetic eye. There is also mention of the prominence that will be given to the forms of religion and godliness, while the actual living out of the principles in the teaching of Christ will be sadly lacking, the professor of Christianity being given to the love of pleasure rather than to the things of God. The amassing of great wealth, and the consequent labor troubles are very clearly and unmistakably spoken of, as is also the general warlike preparations and conditions that will obtain among all the nations of earth. Even the elements of nature and the very earth itself have their story to tell amid the great chorus of voices which are summoning the universe to witness the dying agonies of everything that pertains to injustice, evil, and sin.

As these fulfilling prophecies are seen and embraced they will fix the countenance in a gaze of exultant joy upon that glorious luminary of hope that pierces the very portals of heaven with its beams of light and happiness; yes, these same prophecies will aid us by the sublime flights of faith to behold the marshalling of the armies of the angels of the Lord as they are making their majestic marches and countermarches before the reviewing stand of the King of kings and Lord of lords, preparatory to attending Him on the consummating mission of sounding the resurrection trumpet and conferring immortality upon every one who is ready to receive the rich gift of heaven.

When this evidence comes fresh to you from the book of God's Word, it will make an impression on your mind. It will, in all probability, present before you some duties to perform that may not seem altogether pleasant at first. And if you are not careful you will find yourself seeking to "argue the case" so as to make it appear to yourself that these things that God is giving to you are not true, and that after all the end of time and the coming of Christ is not so near. Some neighbor or friend, who has not seen the light of God's Word, or who may be resisting that light, will more than likely come along to help you to argue yourself away from the evidence that is so striking and so impressive. But God sends His Spirit to "guide you into all truth," and this messenger that invariably comes with every text of scripture that is allowed to enter the mind will be speaking to you continually in a voice so low that no bystander can hear it, yet it will be so impressive in your own heart and mind that it will be the sounding of a trumpet in the depths of your soul. It is to this combined voice of God's Word and God's Spirit that you are entreated to give heed. These entreaties and evidences from God's Word and through the voice of His Spirit have come to you. You know the pressing weight of their convicting power. This is an evidence that God placed clear beyond the power of mortals right in the very innermost recess of the citadel of your private self. If it is slighted it will be the hardest thing that you will have to meet in the great day of judgment that is even now right upon the world. There may be safety in slighting some of the sayings of men, but when the great Father of us all, even though unseen by the natural eye, speaks to us so plainly that we know of a surety that it is He, it is for our eternal good and everlasting joy that we should attentively listen.

The Good News of the Kingdom Sent to all the World

CHAPTER TEN

OUR Lord is asked by His disciples, "What shall be the sign of Thy coming, and of the end of the world?" Matt. 24:3. In answering this direct question He gives, as one of the signs of His "coming," the fact that "this Gospel of the kingdom shall be preached in all the world for a witness unto all nations; and then shall the end come." Matt. 24:14. Note how plain the Master makes His statement. "The end" will come when His "Gospel of the kingdom shall be preached in *all the world.*"

But consider what a vast work it is to proclaim "this Gospel of the kingdom" to "*all.*" There have stood Africa, India, China, Japan, and all the rest of the countries of the far East, together with many isles of the sea, peopled with their untold millions of souls, who have seemed to be securely shut away by themselves. Satan, it would seem, had been successful in holding them back from any ray of Gospel light. But nevertheless, the Lord has said that His "Gospel of the kingdom" is to go to every nation in "*all* the world." And when the time arrives for its accomplishment, every barrier is broken down, and God provides the means, wonderful though they may have to be, by which His work is to be accomplished. Japan is loosed, the bands of China are broken, the walls of intolerance are made to crumble, and the isles "wait for His law."

Now just so surely as God has spoken this word there will be something seen in the way of giving the Gospel to the world that will be so prominent as to be decidedly striking to every one who will stop long enough to give it consideration. And just as surely as the giving of the Gospel to the world is to constitute one of the prominent evidences that the time has come for the end, even so surely will it be done in such a way as to show the all-pervading presence of Jehovah moving in the majesty of His power in the midst of the great work.

Several very important elements must come together and combine in such a work as giving the Gospel to all the world. In the first place there must be such a breaking down of the walls of intolerance as will permit the Gospel to enter the various kingdoms and countries of the world; then there must be facilities provided by which all the world can be readily reached. When Providence has thus opened the way for men to go to all the world, by breaking up the foundations of intolerance, and by providing means of travel and communication, there must combine with these elements a disposition on the part of a class of the people to give this world-wide Gospel message. Men must actually be filled with the desire to do the work as well as to see the open doors for doing it.

A combination of superstition, intolerance, and ignorance, had built up such a religious despotism by the time of the Middle Ages that it would seem to any observer that all hope of a Gospel message that was to place the offers of divine pardon and salvation before the whole world was securely cut off. But God had spoken the word and the way must be prepared. So in the midst of the darkness of the sixteenth century there broke out that vast spiritual awakening that gave to a great extent intellectual as well as spiritual freedom to all Europe.

The benign work of those years of Gospel seed-sowing produced men in later times who began to have those strong heart-throbbings for the salvation of every one that could be reached in the whole human family. Heaven's longing desire to rescue perishing men began to kindle unquenchable flames of missionary zeal in the devoted minds of the followers of Christ. Charles Wesley set the world to singing —

"Lord of the harvest, hear
   Thy needy servants' cry;
Answer our faith's effectual prayer,
   And all our wants supply.

"On Thee we humbly wait;
   Our wants are in Thy view;
The harvest, truly, Lord, is great,
   The laborers are few.

"Convert and send forth more,
   To spread Thy truth abroad;
And let them speak Thy word of power,
   As workers with their God.

"And though our bodies part,
   To different climes afar,
Still ever joined as one in heart,
   The friends of Jesus are.

"Oh, let us still proceed
   In Jesus' work below;
And, following our triumphant Head,
   To further conquests go."

The work has proceeded till the whole world stands as one vast congregation listening to the Gospel message. From the frigid zones to the torrid, from frosty Greenland and Siberia to Ceylon's isle and Sahara's burning plains, from healthful climes to venom-infested and disease-breathing swamps and jungles, the story of Christ and the Gospel message is to go and is going. Hearts and doors are opening in every land to receive it; men of every land are giving themselves to the work of giving it; and the continual surrender of souls is bearing witness to the efficacy of the work that is being done. But while some are heeding, others are heedless, and are grieving heaven by turning from the message with stony hearts. God will not compel any to accept; but He will have His invitation proclaimed in every clime "for a witness." Only another touch of divine power is needed, and the giving of the message of the Gospel to all the world will be completed; and then, when that work has been accomplished, according to the promise, "shall the end come."

With these facts in general before us, let us pass to the next chapter and consider more in detail what has been done within the last hundred years to prepare things in the world for giving speedily a world wide Gospel proclamation.

CHAPTER ELEVEN

WE are living in an age of wonders. There have been such marvelous changes and developments during the past century that the world of to-day would not be recognized at all by the men who lived and died here a hundred years ago. Even those who have been dead but fifty years, if brought to life now, could hardly be convinced that this is the planet on which they spent their lives. Just imagine their amazement as they would view our "lightning express trains," our steamships, our electric lights, electric cars, telephones, telegraphs, twine-binders, sewing machines, and all the rest of the endless procession of inventions and discoveries that the rushing activity of this generation has produced. Do you ever stop to consider the marvelous changes and advancements of this time? And have you not sometimes reflected on what it may signify?

The *Scientific American* celebrated its fiftieth anniversary by publishing in its issue of July 25, 1896, an outline history of the great advancement in the way of inventions and discoveries during the past fifty years. But in attempting the task the editor said:—
"The material world *has advanced so rapidly* during the *last half* century, and with a pace so accelerated, that mankind has almost lost one of its most important faculties and one essential to happiness,—that of surprise. . . . The most marvelous developments are taken as a matter of course. The condition of things fifty years ago is seldom pictured to the mind; and all the material blessings which we now enjoy are used as conveniences of daily life, and no more. . . . Notwithstanding the pages of matter and quantities of illustrations, we feel that the task of telling about the progress of a lifetime can at the least be only inadequately performed—so much has been done."

Overland in the '40's.

When we consider these wonderful inventions and discoveries, and take into account that these stupendous achievements have nearly all been made during the lives of men now upon the stage of action, well may we ask, What does it all mean? Why were not some of these things invented in former ages? And why has the development not been more gradual? However, instead of any of these great inventions being made in former times, or there being a gradual development in this field during a succession of centuries, it remained for the last half of the nineteenth century suddenly to produce nearly all of this marvelous change.

Again, it is urged that we should pause to inquire, What does it mean? And why have not the intellectual giants of former days discovered these things, or at least produced some of these modern inventions?

It would hardly seem necessary to mention what modern inventions have done to promote travel and international communication, and how the hitherto secluded countries of the East have thereby been drawn into closer relations with the rest of the world. Some men may see in all this nothing more than a vast material progress. But the Lord has said, "This Gospel of the kingdom shall be preached in *all* the world," and how marked is His preparation for His world-wide work! The nations are being stirred. The shackles of that old exclusiveness are being broken, and the inhabitants of every part of the globe are becoming acquainted with each other, preparatory

A REMARKABLE CENTURY.

to that great and final proclamation of "this Gospel of the kingdom."

The very fact, as has been pointed out in preceding chapters, that Christ has given His sure promise to come again, should be evidence to us that He will have that coming heralded to the ends of the earth. But we see that He does not leave us thus to conjecture. He tells us plainly that "this Gospel of the kingdom" shall be preached for a witness in all the world, and "then shall the end come." God has a time in mind when He will send His Son in person to earth again; and the signs foretelling that much-to-be-desired event must be given to every nation, else they could not have the opportunity to "*know* that He is near."

Overland in the '90's.

With some of the most populous nations groping in heathen darkness, and because of the barriers of religious intolerance isolated from the Christian portion of the world, as they were seventy-five years ago, and with the means of travel and communications existing in those days, how could such a vast work be accomplished? But God has promised to give the Gospel to every nation; and to accomplish such an immense work we would expect to see correspondingly great facilities.

Who can fail to see the marvelous preparations that are even now being made? Those who are wholly absorbed in the things of this life may fail to note the sublimity of the plan that is now being worked out in the wonders of this age; yet here are the facts in striking reality. We should not become so absorbed in the mere use of the unprecedented inventions and discoveries of our day as to lose sight of the divine purpose for which they are so wondrously bestowed upon the world.

In this connection we should observe that *the most notable, the most useful, and the most highly perfected of the inventions of this time are particularly and peculiarly adapted to assist in giving the Gospel message in all the earth.* The printing-press is a marvel of ingenuity and perfection. It has been developed until there is no limit to the printed pages that it may produce. Then, to carry this matter when printed, the "flying express" trains and the "ocean greyhounds" have been provided. In collecting the news and discussions of the world, the printing-press has a most potent companion, the electric telegraph, that simply annihilates time and space in despatching the doings and sayings of all the world to the editor's desk in the twinkling of an eye. The press — the mighty educator — is doing its work. The fast mails are carrying its products to all the world. No one thing absorbs the efforts of the press more than the promulgation of the Gospel of the kingdom. Do you not see what it signifies?

There can be no ground for doubt in regard to the meaning and purpose of the inventions and discoveries that have marked this generation as the wonder of all ages. But read another direct prophecy upon this point: "But thou, O Daniel, shut up the words, and seal the book, even to the time of the end ; many shall run to and fro, and knowledge shall be increased." Dan. 12 : 4.

The command is given to "shut up the words and seal the book." But till what time are they thus "shut up" and "sealed"? "Even to the time of the end." It will be noticed that the scripture does not say "the end," nor "the end of time," but "the time of the end;" that is, a brief period before "the *end*," in which great and striking changes are to take place, by which we are to know that "the end" is fast approaching. That time

A REMARKABLE CENTURY 83

is to be particularly marked by the "many" who "*shall run to and fro*," and, further, by the fact that "knowledge shall be increased."

The book of Daniel, from which the foregoing text is quoted, gives the prophetic outline of the history of the world from the days of the old Babylonian Empire down to the end of time. In the very nature of things the prophecy could not be understood until the events predicted should be sufficiently fulfilled to enable the individual to take up the thread of the prophetic narrative. Hence God's command to the prophet to seal the book till the time of the end—till the time when the prophecy should be sufficiently a matter of history that the meaning of it could be grasped. In other words our Heavenly Father gave the prophet a view of the history of the world, when that history was yet future, and told him to place the divine seal upon it, closing it until the time when it would be needed,—"the time of the end."

The Brooklyn Bridge.

Bible students are quite generally agreed that the running to and fro spoken of in this text refers to a great awakening in the study of the Bible, particularly its prophetic portions, when the time of the end is reached. Doctor Adam Clarke, in commenting on the text, says, "Many shall endeavor to search out the sense; and knowledge shall be increased—by this means. Though the meaning shall not be *fully* known till the events take place; THEN the seal shall be broken; and the sense becomes plain." "Many shall give their sedulous attention to these things," is the manner in which another student expresses it. When the unfolding of events in the things of this world have broken the seal from the prophecy so that men may readily understand it, still it will be necessary for them to give their "sedulous attention" to the words of the prophet in order to see what God has so plainly revealed. It will be necessary to "search out the sense" if we would grasp the majestic sweep of the prophecy.

"This Gospel of the kingdom" that the Master tells us shall be "preached in all the world for a witness," in the very nature of things must embrace a definite and clear presentation of what the kingdom of the Lord is. It must herald to the world the Lord's express revelation concerning the kingdom

The "Lucania."

that He promises in this world-wide Gospel message. "Many shall endeavor to search out the sense," and to fully understand the prophecies that tell us that the kingdom of the King of eternity is at hand. As the prophecies in all their fulness are seen; as a realizing sense of the perfect fitting together of prophecy and history comes into the mind; and, especially, as it is seen that every striking feature that marks the world of to-day has been completely photographed by the prophets hundreds of years ago, the hearts of men will be stirred by a superhuman power to lift their voices like trumpets as they tell to every creature in all the world that the glorious joys of eternity are here. "Sedulous attention" is given, the book is searched, and the message is proclaimed. Such is the program that the Book of books outlines, and

The ship of yesterday

such are the thrilling events and issues that are even now right before the men and women who are upon the stage of action.

How perfectly does this prophecy coincide and combine with the promise that the Gospel of the kingdom shall be preached in all the world. The one is a promise of what shall be done, and the other tells us how men will get their inspiration for such a vast work. By giving their sedulous attention to searching out the sense of the prophecies they will see that the time has come for the end of all things, and the Gospel will be proclaimed to all with the great power that attends the definite knowledge that is based on the sure word of prophecy.

There are some, however, who have thought that this running "to and fro" spoken of by the prophet has an application and a more literal fulfilment in the great facilities for travel and communication that have been developed within the last half century. But while it would seem perfectly clear from a careful study of the text that it has reference to an unusual awakening in the study of the prophecy that was sealed till the "time of the end," yet we have only to look out upon the world to-day to see the literal running to and fro upon the earth. Mankind has ever been inclined to move from place to place, but never before have there been such facilities for travel and communication as have been provided in this generation. The persons are still living who tell us that they well remember when their journeying had to be done on foot, or on horseback, or by the stage-coach. Hence, of necessity, men were quite closely confined to one locality. But how is it now? If it is desired to cross the continent, instead of the journey requiring six months or more, as in the time of our

Ocean liner leaving dock.

fathers, we step on the "lightning express," and in four or five days are whirled from ocean to ocean. By the steel rail, traversed by the "flying" railway palace, every city, village, and hamlet is brought into speedy communication each with the other. To-day the dweller in New York or Boston speaks of a trip to Chicago or San Francisco about as our fathers talked of a journey to a neighboring village or an adjoining county.

The improvement in travel by sea has been equally great. Fifty years ago a ship could accommodate only a few score passengers. These were slowly dragged across the ocean in "cramped, ill-lighted, and stuffy cabins" upon the old-fashioned sailboats or the primitive paddle-wheel steamers that were then just coming into use. But to-day over two thousand persons can have all the accommodations of a first-class modern hotel in one of our large ocean steamships, and they are carried in a few days from shore to shore across the expansive ocean. Thus the nations of all the world are brought together as next-door neighbors.

A great railway station.

With all this provision for travel by both land and sea, and with the great mass of our fellow-men who are continually going from place to place in pursuit of business or pleasure, how complete are the facilities for giving this Gospel of the kingdom to all the world! Who can estimate the millions of people that are at this moment in motion on railway and steamship? The *Railway Age* informs us that the railroad travel in the United States alone for the year 1897 was equivalent to thirteen billion persons traveling by rail one mile each. And it is readily seen from these enormous figures that enough traveling was done in this country during that one year to have given each of the seventy million men, women, and children residing here, a ride of one hundred and eighty-five miles.

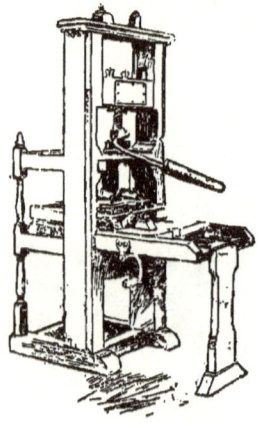

The old "Franklin hand-press."

Further mention, however, should be made of the high state of perfection to which the printing-press has attained. For, as already intimated, it has been and ever will be, a most potent factor in spreading "this Gospel of the kingdom." Although printing has been done for several hundred years, it remained for the last half of the nineteenth century to reduce it to one of the fine arts, and at the same time provide ingenious and rapid presses that are capable of printing several million pages of matter in a single day. The old "Franklin hand-press," with but few improvements and modifications, was the best that had been produced at the beginning of our century. But the first half of this century witnessed some very decided advancements in the printing-press. These improvements, however, were only prophetic indications of what was to be accomplished in the last forty or fifty years.

Franklin's press, which was decidedly useful and a great wonder in his day, stands now in the National Museum simply as a curiosity. Passing down the long list of improvements that have been made in the printing-press since Franklin's time, we are brought to something more marvelous by far than any of the famous "seven wonders" of the ancient world. We refer to the octuple press, invented by Richard M. Hoe. This most ingenious machine has a capacity for printing ninety-six thousand copies per hour, or sixteen hundred per minute, of any of the great eight-page daily newspapers. The paper is reeled off a roll, and travels through the press at the amazing speed of thirty-two and one-half miles an hour. This is a fair speed for a passenger train. The press is constructed so that it prints both sides of the paper as it glides through, and an ingenious attachment automatically cuts apart, pastes, folds, and counts the papers. Two young men have to work quite briskly in taking the papers away from the press as they are printed.

"Imagine Franklin's surprise if he were now awakened."

Robert Fulton.

Samuel F. B. Morse.

Peter Cooper.

Imagine Franklin's surprise if he were now wakened from his short sleep of a hundred years, and brought at once into the presence of this most wonderful perfecting press. What would be his amazement to watch it, acting with all the precision and seeming intelligence of a human being, as it printed, cut, folded, and counted more papers per minute than the historic press he produced could deliver in a whole day!

Without these modern perfecting "presses" the "great dailies," some of them with a circulation of nearly a million every twenty-four hours, and being frequently required to print over a million a day on special occasions, could not, at a merely nominal price, emanate from our large cities to greet the intelligent reading public of our time. And while speaking of the daily newspaper, we should also take into account the modern facilities for printing and circulating magazines, books, pamphlets, and tracts. With all these things before us, is it not forcibly impressed upon the mind that the preparation for placing a knowledge of "this Gospel of the kingdom" before all the world in a very short time is most ample and complete?

But, notwithstanding the far-reaching possibilities of the printing-

A REMARKABLE CENTURY

press, what could it accomplish if the great mass of the people were unable to read, as was the case a century or so ago? And here, again, we may note, as one of the wonders of our time, the world-wide enthusiasm that is thrown into the work of educating all the people, at least so far as to enable them to readily read and write. The *nation* that does not provide a good common-school education for all of its common people is already marked to withdraw in disgrace from the marching columns of progress, while the *individual* who is not able to read at least in his native tongue, is looked upon with pity, and often with disgust and reproach.

Charles Goodyear.

Sir Henry Bessemer.

Here, again, our minds are forcibly drawn back to the prophecy that at "the time of the end, many shall run to and fro, and knowledge shall be increased." A knowledge of this great prophecy that is for this "time of the end" could only be possible in a time when there was a general diffusion of education, so that men might read and understand. How perfectly do the parts of this great prophetic structure come together! The press prints the books, the magazines, the papers, in such abundance that all can have access to them, and then a mighty wave of education places within the

C. H. M Cormick.

reach of all the people the ability and opportunity of reading them.

While considering the marvelous capacity of the printing-press, we should not lose sight of the most ample provision that has been made for gathering intelligence from every nook and corner of the whole earth. It was on May 24, 1844, that the famous message, "What hath God wrought!" was suggested by Miss Ellsworth, and flashed by the electric current from Washington to Baltimore; and since that date the applied genius and business activity of such men as Morse, Edison, Delaney, Stearns, Field, Cooper, Mackay, and others, have not only threaded the several continents of our world with the electric telegraph, but have connected these continents by the ocean cable, so that the inhabitants of the entire globe are made to seem to each other as dwellers of the same village; for the doings to-day of those living in the United States are cabled to the Old World at once, and may be read immediately in the columns of their daily papers; while an account of what is occurring in Europe, Asia, Africa, South America, and even far-off Australia and the isles of the sea, comes gliding over the wires to us, and we are reading all the doings of those distant lands in just a few moments after the deeds are done.

James Watt.

Thomas Edison

The inspired words that were chosen as the first telegraphic message come vividly to mind again; for we may well say, "What hath God wrought!" How marvelous indeed are the preparations that the Lord has made to proclaim to all the world that most precious promise, "I will come again." And with all these modern facilities for communicating knowledge, how literally will God fulfil His Word, "This Gospel of the kingdom shall be preached in *all the world* for a witness unto *all nations.*" God has a precious message for "*all the world.*" It is not a part merely that is to be reached; but *all* are to hear the welcome tidings that Jesus is coming again. How impressive, how abundant, how perfect, are the preparations to give to *all* the good news of our Master's return! The whole world, by means of the railway, the steamship, the printing-press, and the telegraph, are brought into communication *as one* great assembly, and are now hearing the message from God's own Word that the Saviour is about to come.

Cyrus W. Field.

Laying the Atlantic cable.

The facilities for carrying God's message being so abundantly prepared, we should begin to watch for the next step in the divinely complete plan. This Gospel of the kingdom will inevitably "come to the front, and become the theme of world-wide discussion, if necessary, even through the contempt that is placed upon it." Every phase of God's great truth for

The combined harvester and thresher, drawn by traction engine.

these last days will be considered and reconsidered, and men will rapidly range themselves on one side or the other of the great question involved; and when this intense discussion reaches the point where it is an issue in every part of the globe, how swiftly will the Gospel do its work!

Until recently Spain was quietly moving along, attracting but little interest or attention outside her own borders. But no sooner is war declared with the United States than all the world becomes interested in the conflict. In both the Old

World and the New the papers are eagerly sought every morning, and crowds watch the bulletin-boards all through the day to see what are the latest movements of the contending forces. The history of the two countries is studied anew; the dust-covered geographies and maps are brought out, and many who were not aware of the existence of the Canaries, the Ladrones, the Philippines, or the Carolines, are now familiar with the fact that they are islands that for many years have been under the dominion of Spain; and so it is with the dominion and affairs of China, Japan, Korea, Russia, India, Thibet or any of the countries or events that can claim the attention of the public for the time being.

Now, when the spark of divine power shall set all the modern agencies in motion, how swiftly must the Master's last great work be done! Those who have been unfamiliar with the Bible will learn of its contents; they will see the clear evidence that surrounds us showing that the Saviour is about to return; and only a very short time will be required for each individual to come to the place where he will make his final stand for or against the Lord's Christ.

CHAPTER TWELVE

RECALLING again the prophecy of Dan. 12:4, let us study it anew. The prophet states that "knowledge shall be increased," and it should not be overlooked that this is to be in "the time of the end."

As has already been suggested, this scripture foreshadows a general intelligence among the people at the time when the prophecy applies; but for its direct and literal fulfilment we must look for a movement that brings the Bible itself within the reach of every one. For it is the Bible that contains the message and promises of "this Gospel of the kingdom." As we look for this thing in particular we find that among all the great marvels of this marvelous age of material development, progress, and invention, nothing stands out more clearly or more strongly than the facts concerning the vast number of copies of the Word of God that have been printed and circulated during the past few decades.

Notwithstanding the interest that had been awakened in the Scriptures by the Reformation, the beginning of the nineteenth century found Bibles still so scarce, and the price so high, that but very few individuals could afford a copy of the sacred Book; and oftentimes persons would walk miles to have an opportunity of hearing the Bible read.

But in March, 1804, the British and Foreign Bible Society was organized; the American Bible Society was founded in May, 1816; and in connection with these two leading societies, hundreds of auxiliary societies have been formed, all with the one purpose in view of placing the Bible in the hands of all the people in both civilized and heathen lands. Through the combined efforts of all engaged in this work, the Bible, either entire or in parts, is now read in over four hundred languages and dialects. It is being printed at the rate of six million two hundred fifty thousand copies a year; and over three hundred million copies have been circulated since the British and Foreign Bible Society was organized in 1804.

For the first fifteen hundred years of the Christian era only a very few persons could afford a complete copy of the Bible. The Reformation came, however, and awakened a deep interest in it; and while men were able, with the crude printing facilities of those times, to produce a limited number of copies entire, yet they could not nearly supply the demand. The cost of printing and binding with the means at hand previous to this century was ever a strong barrier against placing the sacred Book in the hands of all the people. Then, too, the generous-hearted men had not yet arisen who would devote their lives and their fortunes to the work of giving the Bible to all, and in the familiar language of their native land.

"Fifty years ago . . . grain was cut with . . . cradle-scythe."

But, lo! "the time of the end" arrives; and by a touch of supernatural power the sleepy world that has been dreamily moving along, with but very few improvements in its material life to break the tedious monotony, suddenly becomes intensely agitated. Within the short span of a single lifetime the printing-press is brought to a marvelous perfection; the railway and the steamship within the same time are developed to the point where they seem to carry us from place to place as on the wings of the wind; electricity conveys our thoughts from city to city and from continent to continent with the speed of lightning; and then the Word of God, which is the great fountain of knowledge, is printed by the million, and all these agencies spring forward to swiftly carry it to the nations and tongues of the earth.

How literal, how complete, how marvelous, is the fulfilment of that divine prediction that in "the time of the end" "knowledge shall be increased"! That Word which makes it possible for us to know the promise of the coming One; that Word which reveals to us the evidences by which we may know that we are in "the time of the end;" that Word which gives "this Gospel of the kingdom;" that Word which is indeed a veritable lamp unto our feet, and a light unto our path, disclosing to our otherwise be-

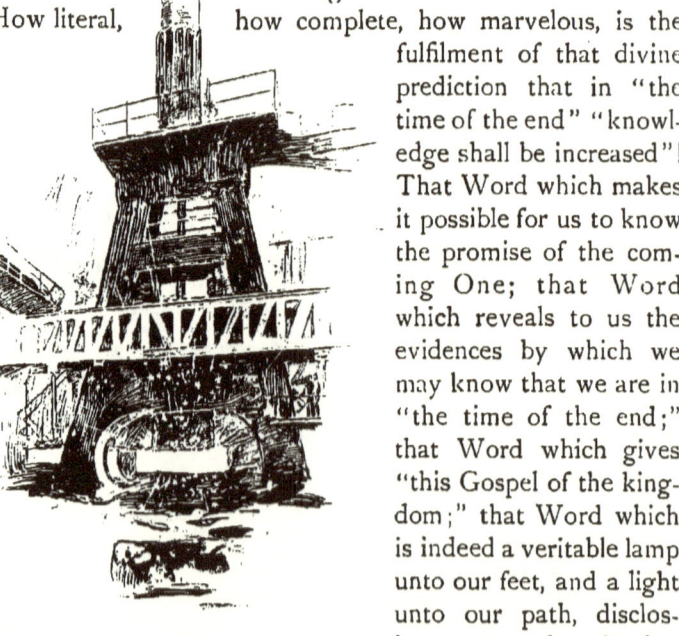

The steam hammer at work.

"The hammer, anvil, and forge."

nighted vision what the marvels of our day really mean —that Word is now, by the multiplied millions, scattered in all the world. Those who have means may purchase it at the most reasonable prices, while the generosity of our great Bible societies has provided it "without money and without price" to those too poor or too indifferent to buy. God has surely done His part. He has fulfilled His prophetic promises so completely that we should be led in wonder and adoration to acknowledge their literal truth.

While mentioning particularly the wonderful inventions of our time which make it possible for "this Gospel of the kingdom" to speedily reach the remotest boundaries of earth, it may not be out of place to note, in passing, what has been accomplished in general in the great field of learning, discovery, and invention. It would be a wearisome task, however, even if space permitted, to make the merest mention of all that has been done. Vast and varied, almost beyond description, are the achievements of this age. Yet the

"Boots and shoes were slowly made by hand."

people are so intent on driving their business or reveling in their pleasures that they are scarcely conscious of the surpassing realities of to-day.

A few contrasts will perhaps serve best to bring the conditions and attainments of this time vividly before the mind:—

The knitting-machine.

Fifty years ago the simple needle and thimble were the implements with which the housewife did her sewing; to-day she has a machine to do this work for her.

Fifty years ago our stockings were knit by hand; to-day a girl with her knitting-machine can knit more stockings in a day than a whole neighborhood of women could have done in those times.

Fifty years ago all our grain was cut with sickle or cradle-scythe, and our hay mowed by hand; to-day the farmer has his mowing-machine, and that marvel of modern ingenuity, the combination reaper and twine-binder, and the combined harvester and thresher.

Fifty years ago our mothers and sisters took the wool and flax, spun the thread, and wove the cloth that made our clothes; now the spinning-wheel and hand-loom are relegated to the curiosity-shop, and the steam loom, with its associated machinery, is doing the work.

"Our stockings were knit by hand."

Fifty years ago the carpenter had to plane his boards, match his flooring, make his doors, sash, and, in fact, work out practically all his building material by hand; now a great variety of wood-working machinery does about all his work for him, with accuracy and workmanlike beauty.

Fifty years ago the hammer, anvil, and forge were the principal instruments for making things from iron; but the forge and anvil have only a modest and obscure corner in the modern shop, while numerous kinds of iron-working machines are rolling out the work.

"To-day she has a machine."

Fifty years ago, with hammer, awl, last, and pegs, our boots and shoes were slowly made by hand; to-day machinery makes our footwear with a speed and deftness that are truly amazing.

Fifty years ago all our writing was done with the pen; to-day the typewriter does it much more neatly and rapidly.

Then we spent our evenings in the dim light of the tallow candle; now the kerosene lamp, gas, or electric light transforms darkness into almost the brilliant light of day.

But, not to make this comparison tedious, it may be said in a word, Let the progress of the past fifty years be destroyed, and we would have taken from us practically such other inventions and discoveries as the telephone, cable and electric street-cars, vulcanized rubber goods, photo-engraving, photo-lithographing, the kodak, the gas engine, the passenger elevator, asphalt pavement, the steam fire-engine, the triple-expansion steam-engine, the Gifford injector, cellu-

"The simple needle and thimble were the implements."

loid, barbed-wire fences, time-locks for safes, kerosene oil and gas wells, machines for making ice, the phonograph, the graphophone, stem-winding watches, the great suspension bridges, steel-frame buildings, ironclad war-ships, revolvers, breech-loading guns, magazine guns, Gatling guns, machine guns, torpedoes, linotype machines, wireless telegraphy, the knowledge of microbes and disease germs, together with a myriad of other things in the medical line, discoveries without number in the general field of science, air brakes, nitroglycerine, acetylene, dynamite and guncotton, Bessemer and Harveyized and Kruppized steel, the automobile and motorcycle, argon, polonium, radium, etc., etc., etc.

"The carpenter had to . . . get out practically everything by hand"

It is useless to enumerate further. So great has been the activity in this field of invention and discovery, so vast have been the achievements, that the mind becomes weary in contemplating the endless array.

"The dim light of the tallow candle."

The remarkable part of it all is that men still living can trace from memory all these great changes and developments that enter into this wonderful age. Mr. Edward W. Byrn, A. M., has well said that "the past fifty years represent an epoch of invention and progress unique in the history of the world. It is something more than a merely normal growth or natural development. It has been a gigantic wave of human ingenuity and resource, so stupendous in its magnitude, so complex in its diversity, so profound in its thought, so fruitful in its wealth, so beneficent in its results, that the mind is strained and embarrassed in its efforts to expand to a full appreciation of it. Indeed, the period seems a grand climax of discovery, rather than increment of growth. . . . The negative conditions of that period extend into such an appalling void that we stop short, shrinking from the thought of what it would mean to modern civilization to eliminate from its life those potent factors of its existence."

"Fifty years ago all our writing was done with the pen."

Standing in full view of all these things, can there be any doubt that we are in the "time of the end"? As we see how literally all the world has been brought together by these modern inventions, can there be any doubt that the Master has made ample provision to have "this Gospel of the kingdom preached in all the world for a witness unto all nations"? And just as soon as the world hears the joyful message of "His glorious appearing," "*then shall the end come.*"

The gladdest of all glad days is almost here. On every hand may be seen and heard the heralds of the morning. And by every one of these heralds we are invited to get ready to sit as joyful guests at the

"To-day the typewriter does it much more rapidly."

"marriage supper of the Lamb." The invitation is now being proclaimed in all the world; and it reads, "And the Spirit and the bride say, Come. And let him that heareth say, Come. And let him that is athirst come. And whosoever will, let him take the water of life freely." Rev. 22:17.

All are invited guests. Will not you allow the sinner's Friend, your Saviour, to robe you in the wedding garment for that feast? "In Thy presence is fulness of joy; at Thy right hand there are pleasures forevermore." Ps. 16:11.

"Sing unto the Lord with the harp; let the sea roar; let the floods clap their hands, and the hills be joyful."

CHAPTER THIRTEEN

THE developments that mark this as the most wonderful age of all time are well known; but men are generally so intent in observing and enjoying the material advancement that has been made that they do not realize that this century has been as wondrously marked by its missionary operations as by its advancement in discovery and invention.

Notwithstanding the fact that the Reformation of the sixteenth century was one of the greatest periods of spiritual activity in the church since the days of the apostles, yet there was connected with it no suggestion or movement worthy of mention, in the direction of carrying the Gospel to the outlying heathen lands. The burden of the Reformers seemed to be to urge the saving Gospel upon the church itself; for the professed Christianity of that time was so formal and dead, so spiritually blind and ignorant, and so full of superstition, that it really stood on a level with, if not below, the non-professing heathenism of India, China, and Japan.

The importance and necessity of sending missionaries to the countries where the Gospel light had not gone, was suggested by individuals at different times, and urged upon the attention of the church; but the way was not yet opened for this work to begin in earnest. God did not have either agents or agencies prepared; for mankind had sunk so low that several centuries of the full blaze of Gospel truth were needed to fit them for the work of evangelizing the heathen world. Such missionary efforts as were put forth during the seventeenth and eighteenth centuries partook in too many instances of the forceful methods that were employed in the darker ages. Speaking of some of the missionaries of the seventeenth century, a historian tells us: "We know that unevangelical means were soon employed, as in Ceylon, where the Dutch governor made the tenure of even the lowest governmental position, and even the governmental protection, conditional upon signing the Helvetic Confession. Thousands pressed to baptism, which was denied to no one who could repeat the Lord's Prayer and the Ten Commandments."

Bible House, New York.

Thus the greater part of the missionary work that was attempted in those times partook more of the nature of politics than of the presentation of the pure, free, saving Gospel of Jesus Christ.

But during the latter part of the eighteenth century the Wesleys, Whitefield, and others were doing their mighty work. The voyages and discoveries of Captain Cook imparted a new interest to what seemed then to be the "far-away" portions of the world, and to the islands of the sea as well. When the nineteenth century entered upon its altogether unprecedented career, Andrew Fuller, William Carey, John Williams, Judson, and numerous other devoted missionaries, with earnestness and intelligent zeal, and the throbbings of Christian love, stood ready to plant the banner of the cross in every dark corner of the inhabited globe.

As those devoted men, with their no less devoted wives, entered upon their great work, observe how rapidly God moved upon other minds to prepare the needed facilities for carrying "this Gospel of the kingdom" with rapidity into "all the world," for a "witness unto all nations." While Carey, Judson, and Williams were planting the banner of the cross in the very strongholds of the barbarous and heathen lands; Charles, and Farn, and Hughes, and Steinkoph, and Owen, and Wilberforce, and Mills, and Boudinot, with many others, were laying the broad and deep foundations for the British and Foreign and the American Bible Societies.

As late as 1777, while the Revolutionary War was in progress, Congress was memorialized to print thirty thousand Bibles to supply the demand. But a lack of both paper and type made it impossible for this work to be done; so the Committee on Commerce was empowered to import from Holland, Scotland, or elsewhere, twenty thousand copies, at the expense of Congress. But they were also unable to carry out this scheme.

In 1794, at the age of ten, Mary Jones, a little Welsh girl, began to lay by all the money she could possibly save, with which to purchase a Bible. In 1800, after six years of careful saving, she found herself in possession of the required sum. She walked twenty-five miles to Bala, the residence of Rev. Thomas Charles, to whom she had been directed. "When she first applied to Mr. Charles, and was told that the few copies he had were reserved for persons who had already made application for them, she burst into tears and sobs. The fond hope of years seemed to be blasted in a moment. These evidences of her sad disappointment led Mr. Charles at length to say, 'My dear child, difficult as it is to spare you one, it is impossible — yes, simply impossible — to refuse you.' And so she obtained the Bible, which, for the sixty-six remaining years of her life, was her most cherished possession."

This was the condition a hundred years ago in the British Isle, the very home of Bible houses and Bible societies. Eighteen hundred years of the Christian era had passed away, and still the vital germs of Gospel truth had been so combated by the gross darkness of superstitious error that it was with the greatest difficulty and sacrifice that one of God's children could procure a copy of His Word.

Bibles in those times, neither in this country nor abroad, were supplied in sufficient quantities or at a price low enough for the poor to possess copies of the Sacred Word; but the Bible societies that sprang into existence during the first two decades of the nineteenth century were not long in providing facilities for placing the Bible in every home of the whole wide world. In 1806 the British and Foreign Bible Society was able to send its first wagon-load of Bibles into Wales. "It was received like the ark of the covenant; and the people, with shouts of great joy, dragged it into the city." But to-day car-load after car-load is shipped from the storerooms of our great Bible societies, and Wales is not alone in rejoicing over supplies of the Book of books.

Missionaries have gone to many heathen tribes that had no literature, and consequently no written language. These faithful messengers of the Gospel have patiently labored until they have reduced these tribal dialects to a written speech, and then have translated the Scriptures into the words that these people can comprehend. And now in every nation, also in the islands of the oceans, in over four hundred languages and dialects, the Bible is being furnished by millions of copies. Over ninety million dollars was expended by our Heaven-appointed Bible societies during the nineteenth century in giving the Scriptures to those who were destitute of the true riches offered in the divine precepts and promises.

What an undertaking it was thus to give the Word of God to all the world! And how miraculous is the success with which it has been performed! All through the dark centuries indestructible and all-powerful truth was only waiting for a sufficient soil to be prepared in which to find a lodgment; and then, towering up in its stupendous growth, it outstrips all the marvels of all the ages.

These favorable conditions were not reached, however, until "the time of the end;" but that time having arrived, the whole world is stirred to perform God's great work. The teaching of the Man of Nazareth and Galilee plows its way through mental rubbish that is piled centuries high.

British and Foreign Bible Society's Building, London.

The light of the eternal day breaks in upon longing hearts in England, in Germany, in Switzerland, and the Gospel enters upon its civilizing, liberating, and elevating work that is to reach "every nation" in "all the world." Bible societies spring up, and millions of copies of the Sacred Volume are speedily prepared. The poor seeker after divine truth need no longer walk twenty-five miles with the careful savings of six long years, only to be well-nigh disappointed in securing the valued treasure. No, indeed! Missionaries, with their hearts all aflame with love for their unfortunate fellow-creatures, gather up the stream of Bibles that pours from the press, and every corner of the world is visited, and the Book of books is offered, yea, urged upon all.

Carey was not afraid to encounter hardships in carrying the Gospel to India; courageous John Williams did not hesitate to plant the standard of the cross on the cannibal islands of the Pacific; Robert Morrison left his friends and native land behind him while he went to China, and devoted his life to giving the Scriptures to that people in their native tongue; and Japan, after a hard struggle, in which many devoted Christian men and women have lost their lives, has opened her doors to receive the Word of God.

Corner in Bible storeroom — British and Foreign Bible Society.

This opening of the doors of progress to receive the Gospel light is not confined to what have been termed these more benighted heathen lands of the distant Orient; but the countries of Europe and western Asia that have refused to discuss matters of religion with the rest of the world, and that have shut away the missionaries who came to bring them light and truth, have one after another been opening their doors. Even Russia, that has been generally considered one of the most despotic and intolerant powers, has bowed her head before the influences with which heaven is flooding the world, and the Czar, thus moved, has, by his ukase of religious toleration, nominally conceded to his subjects the right to follow the dictates of conscience in worshiping God; and also by the greater liberties he has granted to the agencies of the press. Even Tibet is required to come forth from her stubborn seclusion, so that her inhabitants may enjoy their right of the divine invitation to join the throng that will soon be brought into the joys of heaven. Thus nation after nation, island after island, have been entered, until nearly the whole world has the Scriptures of truth. The separating and hindering walls of religious despotism are being overthrown, and the King whose mighty scepter touches every world in all the universe is leveling the way so that His great commission can speedily and surely meet its fulfilment in an accomplished work. "This Gospel of the kingdom" will soon be proclaimed in all the earth, and "then shall the end come."

Do we hear it said that it is just a coincidence that the nineteenth century should have been the great century of missionary activity; that it should have been the great century of Bible societies; that it should have been the great century of the printing-press, so that these Bible societies could have the sacred Book in quantities that are inexhaustible; that

British and Foreign Bible Society, Shanghai, China.

it should have been the great century of the railroad, so that missionaries could have visited every family in every country place, hamlet, village, and city; that it should have been the great century of the steamship, so that every outlying habitable island is reached; also that it should have been the century of every other one of the multiplied wonders of this marvelous age?

Well, it may be best to acknowledge that this is indeed a coincidence; but back of all this stupendous array of coincidences there is the manifest working of the all-powerful hand of Divinity. Stop! Look around you! Is it not evident that "this Gospel of the kingdom" is doing its final witnessing in "all the world"? Is there not a prodigious "increase of knowledge," so vast in its proportions that even our quickened imaginations can scarcely reach beyond it? These are some among the many heralds of the breaking morn.

Bible cart, Japan.

Take time to think of it. The organized Bible societies alone circulated over three hundred million copies of the Bible in that remarkable nineteenth century. They have translated it into more than four hundred languages and dialects; and, too, it should be stated that this does not include the large number of Bibles that have been printed and scattered by private firms. Surely these figures are significant in themselves alone. But when seen in the light of God's prophetic Word, they speak in no uncertain language.

"For the Word of God is quick, and powerful, and sharper than any two-edged sword, piercing even to the dividing asunder of soul and Spirit, and of the joints and marrow, and is a discerner of the thoughts and intents of the heart." Heb. 4:12.
"Being born again, not of corruptible seed, but of incorruptible, by the Word of God, which liveth and abideth forever. For all flesh is as grass, and all the glory of man as the flower of grass. The grass withereth, and the flower thereof falleth away; but the Word of the Lord endureth forever. And this is the Word which by the Gospel is preached unto you." 1 Peter 1:23-25. "For My thoughts are not your thoughts, neither are your ways My ways, saith the Lord. For as the heavens are higher than the earth, so are My ways higher than your ways, and My thoughts than your thoughts. For as the rain cometh down, and the snow from heaven, and returneth not thither, but watereth the earth, and maketh it bring forth and bud, that it may give seed to the sower, and bread to the eater; *so shall My Word be that goeth forth out of My mouth: it shall not return unto Me void, but it shall accomplish that which I please, and it shall prosper in the thing whereto I sent it.* For ye shall go out with joy, and be led forth with peace; the mountains and the hills shall break forth before you into singing, and all the trees of the field shall clap their hands. Instead of the thorn shall come up the fir tree, and instead of the brier shall come up the myrtle tree; and it shall be to the Lord for a name, for an everlasting sign that shall not be cut off." Isa. 55:8-13. Such is the language of our heavenly Father's decree. His Word *shall not return unto Him void.* And just so surely as this is the decree of the Omnipotent One, so sure may we be that the present scattering of the Bible throughout the world is the seed-sowing of the "Gospel of the kingdom." This work of sowing is now well along. The Master says when it is finished, "then shall the end come." He has told us, "The harvest is the end of the world." Matt.

13:39. What a glorious end that will be! It is not the end of joy, but the end of misery, and woe, and despair, and sin; and, while it is the end of all these things, it is also the beginning of the undisturbed bliss of that happy life the confines of which are the farther shores of eternity. What good news this is! Join in the chorus, and swell the song until every listening ear and waiting heart is reached.

Bible boat, Siam.

CHAPTER FOURTEEN

THE prophetic Word is explicit in telling us of the "increase of knowledge" at "the time of the end;" it also tells us of the closing triumphs of the Gospel as it is "preached in all the world for a witness unto all nations." There is a wonderful weight of evidence in those two predictions alone; but still further and more minute particulars are presented in the inspired Book. It is not by disconnected and meager evidence that we are shown that the great day of the Lord is near; but one after another the striking characteristics of the "last days" are pointed out. All may see these things and thus "know," if they so desire, "when He is near."

It seems wonderful that God should have told hundreds of years ago just what many of the people would be saying in the last days; but such is the literal truth. Upon this point carefully read the following scripture: —

"And it shall come to pass in the last days, that the mountain of the Lord's house shall be established in the top of the mountains, and shall be exalted above the hills; and all nations shall flow unto it. And many people shall go and say, Come ye, and let us go up to the mountain of the Lord, to the house of the

God of Jacob; and He will teach us of His ways, and we will walk in His paths: for out of Zion shall go forth the law, and the word of the Lord from Jerusalem. And He shall judge among the nations, and shall rebuke many people; and they shall beat their swords into plowshares, and their spears into pruning-hooks; nation shall not lift up sword against nation, neither shall they learn war any more. O house of Jacob, come ye, and let us walk in the light of the Lord." Isa. 2:2-5.

The first sentence in this scripture tells very plainly when the prophecy will be fulfilled. In the clearest and simplest language we are informed of what "shall come to pass in the last days." Now observe particularly that "*many people shall go and say*" certain things. Do not make the mistake of supposing that God says these things; for He does not. The Lord is simply telling us in advance what "many *people* shall go and say" "in the last days."

The reader will observe that these people say, "Come ye, and let us go up to the mountain of the Lord, to the house of the God of Jacob; and He will teach us of His ways, and we will walk in His paths; for out of Zion shall go forth the law, and the word of the Lord from Jerusalem." These words are spoken by professors of religion. They talk of going to the house of God, and of being taught of His ways.

Continuing, these "people" say further of the Lord that "He shall judge among the nations, and shall rebuke many people; and they shall beat their swords into plowshares, and their spears into pruning-hooks; nation shall not lift up sword against nation, neither shall they learn war any more." The Lord does not tell us that these things that "many people shall go and say" are the truth. He simply tells us that they will say them, and also when they will say them.

It shows that the heavenly Father can read the future perfectly when He tells twenty-five hundred years or more in advance even the sayings of the people in the last days. And this prophecy of Isaiah is repeated almost word for word by the prophet Micah in the fourth chapter of his book, thus showing that God revealed these same things to more than one of His prophets.

Having learned in the foregoing paragraphs what the Lord tells us the people will be saying in the last days, and having produced some evidence in previous chapters to show that the last days are already reached, we proceed to look around us to ascertain if "many people" are even now saying these things as predicted by the prophets Isaiah and Micah.

To some extent a few men at different times in the past have taught that a universal peace and reign of righteousness would prevail on the earth in its present state, and that Christ would come in person to rule over a converted world. But we wait for the dawning of the present century before this doctrine becomes a characteristic belief of "many people." To-day you will hear men eloquently teaching that the age in which we live is the beginning of the great millennium. In the literal words of the prophet, they are saying that a universal peace will make swords and spears no longer a necessity, and that they will be beaten into plowshares and pruning-hooks. They are actually saying, just as the prophets said they would, "Nation shall not lift up sword against nation, neither shall they learn war any more." When the second coming of Christ is mentioned as being very near, the readiest and most popular objection is that "the millennium must come first, and all the world be led through the highways of peace into the blissful state of universal righteousness."

How literally are these teachers fulfilling the Word of God! Instead of their teaching being an evidence that a time has come when peace is to reign over all, and "nation shall not lift up sword against nation," it is one of the unmistakable tokens of the days in which we live; for are not these "many people" *even now* saying just what the all-wise Father said they would be saying when the end of time is at hand?

There can be no question but that thousands of those who have fallen into the snare, and are joining in these "last-day" sayings of the "many people," have taken up the delusion unwittingly, believing that it is the teaching of God's Word. But God's prophetic truth in regard to the condition of the world in the last days is the exact opposite of what the people in large numbers will be saying. How many are the errors and fatal deceptions from which men might be kept if they would only study the Bible with care! It should not be read superficially and only occasionally, but it should be constantly and closely studied; for as we study the Word faithfully, seeking to know only the truth, the heavenly Father sends His Spirit to be our unerring teacher. "Howbeit when He, the Spirit of truth, is come, He will guide you into all truth; for He shall not speak of Himself; but whatsoever He shall hear, that shall He speak; and He will show you things to come." John 16:13.

Returning to the second chapter of Isaiah, the reader is requested to give thoughtful attention to the words immediately following what the "many people" shall be saying. The Lord's words are:—

"Therefore Thou hast forsaken Thy people the house of Jacob, because they be replenished ["filled with customs," R. V.] from the east, and are soothsayers like the Philistines, and they please themselves in ["strike hands with," R. V.] the children of strangers. Their land also is full of silver and gold, neither is there any end of their treasures; their land is also full of horses, neither is there any end of their chariots; their land also is full of idols; they worship the work of their own hands, that which their own fingers have made; and the mean man boweth down, and the great man humbleth himself; therefore forgive them not.

"Enter into the rock, and hide thee in the dust, for fear of the Lord, and for the glory of His majesty. The lofty looks of man shall be humbled, and the haughtiness of men shall be bowed down, and the Lord alone shall be exalted in that day. For the day of the Lord of hosts shall be upon every one that is proud and lofty, and upon every one that is lifted up, and he shall be brought low; and upon all the cedars of Lebanon, that are high and lifted up, and upon all the oaks of Bashan, and upon all the high mountains, and upon all the hills that are lifted up, and upon every high tower, and upon every fenced wall, and upon all the ships of Tarshish, and upon all pleasant pictures. And the loftiness of man shall be bowed down, and the haughtiness of men shall be made low; and the Lord alone shall be exalted in that day. And the idols He shall utterly abolish. And they shall go into the holes of the rocks, and into the caves of the earth, for fear of the Lord, and for the glory of His majesty, when He ariseth to shake terribly the earth. In that day a man shall cast his idols of silver, and his idols of gold, which they made each one for himself to worship, to the moles and to the bats; to go into the clefts of the rocks, and into the tops of the ragged rocks, for fear of the Lord, and for the glory of His majesty, when He ariseth to shake terribly the earth. Cease ye from man, whose breath is in his nostrils; for wherein is he to be accounted of?" Isa. 2:6-22.

Particular and careful study should be given to every one of these specifications. The thought of the reader will, however, be directed here to only a few of these remarkable utterances of Him who sees the end from the beginning. "Therefore Thou hast forsaken Thy people the house of Jacob;" "they please themselves in the children of strangers;" "their land also is full of silver and gold, neither is there any end of their treasures;" "their land also is full of idols; they worship the work of their own hands." These words express God's estimate of the generation when "many" shall say that the time of universal peace and righteousness has come. How different is the picture presented by the unerring One from that which "many people" would fain have us believe!

Notice, further, what God says of the people in this time: "The mean man boweth down, and the great man humbleth himself; therefore forgive them not." Yes, "the *mean* man boweth down," or, in other words, he is saying, as expressed in the third verse of this prophetic chapter, "Let us go up to the mountain of the Lord, to the house of the God of Jacob." But though he goes to the house of God, he still remains a "*mean man.*" He is a base hypocrite. He knows nothing in reality of the pure, unselfish Gospel of Christ that he professes to believe, and yet dishonors by his hypocrisy and deceit. There is no lack of professors. Even "*the great man* humbleth himself." When statistics are considered, there is an immense array of the vast number who are enrolled as the followers of Christ. But God's Word shows that this outward appearance is only a sham. The pure, unselfish character of the real Christ is left out of the lives of the greater part of this multitude of world-loving professors. It is the Word of God that presents these clearly-defined facts, and the reader's own observation presses the conviction home upon the soul and conscience that God is true, and the "many people" to the contrary are wrong.

The Father in heaven will be driven to the extremity of visiting dire punishment upon this base hypocrisy. "The great man" who "humbleth himself" in his deceitful pretensions of piety, and who, by lending his wide influence to the wrong, has led many more into the ways of error, will be overwhelmed beyond the powers of description by the waves of remorse that will break in upon his distressed and ruined soul. The best interests of these sinners themselves will not permit the Lord to allow them to continue in their evil course. There comes a time when divine forbearance no longer leads men to renounce the evil and turn into the pathway of righteousness, and then

God must of necessity arise to put an end to the devouring plague of sin.

Read again the warnings to these "many people" who in "the last days" shall be teaching "peace and safety" to the world, when their voices should be sounding the trumpet notes of truth. God says:—

"Enter into the rock, and hide thee in the dust, for fear of the Lord, and for the glory of His majesty. The lofty looks of man shall be humbled, and the haughtiness of men shall be bowed down, and the Lord alone shall be exalted in that day. For the day of the Lord of hosts shall be upon every one that is proud and lofty, and upon every one that is lifted up; and he shall be brought low. . . . And the idols He shall utterly abolish. And they shall go into the holes of the rocks, and into the caves of the earth, for fear of the Lord, and for the glory of His majesty, when He ariseth to shake terribly the earth. In that day a man shall cast his idols of silver, and his idols of gold, which they made each one for himself to worship, to the moles and to the bats; to go into the clefts of the rocks, and into the tops of the ragged rocks, for fear of the Lord, and for the glory of His majesty, when He ariseth to shake terribly the earth." Isa. 2:10-21.

How clearly and graphically does this bring us face to face with "the day of the Lord of hosts"! The scenes of that great day are vividly depicted. It is stated that men will then cast away their "idols of silver" and "idols of gold, . . . to go into the clefts of the rocks, and into the tops of the ragged rocks, for fear of the Lord, and for the glory of His majesty, when He ariseth to shake terribly the earth."

God's message to those living in "the last days" is surely very different from the doctrine of the conversion of the whole world and a universal peace. But bear in mind that for more than twenty-five hundred years the heavenly Father has been telling the world of the delusive teachings of this time. All about us to-day is the multitude whose very words are a strikingly literal fulfilment of this remarkable prophecy. The Lord has taken pains to tell us these things in advance. He not only wants us to *know* when we are near the end of time, but He seeks to shield us from falling into the snare of following the "many people" rather than the Word of God.

It is a most marvelous thing that in the providence of God, nearly the whole world to-day has His Word to read. It is also a marvel that so many who profess to believe that Word do not study it sufficiently to understand its teaching, and thus be saved from the deceptive doctrines against which such faithful warnings are given. There is, perhaps, no one thing that is more universally believed than that the world is to reach a time when every nation will be resting in a settled and abiding peace; and it is an equally world-wide notion that during this all-pervading peace every sinner will be converted to God. But if men would only read and believe the Bible, they would find that these sayings of the people are false. Instead of their leading us to look for good times in this life, we should see in them one of the striking signs that the day is at hand for the great and final destruction of the sin with which this world is deluged. Every one of the senses is impressed with the awfully increasing depths of crime and wickedness that are devastating our once fair earth; and the gathering of the greatest armies and navies that the world has ever dreamed of is no indication of a world-wide peace.

A single parable of the Master is sufficient, if read and believed, to dispel completely this delusion of a universal peace and the world's conversion. The parable reads thus:—

"The kingdom of heaven is likened unto a man which sowed good seed in his field; but while men slept, his enemy came and sowed tares among the wheat, and went his way. But when the blade was sprung up, and brought forth fruit, then appeared the tares also. So the servants of the householder came and said unto him, Sir, didst not thou sow good seed in thy field? from whence then hath it tares? He said unto them, An enemy hath done this. The servants said unto him, Wilt thou then that we go and gather them up? But he said, Nay; lest while ye gather up the tares, ye root up also the wheat with them. Let both grow together until the harvest: and in the time of harvest I will say to the reapers, Gather ye together first the tares, and bind them in bundles to burn them; but gather the wheat into my barn." Matt. 13 : 24–30.

There need be no mistaking the lesson that this parable is designed to teach; for the Lord Himself interprets it in the following explicit words:—

"His disciples came unto Him, saying, Declare unto us the parable of the tares of the field. He answered and said unto them, He that soweth the good seed is the Son of man; the field is the world; the good seed are the children of the kingdom; but the tares are the children of the wicked one; the enemy that sowed them is the devil; the harvest is the end of the world; and the reapers are the angels. As therefore the tares are gathered and burned in the fire; so shall it be in the end of this world. The Son of man shall send forth His angels, and they shall gather out of His kingdom all things that offend, and them which do iniquity; and shall cast them into a furnace of fire; there shall be wailing and gnashing of teeth. Then shall the righteous shine forth as the sun in the kingdom of their Father. Who hath ears to hear, let him hear." Matt. 13 : 36–43.

Any one may understand this divine explanation of the parable. The wheat represents the good, and the tares the bad; *both are to grow together till the harvest; and the harvest is* the end of the world. Those who give heed to these words of Christ, will have no room in their minds for a belief of the error, even though "many people" proclaim it, that this whole rebellious, wicked world shall nestle in the folds of peace, while arrogant and defiant sin makes a voluntary and unconditional surrender.

But, notwithstanding the plain evidence to the contrary, there will still be many who will continue to chant the fatal error. The thing for you and me is to believe the Bible, and seek to lead as many as possible from mistaking the sayings of a deluded people for the voice of the God of truth.

An apostle also tells of some other things that the people will be saying in the last days. His words are as follows:—

"Knowing this first, that there shall come in the last days scoffers, walking after their own lusts, and saying, Where is the promise of His coming? for since the fathers fell asleep, all things continue as they were from the beginning of the creation." 2 Peter 3:3, 4.

The signs by which the heavenly Father designs that we may "*know*" when the end of time is at hand are appearing all around us. There are some who will see these tokens of the approach of the great day of God, and will urge them upon the attention of the people. But instead of every one being good and a friend of the Messiah, and rejoicing at the thought of His return to earth, "there shall come in the last days scoffers, walking after their own lusts, and *saying*, Where is the promise of His coming?"

Perhaps these very ones who are scornfully saying, "Where is the promise of His coming?" are professors of His name; for Isaiah has told us of the "mean man" who will be making pretentious visits to the house of God, while he is at the same time advocating pernicious errors. Those who would really follow the Master, must indeed be on their guard. When the scoffer is met, instead of being discouraged by his derision, try to win him from his errors and lusts. And never lose sight of the fact that those who cling to their sins and scoffings, regardless of all that divine love can do for them, serve to make up a part of the monumental evidence by which we "know" where we are in the stream of time. When the scoffer makes the remark, "Where is the promise of His coming?" do not cower before his ridicule nor allow it to disturb you. See his remarks in their true light. Recognize in what he is saying the unmistakable fulfilment of prophecy right in your hearing and before your very eyes, and with all the love that is born of the great sacrifice of Christ seek to exercise that delicate skill in the use of your words and in what you do that will win him from the wrong, and turn his face to the great blazing light of prophetic truth.

None but God could be so minute in describing the distinguishing characteristics of a particular age; but see how definitely His Word delineates the many features that mark this time. Even things that the people will be saying are pointed out. What marvelous foreknowledge does the Lord possess!

You have heard the "many people" who are saying that "nation shall not lift up sword against nation, neither shall they learn war any more;" you have also observed how readily, and to what an extent, the scoffer is saying, "Where is the promise of His coming?" Nothing seems to be a more favorite subject of ridicule with many than the coming of the Saviour. You have observed these things. Possibly you may be among those who have been repeating these prophetic sayings. But did you ever consider that even these sayings of the people are among the unmistakable evidences that mark this time?

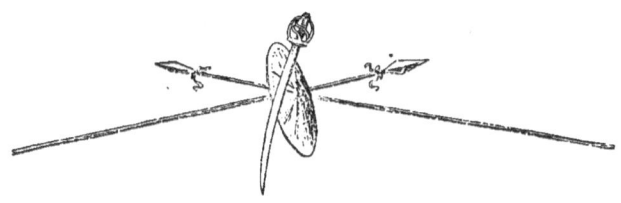

THE PREVALENCE OF CRIME — A SIGN OF OUR TIMES

CHAPTER FIFTEEN

INSTEAD of peace and righteousness filling the earth before the coming of the Lord, the Bible evidence is all to the contrary. We have seen that "many people" are teaching the doctrine of a millennium of peace and goodness; but a careful examination of God's Word is the only means of reaching the truth. Men may falsify even when their intentions are good, but the Word of God makes no mistakes. Hear what it says:—

"As it was in the days of Noah, so shall it be also in the days of the Son of man. They did eat, they drank, they married wives, they were given in marriage, until the day that Noah entered into the ark, and the flood came, and destroyed them all.

"Likewise also as it was in the days of Lot; they did eat, they drank, they bought, they sold, they planted, they builded; but the same day that Lot went out of Sodom it rained fire and brimstone from heaven, and destroyed them all. Even thus shall it be in the day when the Son of man is revealed." Luke 17:26–30.

This scripture shows that the Saviour has selected the two most corrupt periods in the world's history as illustrative of

"The same day that Lot went out of Sodom."

what we are to see "in the day when the Son of man is revealed." The evil condition of the world in "the days of Noah" is very clearly set forth in another scripture. Of that time it is said, "God saw that the wickedness of man was great in the earth, and that every imagination of the thoughts of his heart was only evil continually." Gen. 6:5.

Then in Noah's time, no matter what the views of the people may have been, "God saw that the wickedness of man was great in the earth." The alarming darkness of the picture is shown still more fully by the further statement that "every imagination of the thoughts of his heart was only evil continually." Such was the condition in that time. And when men have sunk to so great depths in the pit of degradation that there is in the mind no pure and holy desire, when *"every imagination of the thoughts"* of the heart is *"only evil"* and that *"continually,"* what could be worse?

If we have been fondly cherishing a contrary view, it may not be pleasant at the outset to contemplate these facts; but it is always best to be right first and above everything else, and in the end it will be seen that the way of truth leads to the only real happiness. Then do not forget that the Lord tells us that "as it was in the days of Noah, so shall it be also in the days of the Son of man."

But we have not read all that is said of the wickedness in the days of Noah. It is further stated that "the earth also was corrupt before God, and the earth was filled with violence. And

God looked upon the earth, and, behold, it was corrupt; for all flesh had corrupted his way upon the earth." Gen. 6: 11, 12.

"The earth was filled with violence," and "all flesh had corrupted his way upon the earth." Such are the expressive utterances of this scripture with reference to the condition of society in Noah's time. Because man had become so corrupt, so degraded, so vile, God was obliged to destroy the race by

"As it was in the days of Noah."

the flood. The infinite kindness of Infinite Mercy could devise nothing that would save that corrupt people. Goodness no longer appealed to them. The right, the pure, and the holy was only a subject of ridicule and contempt; and if we will believe the Word of God, we may know that "as it was in the days of Noah, so shall it be also in the days of the Son of man."

Every person must carry the conviction, whether he will

freely acknowledge it or not, that our day and generation is as remarkable for its corruption and violent crimes as it is for its wonderful inventions and material progress. It would be useless to wander at length through the maze of statistics in order to show the alarming progress that evil is making. All have the unmistakable evidence about them continually that wickedness in its darkest forms is taking complete possession of this whole world. As Charles B. Spahr, Ph. D., expresses it: —

"Upon matters coming within its field, the common observation of common people is more trustworthy than the statistical investigations of the most unprejudiced experts. Social statistics are only trustworthy when they show to the world at large what common observation shows to those personally familiar with the conditions described."

Ask yourself the question candidly and seriously, "Have I not been alarmed because of the robberies, the murders, the drunkenness, the dishonesty, and the many other crimes that are seen on every hand?" This is an age in which corruption in political and social life is simply appalling. If we look to the rising generation for help, we find no relief; for even our little boys and girls in large numbers are becoming expert criminals. The facts upon this question are so open that common, every-day observation is really all we need to show us the true condition of our times.

Such men as W. Douglas Morrison, who has made a careful and exhaustive study of criminals and the causes that produce them, with the one thought in mind of suggesting remedies by which the evil may be abated, testifies that "the amount of crimes committed, whether by juveniles or adults, *is always largely in excess* of the amount of crime recorded in the most complete and elaborate public returns." See "Juvenile Offenders," p. 2, D. Appleton & Co.

The same author, speaking from the view-point of "a wide

experience of the criminal population," says: "One of the formidable problems confronting civilized communities at the close of the present century is the problem of habitual crime. It is perfectly well known to every serious student of criminal questions, both at home and abroad, that the proportion of habitual criminals in the criminal population *is steadily on the increase, and was never so high as now.* In almost every official document dealing with penal administration, this unsatisfactory state of things is both admitted and deplored."—*Id., Preface, p. 5.*

Writing from his office in London, Mr. Morrison says further: "Whether we look at home or abroad, whether we consult the criminal returns of the Old World or the New, we invariably find juvenile criminality exhibiting a distinct tendency to increase. It is a problem which is not confined to any single community; *it is confronting the whole family of nations;* it is arising out of conditions which are common to civilization."—*Id., Preface, p. 8.*

Upon this subject of the criminality of our time the *Catholic Mirror* says editorially:—

"In an article recently, Professor Andrew D. White, who is not given to sensational statements, draws attention to the *extraordinary increase of crime throughout the country.* That there is such an increase, no statistics are needed to show; for we have proof of it, such as can scarcely have escaped the attention of even careless readers, in the daily papers. Shocking occurrences are chronicled—murder in all its forms, robbery, felonious assaults, and every kind of vicious manifestation."

The several foregoing quotations are from gentlemen who are not only eminent for their education, wide experience, and public services, but who are decidedly optimistic in their general views; hence their statements would not be overdrawn, and are entitled to the most candid consideration.

Similar statements equally as strong as the foregoing could

THE PREVALENCE OF CRIME A SIGN OF OUR TIMES   133

be quoted at length from numerous other sources, but it is unnecessary. The reader's own personal observation enables him to know that crime is increasing rapidly, and has already reached a terrible stage.

How heart-sickening is the fact, disclosed by the criminal records of the day, that even women, young girls, and little boys, as well as men, have become so lawless and vicious as to commit the darkest crimes, even to audacious highway robbery and the foulest murder! Any one knows that these records chronicling, as they do, such a variety of crimes, may be found in our daily papers three hundred and sixty-five days out of every year. How clearly and completely are the prophetic words of our Saviour thus fulfilled before us!

Reader, as you see this constant outbreaking of crime all around you, are you not forcibly reminded of the inspired description of Noah's time? "God looked upon the earth, and, behold, it was corrupt; for all flesh had corrupted his way upon the earth, and God said unto Noah, The end of all flesh is come before Me; for the earth is filled with violence through them; and, behold, I will destroy them with the earth." Gen. 6: 12, 13.

In considering these inspired words, do not overlook the fact that "as it was in the days of Noah, so shall it be also in the days of the Son of Man." Luke 17: 26.

The reader may have believed heretofore that the world will march on to a great millennium of righteousness and peace before the Saviour's coming, but still the mind must often have been disturbed by the lack of harmony between the peace-millennium theory and the appalling facts concerning the criminality that, like a malignant plague, is breaking out everywhere. Some theories and the facts may fail to harmonize; but God's Book and the facts will never fail to be in unison. We should study the Bible; we should believe it and rely upon it fully, for we shall need its perfect light to guide us through the perils and amid the darkness of these last days.

CHAPTER SIXTEEN

A PRACTISE has grown up within the last few years of presenting technicalities and various quibbles in courts, so that criminal cases are carried from one tribunal to another, until the guilty are finally set free without receiving the just and lawful punishment that their evil deeds deserve. The current writings of prominent lawyers and judges make frequent mention of this fact, but no human language expresses it so forcibly as the inspired prophet. Hear what he says:—

"Our transgressions are multiplied before Thee, and our sins testify against us; for our transgressions are with us; and as for our iniquities, we know them; in transgressing and lying against the Lord, and departing away from our God, speaking oppression and revolt, conceiving and uttering from the heart words of falsehood. And judgment is turned away backward, and justice standeth afar off; for truth is fallen in the street, and equity can not enter. Yea, truth faileth; and he that departeth from evil maketh himself a prey; and the Lord saw it, and it displeased Him that there was no judgment." Isa. 59 : 12-15.

There may have been times and places since Isaiah uttered this prophecy in which judgment was "turned away backward," and justice stood "afar off," because "truth had fallen in the streets," and equity could not "enter;" but never has it been so literally and universally true as to-day; and all these prophetic utterances concerning the children of Israel in the old dispensation, while they doubtless had a partial and incidental fulfilment in those times, are yet especially applicable in these last days. For, speaking of ancient Israel, the apostle says:—

"Now all these things happened unto them for ensamples; and they are written for our admonition, upon whom the ends of the world are come. Wherefore let him that thinketh he standeth take heed lest he fall. There hath no temptation taken you but such as is common to man; but God is faithful, who will not suffer you to be tempted above that ye are able; but will with the temptation also make a way to escape, that ye may be able to bear it." 1 Cor. 10:11-13.

Then "*all* these things happened" unto the Israel of old for "ensamples," and "they are written for *our* admonition, upon whom the ends of the world are come." There is no necessity for mistake here. All we need to do is faithfully to consider and heed what these scriptures say.

There is another scripture that it will be well for us frequently to study. It says: "Woe to the inhabiters of the earth and of the sea! for the devil is come down unto you, having great wrath, because he knoweth that he hath but a short time." Rev. 12:12.

Satan manifests "great wrath" when "he knoweth that he hath but a short time." He profits by all his experience in all the past ages in leading men to commit sin. As his time grows shorter and shorter, he becomes more and more enraged; and those who do not resist his influence by relying upon God and the power of His Word, are taken possession of by his satanic cunning. Thus will men be transformed into demons to do deeds of injustice and cruelty that will cause an involuntary shudder from all who have not closed their hearts against the tender influences of God's merciful Spirit. We see the beginnings of the evils now. What will be the state of things when to its extreme limit it is true that "truth faileth; and he that departeth from evil maketh himself a prey"!

The reader has doubtless been impressed to some extent at least by the lack of justice among men; but how many have opened their eyes wide, so that they can see the true condition of our world? How does the heart grow sad and sick at the contemplation of the enormous degree to which "judgment is turned away backward, and justice standeth afar off"!

To an alarming extent our cities are passing under the control of the corrupt and criminal classes. In saying this I am not confiding to the reader a secret, but am simply stating a fact that hundreds of tongues and pens are discussing. What to do with the great cities is one of the most discussed and perplexing questions of the age. The reason for this is that the political "boss" has taken possession of the city government, and persistently and effectually holds it in the interest of his friends, who subsist upon that which may be secured by fraud or otherwise, through the "political machine."

It is a source of gratification and thankfulness that there are still some honorable and honest public men. Were it not for the influence of the sterling integrity of these, who can picture what our world would be? But how long can these faithful guardians of official uprightness hold in check the tides of evil that come rolling in? When the last barrier is swept away, and, as in the days of Noah, this earth, in its private citizens and public officials as well, is wholly given to evil, a merciful and just God could do nothing short of coming in person to destroy the world in its iniquity. In the past, when portions of the world have become irredeemable Sodoms of corruption, it has been the invariable course of our divine Father to visit them with destruction. And when the whole world reaches like depths of wickedness, He can not be consistent without following His usual plan.

Let the reader turn his back upon sentiment, and look at the facts as they actually exist. For certainly there is as yet no sentimentalism that can so completely benumb the perceptibilities that the true condition of the world may not be seen.

It is a common saying that money carries with it all the influence needed to blind the eyes of justice and defeat the purpose of properly enacted law. The records of courts and legislatures show many tracings of the influence of money, both in the enactment of law and in the execution of laws already enacted; and if all that the records do *not* show could be revealed, many more immense volumes would undoubtedly be required to tell the story. But it seems to pass without serious contradiction that great combinations of capital work together to control elections and enact laws that suit their purposes; and if some are brought before the bar, there is a process of delays, quibbles, and appeals from one court to another, until justice is turned away, and evil and oppression for the time at least stalk about in haughty triumph.

With these corrupting influences at work in legislatures and courts, is it any wonder that the police force of our large cities should also become infected with the evil contagion? The extent to which they are affected may be judged somewhat from what was brought to light by the Lexow Committee in New York City during the years 1894 and 1895. Similar exposures have been made more recently, but this one in New York is taken because that city stands as the great influential commercial head of this nation. Complaints had become so strong against the official corruption of the great metropolis of the New World that the New York Senate appointed a committee, with Mr. Lexow at its head, to make an investigation.

The committee held seventy sittings, and its proceedings were all made public through the papers at the time, and afterward published in five large volumes of eleven hundred pages each. It would not be proper nor profitable to conduct the reader through all that mire of corruption; but in brief it may be stated that it was proved conclusively upon sworn testimony that many of the politicians, the police, and the magistrates were confederate with the criminals and promoters of vice, and were dividing their spoils on a regular percentage basis. This gross evil and injustice was not confined to a few subordinate policemen; but the whole force, from captains down, was found to be very largely affected by this collusion with the perpetrators of crime.

They had the matter so thoroughly organized that the thief or confidence man could lure his victim into a saloon or some other den, and without fear of molestation proceed to rob him. A complaint would be lodged at police headquarters, and a detective sent to hunt out the criminal and bring him to justice; but the detective himself would be a part of the organized banditti, and of course know the best way *not* to find the thief. If, by force of unavoidable circumstances, the police were compelled to arrest one of these thugs, then the magistrate would come in to play his part; and as all hands had already received their proportionate share of the plunder, the thief or confidence trickster would be turned loose again just as soon as possible, so that he might go in quest of more victims to despoil. And thus this conspiracy would continue its diabolical work.

Most of the readers of this book doubtless know about that revelation of the most shameful corruption in the city of New York,—that city which ought to be one of the crowning glories of the great American commonwealth. But some may not be aware of the scandalous crimes that were committed in common between thieves, assassins, confidence men, and those who were entrusted with the high responsibility of guarding the peace and good order of the city. Those who have lived in such happy seclusion that even the rumors of the prevailing wickedness of this age have not reached them, may be incredulous. They may think it is impossible that such things exist. They will ask in surprise and horror, "Do you mean to say that a police officer can not always be trusted? Is there a possibility that he may be in a secret confederacy with the murderer and the highwayman?" It is appalling to think of it; but such is the literal condition in that great center of commerce, art, and education, the metropolis of the republic and the second city in size and importance in all the world. And since the mother city has set the diabolical example, it is not to be wondered at that so many other cities, towns, and villages, like Steffens' characterization of Minneapolis, St. Louis, Pittsburg, and Philadelphia, have been marching to the intoxicating quickstep music of fraud and vice and crime.

So thoroughly is this system of criminality organized and worked that a collector is appointed to exact the bribes and blackmail, and pay over the proper proportion to the police captain and his associates in this nefarious work. The following are some of the amounts regularly collected by the policeman of New York City as the price for keeping his official eyes closed, and for doing all within his power *not* to catch the criminal, but to help him to get away: Pool-rooms, from $50 to $300 a month; policy-shops, from $20 to $25 a month; liquor-dealers, $2.00 a month; prostitutes, from 50 cents a day to $1.00 a week, each; houses of ill-fame, from $10 to $50 a month.

In the pool-rooms and policy-shops,—and they are usually in the back part of some saloon,—every form of robbery is concocted and carried out. The city is districted, and each thief and confidence man has a given territory in which to work, and if in plying his infamous business one of them, either by chance or design, gets out of his prescribed limits into the territory of another, he is promptly notified by the police in that section that he must desist, or be "run in."

As we might naturally expect, in operating such a system

of iniquity, policemen are appointed and promoted, not on account of bravery or any other peculiar fitness for the responsibilities of the office, but because, according to the slang of politics, they have a "pull." But notwithstanding the "pull," they have to pay for the office. The price, according to the testimony before the Lexow Committee, that a police captain has to pay for his appointment to office is $15,000. This money goes to the "ring" politicians, who use it according to their corrupt desires in perpetuating their office and power; and of course the captain expects to have it returned with usury by the hand of his subordinate associates in crime. What a system! What depths of debauchery and wicked injustice are reached!

Space can not be given to the recital of the long story of oppression and worse than highway robbery that are carried on under this high-handed system of iniquity; but a representative case may help to a fuller understanding of the awful depths of the pit of evil, which now exists. Mrs. Urchittel, a Russian Jewess widow, had a most sad experience while under the heel of this cruel tyranny. We will let her tell, in her own simple language, her story of sorrow and oppressive injustice. As found in the Lexow Report it is as follows:—

"In 1891 I came to New York, a widow with four children; my husband died in Hamburg. Being without means, I applied to the Hebrew Charities on Eighth Street for help, and they were kind enough to support me for starting a boarding-house in 166 Division Street, and gave me for furniture and other necessities, and besides $60, sent immigrants to my boarding-house. My business was increasing daily, having thirty to thirty-five persons every week, and in eight months I saved $600. I worked hard, indeed; but I did it gladly, knowing that this will enable me to support my children, the orphans.

"The immigration having been stopped, I had to give up boarding business; and applying again to the Charities, they supported me again, giving me $150, and sent me to Brownsville, where I bought a restaurant and made a nice living. But having the misfortune to lose one of my beloved children, I left Brownsville, after staying there but a little time, and came back to New York.

"I bought a cigar store in 33 Pitt Street, corner of Broome, for $175, and gave the landlord $40 security, and supplied more goods for $50. On the second day of my taking possession of the store, a man came in and bought a package of chew tobacco for five cents. A couple of days later the same man came in, asking me for a package of chew tobacco, to trust him, which I refused, excusing myself; being recently the owner of that store, I don't know anybody of that surrounding. I can not do it. He took then out a dollar of his pocket, and gave it to me for changing; and having no small change, only pennies, which he wouldn't take, I sent my little daughter to get other coin for the dollar, and handing same to the man, I felt a tickling in my hand caused by the quarter of the dollar in the hand of the man, and I said good-by to him.

"On the evening of that day another man came in the store, and told me that the man who was before asking for chew tobacco without money is a detective, and that he has a warrant to arrest me, and I can avoid the trouble by giving the detective $50, and refusing to do it I will be locked up, and my children taken away from me till the twenty-first year. Not knowing to have done anything wrong, I laughed at the man, and told him that I wouldn't give a cent to anybody, and if that man should come in again, I will chase him out with a broom.

"The other night, at eleven o'clock, the children being asleep already, the same man who asked me to trust him the chew tobacco, and after which I learned he was a detective named Hussey, came in with another man, who took away my cousin that came to see me in that night, and the detective remained with me alone in the store. He told me then that he knows that I keep a disorderly house, and saved $600 of that dishonest business. If I wanted to escape being arrested, he wanted $50. I opposed to his assertion, and protested against his wanting money of me, saying that I ever made a living by honest business; but he wouldn't listen to me, and in spite of my protesting and the crying of my children, I was forced to leave my store and follow him.

"As we were two blocks away, we met Mr. Hochstein, and, crying, I told him all my trouble, and how I don't know anything about the false accusations. It was of no avail; Mr. Hochstein told me that the detective wants $75, but he will try to settle it with $50, but without any money nothing can be done for me; and gave me also his advice, to pay $10 monthly to the detective, I wouldn't be troubled at all, and that I should resume my business unhindered. I repeated again that I don't know anything about dishonest business, but it was no use talking more.

"I was dragged from corner to corner till three o'clock in the morning, insisting that I had money with me, $600, I kept it in my stockings. Weary and tired out, I sat down at the corner of Essex and Rivington Streets, at a dry goods store, and took off my stockings, showing that I had no money in them. 'If you don't want to give the money,' said the detective to me, 'I can't help it; you must follow me to the stationhouse.' Being convicted that it is impossible that I should escape without giving money, I took out $25 of my pocket, the only money I had, and handed them over to the detective standing by a window, which money was parted between Mr. Hochstein and himself, he taking $13 and Hochstein $12.

"They went with me to Essex Street, and, sending me in through a gate in the house, where I was kept about two minutes, they sent me home after with the warning to be prepared with $50. At seven o'clock in the morning the detective, Hussey, came to my store asking for the money. I cried again and begged him to let me go, that I am not able to give him any more money; but he didn't want to hear me any more, and I had to follow him. By the signal of a whistle a man came near me, and the detective gave me over to him with the remark not to let me go till I have the $50. The name of that man is Mr. Meyer. I went with him to Mr. Lefkovitz, manufacturer of syrups, 154 Delancey Street, and to Mr. Frank ———, for selling the store even for the $50; but they didn't want to buy it, seeing the man after me and fearing trouble. After trying in vain to sell the store, the detective said to Mr. Meyer: 'That bad woman don't want to give the money. Take her to the court.' And I had to stay at the trial.

"Two bad, disreputed boys were engaged by the detective, Hussey, for witness. The one said that he gave me fifty cents for gratifying him, and the other said that he would give me forty cents, and I did not agree, asking fifty; and thus I was detained in default of $500 bail. Having been sitting in the court, the detective, Hussey, came in to me on the same day at four o'clock P. M., and told me that my children are already taken away from my house, and if I can give him the $50, he can help me even now.

"Hearing the distress of my poor children, I cried loudly, and a lady took me to a dark room, where I was locked up. Unable to procure bail, I was imprisoned for three days, and sent after to the Tombs, where I had to stand trial.

"There were about fifty persons to witness that I had always made an honest living; but they were not asked at all, and being wholly unable to understand the English language, I couldn't defend myself. The lawyer who was sent from the Hebrew Charities, came too late, and had to give only the certificate of the society, testifying that I was supported by them, and led a decent living. But this came too late.

"I was fined $50. My brother sold my store for $65, and paid the fine.

"I ran then crazy for my children; for I didn't know where they were. Meeting the detective he told me that they are in the hands of a society in Twenty-third Street. I ran there, but no one knew of my children. Finally, after five weeks, I received a postcard of my child, that the children are at One Hundred and Fifty-first Street and Eleventh Avenue, and when I got there, and begged to give me back my children, none would hear me.

"Grieved at the depth of my heart, seeing me bereaved of my dear children, I fell sick, and was lying six months in the Sixty-six Street hospital, and had to undergo a great operation by Professor Mundy. After I left the hospital, I had the good chance to find a place in 558 Broadway, where I fixed up a stand by which I am enabled to make a nice living, to support and educate my children. I went again to Twenty-third Street, begging to release my children, and that was denied again. My heart craves to have my children with me.

"I have nothing else in the world only them. I want to live and die for them; I lay my supplication before you, honorable sir, father of family, whose heart beats for your children, and feels what children are to a faithful mother. Help me to get my children. Let me be mother to them. Grant me my holy wish, and I will always pray for your happiness, and will never forget your kind and benevolent act toward me."—*Proceedings of Lexow Committee, vol. 3, pp. 2, 961-964.*

It would seem that the knowledge of having perpetrated such deeds of inhuman and worse than barbarous cruelty would cause shame, remorse, and indignant self-condemnation, and that even a demon would be led to forsake with disgust such injustice and oppression. But such is not the case. We are in the time that corresponds to the days of Noah, and the wickedness of man is "great in the earth," and "every imagination of the thoughts of his heart" is "only evil continually."

The case of Mrs. Urchittel is by no means an isolated one. The committee reported that "many cases of similar oppression are found on the record." They also say in this report:—

"Oppression of the lowly and unfortunate, the coinage of money out of the miseries of life, is one of the noteworthy abuses into which the department has fallen. . . .

"The evidence of many witnesses shows the existence of a wonderful conspiracy in the neighborhood of Essex Market police court, headed by politicians, including criminals, professional bondsmen, professional thieves, police, and those who lay plots against the unwary, and lead them into habits of lawbreaking, or surround them with a network of false evidence, and then demand money as the price of salvation, and if they do not receive it, drag their victims into court and prison, and often to a convict's cell."—*Proceedings of Lexow Committee, vol. 1, pp. 43, 44.*

After reviewing this system of crime, Mr. Stead tersely remarks: "Is it any wonder that the Lexow Commission reported under the head of 'Brutality' as it existed in the police force, 'This condition has grown to such an extent that even in the eyes of our foreign-born residents, our institutions have been degraded, and those who have fled from oppression abroad have come here to be doubly oppressed in a professedly free and liberal country'?"—*Satan's Invisible World Displayed, p. 144.*

It was fondly hoped by many that the exposures by the Lexow Committee of this sink of corruption would produce a public sentiment that would sweep it from the earth; but these high hopes have not been realized. The subject was discussed quite freely at the time, but as yet no reformation has been reported. During the sixties, "Boss" Tweed was perpetrating fraud and scandals as leader of his political ring in New

York that created even a greater sensation at that time than these more recent exposures through the Lexow Commission. Tweed was finally arrested and lodged in jail, where he died. It was said that his criminal extortions had brought him, as his share, a fortune of $20,000,000. He was living like an ancient Persian prince when he was taken into custody. It was supposed that his "ring" was broken up, and with it the evil destroyed; but the seeds of corruption had been sown, and the facts show that the crop is still most amazingly prolific.

The New York *Tribune* evidently has not seen any improvement in that city or the country at large, as witness the following from its issue of January 11, 1898:—

"The practise among burglars and highwaymen of using torture to compel their victims to tell where they have hidden their money seems to be on the increase, and thieves appear to be even more ready now with knife or pistol than they were in former years. It is painfully evident that murderous criminals now feel less fear of punishment in many parts of the country than they felt in the eighties or the early nineties."

A committee was appointed by the Illinois Senate to make investigations in Chicago similar to those made in New York by the Lexow Committee. In the New York *Sun* of January 27, 1898, may be found a brief report of some of the work done in Chicago by this committee. The report is headed "Corruption in Chicago," and shows that the condition of that great city is by no means better than was found to be the case in New York. The same issue of the *Sun* heads another article—

CHICAGO'S HOLD-UP RECORD.

Two Men Try to Rob a Saloon in Charge of a Woman.

POLICEMAN DISGRACED.

The "disgrace" of the policeman consisted in first "holding up" two men and demanding their cash, and afterward being discharged from the police force because of "conduct unbecoming an officer." It was such "unbecoming conduct" as this that led the head of the Chicago police, when before the investigating committee, to "apologize for the thugs and toughs who had been appointed as members of the police force since he was made chief."

At about the same time that this investigation was being conducted in Chicago, a number of clergymen in Philadelphia were probing the evils there; and, according to the New York *World* of January 28, 1898, the Quaker City was found to be worse than New York had been. The ministers testified that there was plenty of evidence to show that the police of that place, too, were in league with the criminals. Following these exposures have been the more recent one in St. Louis, that has attracted international attention, as well as lesser ones in Minneapolis, San Francisco, and elsewhere.

These evils are not confined to the cities of the United States, as is very well known. From time to time the periodicals of the day are telling us of the corrupting influences that are leavening the cities of the Old World as well. During the latter weeks of 1898 the papers were reporting and deploring the frauds and crimes that were being committed by high officials in the city of London, "the great metropolis of the world." The reports showed, among other things, that the same scandalous crimes were being carried on there under the cover of official protection and collusion that the Lexow Committee discovered and exposed in New York.

Not being content with these despicable methods of cruelly extorting money from the poor and defenseless, business enterprises have been launched by smooth-tongued "promoters," and millions of dollars have been taken from the wealthy in both the Old World and the New through misrepresenting the earning capacity of fictitious speculative corporations. Men supporting titles and holding positions that should carry with them a dignity that would not stoop to such practises, have assisted the "promoter" by lending their names and influence to extort money from those seeking places to invest their means.

During the year 1897, sums aggregating $11,154,530 were embezzled in this country alone; and of this money more than three and a half millions were taken by public officials. This of course represents public funds that were taken outright, and the embezzlers caught at their deeds; but when so much is stolen in this way, it is not to be supposed that all are found out; and those who are arrested have such resources in bribes, lawyers' technicalities, pardons, etc., that it is difficult for justice to be secured.

The lord chief justice of England, on Lord Mayor's day, November 9, 1898, during a brief address, pointed out some of the frauds and embezzlements that are such a menace to the people of Great Britain; and, after speaking of the evils that were being committed by men in high positions, he stated that careful official research showed that corporation officials had embezzled £28,159,482, or about $140,000,000, during the seven years ending with 1897. He said, "These figures relate only to companies wound up compulsorily." And, after mentioning other cases that were not taken into account in the foregoing figures, he adds that if these latter companies are reckoned among the rest, "the loss to the public is enormous." Thus Great Britain's defalcations that are sought out and reported average about twenty millions annually. These figures seem "enormous" enough, but still they show only a part of the depths of the yawning abyss of crime.

It is a noteworthy fact that, whether it is across the water or in this land of America, when honest, thinking men meet to-day, one of the uppermost topics of discussion is, "What shall we do to stay the avalanche of criminality that is coming down upon us?" There are criminals in high stations and criminals in the back alleys and gutters — criminals have stolen influential offices of state, and climbed into the judgment-seat. "What can be done?" is the anxious query.

Not the least interesting, or, more properly stated, the most amusing, if not so fraught with evil, among the facts brought out in connection with this epidemic of crimes are the conscientious scruples that some of these monstrosities of evil have. For instance, one police captain said he was a Christian, and therefore did not want to receive any of the blackmail extorted from prostitutes. He would receive his share of the sums extorted from the poor victims in policy shops, or that which was taken by the highwayman; but when it came to receiving a share of the spoils gathered from the houses of ill-fame, his conscience was too tender to receive it. We may smile at this, and yet it is a serious matter to this depraved officer of the law. And when we see that men can sink so low, and still, even in the society of their corrupt associates, flaunt their counterfeit piety and diseased conscientiousness, it shows that the cunning of Satan can even make a man believe that his despicable crimes may all be covered by some act of feigned piety.

The foregoing pages take only the briefest and most limited survey of the increasing injustice of our time. Nor has it been the design of the author to always select the most recent or the most unrighteous deeds from this political and social mire of the present days. It has been the design to select representative cases that mark the fulfilment of these prophecies. The reader has no doubt been compelled to see and hear much more of it; for it is distressingly prevalent everywhere. The important question is, What does it portend?

Surely the evils in Noah's time could not have been much greater or darker than those which are cursing the world to-day. Most literally are we in the time when "judgment is turned away backward, and justice standeth afar off; for truth is fallen in the street, and equity can not enter. Yea, truth faileth; and he that departeth from evil maketh himself a prey; and the Lord saw it, and it displeased Him that there was no judgment." Isa. 59:14, 15.

Looking to this world, the prospect is gloomy enough indeed; but there is a gleaming of light. It is not centered in this corrupt earth, however, but it is shining from that Book which holds forth the promises of the Coming One. All hail to this glorious light of eternal day! Justice in the earth is hard to find; but justice from on high is about to strike. Who, with a knowledge of the facts, can expect that it will be long delayed?

THE EARTH FILLED WITH VIOLENCE

CHAPTER SEVENTEEN

IT should be particularly noticed that in speaking of the days of Noah the record says: "The end of all flesh is come before Me; for the earth is filled with violence through them; and, behold, I will destroy them with the earth." Gen. 6:13.

At that time the land had become "filled with violence," and God found it necessary to destroy the earth. The misery, the oppression, the vices and crimes that abound when everything is given up to evil, would of course, if time were given them, work out the destruction of the whole race; but it would be amid prolonged tortures and indescribable anguish, from which no possible good could result. Hence the divine destruction of such abandoned evil, when viewed from the correct standpoint, is the measuring out of infinite mercy.

The agencies are actively working which must soon produce the terrible condition of which it will truly be said "the earth is filled with violence." Who has not been impressed by the rapidly-increasing tendency toward "mob law"? Day by day the record comes to us of some poor wretch who, without the benefit of either judge or jury, is taken with "violence," and brutally and inhumanly put to death. Leading jurists and

statesmen, viewing this increasing tendency to mob "violence" in dealing with crime, regard the situation with grave apprehension. The Hon. I. C. Parker, judge of the United States District Court for the Western District of Arkansas, says:—
"When we go to the facts, we find that during the last six years there have been 43,902 homicides in the United States, an average of 7,317 per year. In the same time there have been 723 *legal* executions, and 1,118 *lynchings*. These startling figures show that crime is rapidly increasing, instead of diminishing. In the year 1895, 10,500 persons were killed, or at the rate of 875 per month; whereas in 1890 there were only 4,290, or less than half as many as in 1895. This bloody record shows a fearful increase of the crime that destroys human life. . . . *We can easily recognize that the greatest evil of any civilized age is confronting us*, not only in the shape of crimes committed by individuals, but also of crimes committed by masses of men who are endeavoring by bloody and improper means to seek a remedy—I mean those who band themselves together as mobs to seek that protection which they fail to obtain under the forms of law."—*North American Review, June, 1896.*

Judge Parker in the same article states his opinion as to the cause of this increase of murder and mob violence. He says: "The criminal law and its administration have rather fallen into disgrace. . . . It is largely because of the corrupt methods resorted to to defeat the law's administration, and because courts of justice look to the shadow, in the shape of technicalities, rather than to the substance, in the shape of crimes. . . . Now, the condition is so serious—*and it is growing more so all the time*—that there must be some remedy. . . . The cause of this condition springs in part from a morbid, diseased public sentiment, which begets undue sympathy for the criminal, and has none whatever for his murdered victim. It grows out of the indifference of the people to the enforcement of the criminal law. It arises from corrupt verdicts begotten by frauds and perjuries. It arises from the undue exercise of influence, either monetary, social, or otherwise, so that juries are carried away from the line of duty."

The foregoing statements were made after a careful and exhaustive study of the subject. The judge has had unexcelled opportunities to scan the whole field, and learn the true state of affairs, and he has stated simple facts that men and women everywhere are affirming and deploring. In harmony with the foregoing from Judge Parker is the following statement of Judge Elliot Anthony, president of the Illinois State Bar Association, in his address at its annual meeting, Jan. 24, 1895, at Springfield, Ill.: —

"There is dissatisfaction everywhere throughout the country in regard to the methods adopted and the course pursued by our courts in dealing with the violators of the law, and it is but little wonder that the people in some of the oldest portions of the republic have at times become exasperated at the trifling and juggling which are allowed, and have wreaked summary vengeance on thugs and assassins, to the disgrace of civilization and the age in which we live."

Following these statements, the words of the lord chancellor of England, as reported in the London *Times* of Nov. 10, 1898, are forcible and to the point. He says: "There is nothing which will so dissociate men, which will drive nations to madness so quickly, as the belief that the justice of the country is not honestly and impartially administered."

The statements of these leading jurists are not given to prove facts, but to state facts that every one knows are in existence all about us at this very time. Not only is it known that these facts exist, but it is equally as well known that the wrong conditions pointed out are spreading and deepening with an alarming rapidity.

Who can know these things without being deeply impressed

with the truth that we are indeed living in days that answer fully to the Bible description of the time of Noah? Common observation is all that is required to enable us to know that they are true. A detail of facts and statistics is not necessary in order for us to see and understand the condition of things about us.

The mobs that rise up like armies in various parts of the country almost every day show the violent tendencies of the times. There is a regular epidemic of lynchings. The spirit of anarchy has so taken hold of the minds of a small class that no reigning monarch or other ruler, be he ever so upright and kind in his administrations, is safe from the plots of skulking assassins who lurk at every turn to catch an opportunity to take the lives of the ones standing at the head of governmental authority. The vast number of kings and rulers who have fallen victims to this reign of lawlessness, during recent decades, in both this country and foreign lands, is among the silent witnesses to the growing violence of our times. And this turbulent rioting spirit is increasing very rapidly, and shows that the restraining bands of law and order are being consumed by the fires of unbridled hatreds and revengeful emotions.

A condition of discontent pervades the world, and these clamoring elements are constantly breaking loose with ever-increasing "violence." There is no power that will continue to restrain them for any great length of time. There have been social problems in the past, but never have they appeared in such vast and alarming proportions as now.

At the beginning of the year 1898, Bishop Newman said: "This is the most unsettled condition of the world since the crucifixion of Christ. . . . The stability of government is no longer a fact. Change is in the atmosphere. It is just as true now as a thousand years ago, 'Thou knowest not what a day will bring forth.' . . . Statesmen are at their wits' end. Philosophers speculate in vain."

The forcible truth of Bishop Newman's statements may be more fully realized by briefly calling to mind some of the events that followed within a few months from the time he wrote the foregoing. First it might be well to mention that there is scarcely a nation that was not in a quarrel with some other nation during the year 1898. The United States not only quarreled but fought with Spain. England had trouble with Russia, Germany, and France. France and Germany had difficulties to settle; and so complicated are the questions involved in these difficulties among the great powers of Europe, that, if war breaks out, it seems highly probable that all the world will be drawn into the conflict.

Then look at the domestic troubles that are perplexing these governments. The ink with which Bishop Newman wrote was hardly dry before there was rioting in Algiers. The great strike of the engineers in England had been going on for several months. Revolution was smoldering in France over the Dreyfus case; and it is evident that numerous causes are at work there that may at any time result in another Reign of Terror. Spain was on the verge of a revolution at home while she was at the same time warring with the United States; there was serious rioting in Austria-Hungary, and the conditions were such in the Austrian Empire that Austria's rulers dared not undertake to assist their kinsmen in Spain, for fear that, if their army were taken from home, there would be a general revolt of the people. Italy had her bread riots, and four hundred persons are reported to have been killed and a thousand injured in the conflict of a single day; and the reader will recall the riots in China, the Moslem revolt in Central Asia, the uprisings in Africa, South America, etc., etc.

In the countries where there have been no uprisings or riotings in recent months, there may be found the seeds of discontent that are liable to produce disturbances any day. For instance, in Germany members have been elected to the Reichstag by twelve different political parties, with a marked increase in favor of the Socialists. Who can estimate the discontent in a country that has so many different political creeds, and each working to produce reforms that all assert are sorely needed? Is it to be wondered at that Germany had five hundred seventy-eight strikes during the year 1897?

Nor is it in Germany alone that there are numerous political parties struggling for the supremacy, and strongly voicing their disapproval of existing conditions. Every nation has them; and where so many factions are working, and all at cross purposes with each other it must be evident to any one that this seed sowing will soon produce a harvest of anarchy and violence. Many think that these conditions betoken a great revolution that will purify the world; but a revolution of purification could never come out of such a sea of discord and strife. For not only is society broken up into these warring factions, but there is such a prevalence of immorality and criminality that the only result that could come from the breaking loose of such forces would be the absolute chaos of anarchy itself. The restraining hand of the Almighty is the only power that keeps these forces from breaking loose and flooding the world with a deluge of destruction. So we may well sing praises to the Most High that it is His divine plan to send His Son to earth to cut this prospective reign of terror short in its mad career, and thus keep it from reaching the possible limits of its direful harvest.

In all the world may be found, as Mr. Chauncey M. Depew terms it, "the century-vexing problem of capital and labor." There is an irrepressible strife between these two camps. We may seek to minimize it by words; but the evil growth is there, nevertheless, and sooner or later the world-wide struggle will begin. Money has been used to defeat justice; it has been used to control elections and legislatures. Fortunes have been accumulated that rival the stories about Midas and Crœsus; and over against these colossal treasures and their possessors may be seen the gathering legions of organized labor as well as the army of the poverty-stricken and destitute.

In every strike it may be seen that "violence" is becoming more pronounced. The hatred that is being cultivated against trusts, corporations, and the individual possessors of great fortunes, is growing deeper and more vengeful. The reports tell of some strikers who clubbed and stoned an agent of a corporation until the man was supposed to be dead. The police finally succeeded in rescuing his body, and he was laid out upon the court-house lawn to await the action of the coroner. The man moved his head, and thus showed signs of life, whereupon a person from the mob jumped on his body and began to stamp and kick him. How strikingly does this represent the growing "violence," for this case merely illustrates the general condition!

Briefly reviewing the situation, we find that the love of money is corrupting the age. The judge is blinded by bribes. The legislator is elected by the corrupt use of money. Money is freely used to influence the making of laws. With these evil influences working so extensively in what are called the higher circles, composed of the wealthy and influential members of society, is it to be wondered at that town and city politicians should learn the lesson, and put it into active operation? Need we be surprised that the city has its corrupt politicians, its dishonest and criminal policemen, and its magistrates who will not protect the oppressed, and who seek a bribe to influence every decision? And when the magistrate or judge will free the robber and assassin for a gift of money, it is but a natural consequence that murders and robberies should become more numerous and daring.

In short, society to-day is a school that is filling the world with criminals, and the fact should not be passed by that a flood of pernicious literature is a mighty factor in this debasing work. Especially does this literature pervert the minds of boys and turn them into the downward road of criminality while they are yet children. It is no uncommon thing to read of lads still in their teens who commit robberies, murders, and all the rest of the crimes.

Now, in the very nature of things, all of these corrupting practises of this time are drowning the sense of justice. The world is driving headlong into that time when "every imagination" will be "only evil continually;" and who can conceive the extent of the "violence" with which the earth will be filled when the harvest of sin is fully ripe?

The Lord looked down the ages to these last days. He has shown in advance what the culminating works of sin will be. He has taken pains to unmask it, and in every way possible to warn us against the evil, while He freely offers us the good. Many of the poor souls who are floundering in the lowest depths of the dark sins of this time do not know that the Saviour still loves them. They are not acquainted with the truth that He died not only to save them, but to make the depths of His love more manifest to them.

In these last days truly "the earth is filled with violence." Though this violence has not yet broken out with all its malignant terrors, nevertheless the seeds of the evil are rapidly growing into a prolific harvest. But "the days of the Son of Man" are at hand. He will separate sin from the hearts of all who will yield to His moulding touch, and He will fashion them into jewels of His grace. Then in that near day of His coming it will be a joy to be made like Him; for we shall see Him as He is.

CHAPTER EIGHTEEN

THE Saviour makes mention of the "days of Lot," as well as the days of Noah, to represent the depths of vice that would be reached in the last days. Let us read His words again: "As it was in the days of Noah, so shall it be also in the days of the Son of man. They did eat, they drank, they married wives, they were given in marriage, until the day that Noah entered into the ark, and the flood came, and destroyed them all. Likewise also as it was in the days of Lot; they did eat, they drank, they bought, they sold, they planted, they builded; but the same day that Lot went out of Sodom it rained fire and brimstone from heaven, and destroyed them all. Even thus shall it be in the day when the Son of man is revealed." Luke 17:26-30.

The Word of God tells us that in the "days of Noah" "every imagination" of man's heart was "only evil continually;" and since these same depths of evil imaginings will prevail again at the close of time, it should not be a matter of surprise that the corrupting vice of Sodom as it was in "the days of Lot" will break out as a debasing plague.

The grossest sin of Sodom was her abandoned licentiousness. When we wish to describe the very lowest sink of licentious lust, we speak of it as a "veritable Sodom." The depravity of mankind was manifested in that wicked city in its most shameful and vilest forms. It is sad to know that the human race, excepting those, of course, who resist the influences of Satan, will again be led by him into such gross sensuality; but such is the prediction of the Word of God, and it will be fulfilled.

In 1895 it was estimated that there were between forty and fifty thousand prostitutes in the city of New York alone; and there is no evidence that New York is worse in proportion to its population than other cities. When there is such a vast multitude of women who support themselves by their life of shame, who can estimate the thousands of men who are sacrificing their virtue and manhood at the shrine of lust? It is usual to count only the women; but for each woman who lives as a public prostitute, there are, in the very nature of things, several men who are the companions of her vice.

The prevalence of licentiousness is only too apparent. The evidences of the existence of houses of shame are not disguised, but are open and apparent. It would seem that our boasted civilization should sweep such disgusting spectacles away, as too loathsome to be endured; but legislatures and city councils, at least to the extent of a majority, look upon the prostitute as a necessity. Age-of-consent statutes have been enacted that allow men to seduce the merest little girls to their ruin, with no fear of legal penalties to deter them.

It is a mystery how grown-up men — the fathers of little girls — can stand up in the legislative assemblies, and seriously propose and enact such laws. How can it be possible that men are so lost to the sense of shame, even if their sense of justice is gone, that they will support the idea that a child in her "teens" may "consent" to abandon her virtue, without being first deceived by a base libertine? Why, a child of such tender years can not comprehend what she is doing. She does not as yet have the mental development that will enable her to look down the awful road into which the cruel, lustful seducer is turning her childish and innocent feet. "We are in the full blaze of the great enlightenment and humanitarian civilization of the twentieth century!" Yes, that is the boast of this age. But, nevertheless, can any one imagine that Sodom could have done much worse than first to make such great pretensions, and then deliberately make laws that would shield the villain of lust in ruining little girls? No child can give her consent to such vice, and realize its enormity; and such age-of-consent laws are nothing more than a legal protection to vice, while, with Satanic cunning, it hurls the innocents into shameless ruin.

There is a regular traffic in young girls; and that is one reason why these age-of-consent laws can still hold their place on our statute-books. Men of wealth who frequent the house of shame will pay a big premium to get young and innocent girls for their vile purposes. So the brothel sends its agents out to find little girls who are just entering their teens. Sometimes these innocents can be lured away by childish gifts; sometimes, if they are a little older, the villains make love to them, and propose to marry them; and finally the unsuspecting child is enticed into her life of misery and ruin.

Only demons could inspire such work, and only men who are under the beguiling influence of demons would yield themselves as agents to do it.

But, you ask, how can such evils be carried on in a civilized land? Why is not the law invoked, and the evil stopped? Here, again, is where the corruption of the officers of the law serves these vile persons in carrying on their traffic of shame. The laws in most localities are against houses of ill-fame; but the policeman is bribed, or perhaps it would be nearer the truth to say that the policeman takes it upon himself to license vice and sensuality. Upon this subject the Lexow Committee reported:—

"The system had reached such a perfection in detail that the inmates of the several houses were numbered and classified, and a ratable charge placed upon each proprietor in proportion to the number of inmates, or in cases of houses of assignation the number of rooms occupied and the prices charged, reduced to a monthly rate, which was collected within a few days of the first of each month during the year."

In the "Proceedings of the Lexow Committee," vol. 1, pp. 33-36, may be found a full account of how this collusion between the police officers and the brothels is carried on. And from this report it is seen that the police of New York—and New York is not worse than many another large city, as has already been shown—are more than partners of the mistresses of the brothels. These officers assume control, and levy a regular monthly tax of from $25 to $50 from each disorderly house; and in another part of the committee's report they state that each woman who goes on the street to solicit has to pay the policeman from fifty cents to a dollar a week, in addition to this monthly tax. Then, when the mistress opens her house of shame, she has to pay the police captain $500 as an initiation fee, and this fee of $500 has to be paid over again every time a new captain comes in by exchange from another precinct. Worse than all, if the fallen woman seeks to abandon her life of shame, the officer refuses to allow it, holding her in her chains of vice through fear of official persecution.

Does not a knowledge of these horrible facts cause the heart to burn with indignation? Does it not make one feel ashamed that he belongs to a race that has sunk so low?

With the police force financially interested in the perpetuation and increase of prostitution, it is easy to see why it is so hard to protect young girls from being dragged into the corrupting evils of the brothel. Agents are sent out everywhere to be on the lookout for victims to lure into the dens of vice; and oftentimes the very blue coat that is appealed to for protection will only help to make the ruin of the victim all the more secure. Thousands of the young women who are held in houses of ill-fame have been decoyed there, and are kept against their will, a thing that could not be done if officers were faithful to their high duties and responsibilities.

Did it ever occur to the reader that the greed for money, on the one hand, and the great destitution, on the other, are powerful factors in producing this wide-spread licentiousness? In our cities the so-called "merchant prince" in many instances pays his girl clerks starvation wages, and then deliberately teaches them to "make up the lack" by giving themselves as concubines to the respectable (?) libertine. This statement seems too shockingly disgusting to be true; but it is, nevertheless, a fact. I will subjoin some statements that will bring this matter more forcibly before the reader than anything I can write.

Rev. Louis A. Banks, in his book "White Slaves," has a chapter on "The Relation of Wages to Morals," in which he says:—

"I received a letter from a gentleman in Conway, N. H., this week, who writes, not knowing that I was intending to discuss this question: 'After you have given the sweating system one round, can you not take up the question of the girls working in the big stores? I have just heard a well-authenticated account of a man high in authority in one of the largest stores, suggesting the way to ruin to a young girl from the country, who said, when she learned what her wages were to be, that they would not be sufficient to give her a bare support. This not only shows the attitude of these wealthy merchants to the souls of their working-girls, but it shows that they are conscious of their attitude, and have deliberately chosen to take it.' I am told, upon undoubtedly credible testimony, that another young woman who came to Boston from the country, and sought work in several stores, was so outraged at the vile suggestions which were made to her about means of adding to her salary, that she went back to the house of her friend — a lady of as high standing as any in the city — and cried and sobbed all night long. She said she would beg or starve before she would submit herself to such outrage again.

"It is impossible to turn these incidents aside as exaggerations. They are horrible, I know; but the most horrible thing about them is that they are true."—*Pp. 130, 131.*

Some time since the New York *World* contained a most touching and pathetic appeal from a young man, who, on account of continued illness, had lost his position, and was unable to protect the young lady he had chosen to make his life companion. The appeal reads as follows:—

"In the interest of humanity I beg you will find space for this appeal—an appeal for protection for a young girl struggling against heavy odds in the battle of life—an appeal for some one to show her that vice is not always triumphant over virtue; for some one to prove that it is not always necessary for a penniless girl to sacrifice purity and honor to gain a livelihood in this modern Babylon.

"I seek only the protection of some Christian family or home for one who will not be a burden, for one whose own life has become burdensome to herself from the continual persecutions she has had to resist, even in private houses and other places where her lot has been cast while striving to earn a living, and who even now is in daily peril of contamination under circumstances where the word of a defenseless girl would be powerless against the machinations of conscienceless fiends. What mother will stretch out her hand to save this unprotected daughter, not for charity's but for mercy's sake?"

The editor of the *World* said concerning the foregoing appeal:—

"It is a cry of distress from one of the humble orders of life, and is the more moving and instructive because such cries are usually suppressed by the conditions which cause them. *There are doubtless thousands of similar cases* of young girls driven by the stress of poverty to hold perilous positions, and to continually expose themselves to repeated temptations of their remorseless employers. It is small wonder that under the prolonged strain, subjected to all forms of enticement and even intimidation, human nature often wearies of the protracted efforts of resistance, and the victim falls at last a prey to the crafts and assaults of a treacherous sensuality."

That the pollutions of lust are not confined to this country may be seen from the following statement from Lady Henry Somerset in regard to the condition of London. Speaking of the drink habit, so universal in London among women and girls as well as men and boys, she says:—

"It is impossible to overrate the influence, the soul-destroying influence, this has had upon the homes of the poor; for it is by this, I am convinced, that the idea of right and wrong has come to be hopelessly confused when it is not absolutely lost. It is *not uncommon* to find a mother who since marriage has been a faithful wife, and perhaps before that a virtuous girl, looking on with indifference while her daughter 'goes on the streets,' and is lost in the unnumbered legion of victims hourly sacrificed to the demon of vice. She may regret the fact, as a mother in a wealthier station might regret her daughter marrying beneath her; but there is no shock, no natural horror, at the wanton marring of God's fairest handiwork, a woman's soul. In our long worship of mammon, the shame of poverty and the shame of sin have got confused. To the poor in their misery the burden of disgrace is but a slight addition to the load they already carry."—*January, 1892.*

The foregoing quotations state the facts as every well-informed person knows them to exist, and they could not be stated in more chaste, and at the same time clear and forcible language. It is not necessary to produce further testimony to show the conditions of sensuality that exist. Indeed, it would hardly seem necessary to produce any testimony other than to cite the scriptures that tell of the conditions that God said would obtain in this time, and then ask the individual to look around at the state of things as every one knows it to be. Even the fences by the roadside, the walls of public buildings, and the columns of nearly every paper in the land, face us constantly with ingenious advertisements of nostrums offered as a panacea for the numerous diseases produced by sensuality. Such extensive advertising costs large sums of money, and it would not be continued if it did not pay; and the thing that makes it pay is the prevalence of the debasing and disease-producing sins of Sodom. If no other evidence was given, there is enough in this one item of the extensive advertisements of remedies for these vile diseases, to show how full of vice the world must be.

Can there be any doubt that we are living in the days on which the Saviour fixed His prophetic eyes when He said, "As it was in the days of Noah; . . . likewise also as it was in the days of Lot; . . . even thus shall it be in the day when the Son of Man is revealed" (Luke 17:26-30)?

And how forcibly do the words of the prophet Hosea come to mind:—

"Hear the word of the Lord, ye children of Israel; for the Lord hath a controversy with the inhabitants of the land, because there is no truth, nor mercy, nor knowledge of God in the land. By *swearing*, and *lying*, and *killing*, and *stealing*, and *committing adultery*, they break out, and blood toucheth blood. Therefore shall the land mourn, and every one that dwelleth therein shall languish, with the beasts of the field, and with the fowls of heaven; yea, the fishes of the sea also shall be taken away." Hosea 4:1-3.

"Swearing, and lying, and killing, and stealing, and *committing adultery*" have broken out, and truly "blood toucheth blood." Sodom, with its vile pollutions, is being reproduced all about us. And who can estimate how soon it must be decreed that the pure eyes of God can endure the scene no longer? The Lord made an example of Sodom anciently; there can be no

"He that is without sin among you, let him first cast a stone at her."

mistaking His purpose in dealing decidedly with this modern Sodom that has spread its corrupting vices over the entire world. At that time His dealing was with a single city in one locality, but in this time His dealing is to be with all the inhabitants of the earth at the second coming of His Son. How cheering the thought that Jesus is soon to come and bring this reign of sin to an end!

But those who are found corrupting themselves at His coming, will be destroyed by the brightness of His holiness and purity, that will be so gloriously revealed in that day; and so He has faithfully pointed out all these things, in order that we may know and avoid the dangers of these times, and be ready to meet Him. Now He is yearning over every sinner, no matter how vile and polluted, and is earnestly calling each one to repentance, that He may purify his heart, and clothe him with the white garments of righteousness.

The sinner who has plunged to the very lowest depth still finds in Jesus his Friend. "For we have not an High Priest which can not be touched with the feeling of our infirmities; but was in all points tempted like as we are, yet without sin. Let us therefore come boldly unto the throne of grace, that we may obtain mercy, and find grace to help in time of need." Heb. 4:15, 16.

Think of it, O soul burdened with a load of sin! Jesus so loves you that He took upon Himself our flesh,—this flesh that is so full of the tendency and desire to sin,—and all this that He might "*be touched* with the *feeling* of our infirmities." So, then, tempted and sinful one, whoever and wherever you are, the Lord of glory is "touched" with your feelings; and when every earthly friend has forsaken you, know that He is ever your Friend. He knows all about your difficulties and trials; and since He knows your case so perfectly, if you will only trust Him, He will administer just the consolation and help that are needed.

The scribes and Pharisees of old, with their manufactured dignity and sham holiness, "brought unto Him a woman taken in adultery," and asked Him what should be done with her. She stood trembling before Him, and no doubt expected to hear Him condemn her to death; but the Pharisees, with the pure and discerning eye of the Master piercing the inmost secrets of their hearts, were told, "He that is without sin among you, let him first cast a stone at her." Conscience-smitten by the irresistible sense of their guilt, they began one by one to steal away from His presence. When she whom they thought too vile to live was left alone with her Lord, He asked her, "Hath no man condemned thee? She said, No man, Lord. And Jesus said unto her, Neither do I condemn thee; go, and sin no more." See John 8: 3–11.

When Jesus said to that fallen woman, "Go, and sin no more," there was power in that word both to cleanse her from all past sin, and also to keep her from falling again so long as she continued to trust the Lord. Jesus hated sin worse than it was possible for those Pharisees to hate it; but He knew how to separate the sin from the sinner, and to speak peace to the burdened soul by saying, "Go, and sin no more."

He is coming very soon to destroy all evil, and at that time, if wickedness is still found in our hearts, the only thing for us will be destruction, with our sins. But, O, He is now inviting us to come to Him, confessing our sinfulness, that He may cleanse us, and make us so pure that we may greet Him with rejoicing when He comes!

"To-day if ye will hear His voice, harden not your hearts."

CHAPTER NINETEEN

THE question is asked, "When the Son of man cometh, shall He find faith on the earth?" Luke 18:8. The very form of the expression shows that the Saviour's question is an emphatic statement of the great lack of genuine faith among those living at the close of time. This fact is further confirmed by His answer to the question, "What shall be the sign of Thy coming, and of the end of the world?" The Master says, "Because iniquity shall abound, the love of many shall wax cold." Matt. 24:3, 12. Then a great lack of faith, the abounding of iniquity, and the love of many waxing cold, are sufficiently prominent in the last days to be mentioned as among the signs of the Saviour's coming.

Another scripture is to the point in this connection. It reads: "This know also, that in the last days perilous times shall come. For men shall be lovers of their own selves, covetous, boasters, proud, blasphemers, disobedient to parents, unthankful, unholy, without natural affection, truce-breakers, false accusers, incontinent, fierce, despisers of those that are good, traitors, heady, high-minded, lovers of pleasures more than lovers of God; having a form of godliness, but denying the power thereof; from such turn away." 2 Tim. 3:1-5.

This scripture tells us plainly that "perilous times shall

come," and just as plainly does it say that these perils shall be "in the last days." No matter what our views may have been to the contrary, we should now surrender to the statement of God's Word. What God says of the case is correct; what He has pointed to as signs of the end will surely appear, and we may see them if we will.

There is another point in this text quoted from Timothy that we must not pass by. The apostle not only tells us that "in the last days perilous times shall come," but adds, "*For* men shall be lovers of their own selves," etc. The word "for" in this connection is equivalent to "because." Then the perils of the last days are brought about "for," or "because," men are so filled with covetousness, pride, and all the rest of the long list of the sins mentioned in this text. Note particularly that the text says that those engaged in these sins of darkest hue, are at the same time "having a form of godliness, but denying the power thereof." The world does not have a "form of godliness." Only a backslidden church could be in such a condition — a church filled with "lovers of pleasures more than lovers of God." When the things mentioned in this text appear, we may know that the "last days" are reached. For these days will be made "perilous" by the prevalence of evil. "Iniquity shall abound," and over all the mass of sin those who, by a lack of faith in God's Word, are denying His power, will throw the hypocritical robes of a "form of godliness."

With these quotations from Matthew, Luke, and Paul agrees the statement of Peter: "Knowing this first, that there shall come in the last days scoffers, walking after their own lusts, and saying, Where is the promise of His coming? for since the fathers fell asleep, all things continue as they were from the beginning of the creation." 2 Peter 3:3, 4.

As the doctrine of the second coming of Christ is preached, there will be "scoffers." And, to be sure, since they are "walking after their own lusts," they will say in derision, "Where is the promise of His coming?" But the believer in the sure Word of God will not be affected by these scoffers, except to see in them the evidence of the Master's coming, and, in pity for them, to work and pray that their hearts may be touched by divine grace, and turned away from their scoffings to a Saviour's tender love.

How faithfully do these scriptures disclose the perils of the "last days"! How pointedly they tell us that sin shall be glossed over by the "form of godliness;" that faith will be almost wanting; that the "love of many shall wax cold"—and all because "iniquity shall *abound;*" and that amidst it all will be found the "scoffers," making light of the "promise of His coming"!

With these scriptures before us, telling us so plainly that in the "last days" "godliness" will become a mere form among the great multitude, we have only to look about us to see the literal fulfilment.

The thing that we naturally expect when we go to the house of God is to hear the preaching of the Gospel "in the demonstration of the Spirit and of power." The theme that should be dwelt upon is the "Lamb of God, that taketh away the sin of the world." But in how many of our churches is the preaching of the simple Gospel sadly lacking! I have met hundreds of people, representing all our various denominations, who recognize and deplore this fact.

But why this lack of power in the church? Why do we see only the "form" when we should expect to find the life and power belonging to the Master's church? There is one little statement in a text already quoted that furnishes the answer. Observe that it is said of those who have this "form of godliness, but deny the power thereof," that they are "lovers of pleasures more than lovers of God." The pleasures that God offers are soul-satisfying, real, substantial and abiding. They are filled with indescribable joys, and leave behind them only pleasant memories; and mingled with these pleasures is that joy of the Lord which comes from helping those who are in need. It is to deny self, and do right. There is an infinite joy and an eternal satisfaction in following the Lord's way. But by those living in the last days the transient pleasures of the world are chosen instead; and to such an extent is their pleasure-seeking carried, even while maintaining a "form of godliness," that it marks one of the distinctive signs of our times. Seeking for pleasure for the mere sake of selfish enjoyment has ever been the pursuit of the world; but now the craze takes possession of the church, and plunges it also into the ephemeral and delusive pleasures of time and sense.

Who is there to-day that has not been impressed with the efforts made by so many of the churches and in so many places to supply amusement? This is done, of course, ostensibly to "raise money for the cause," or "to attract the young people in the church." Rev. Mr. Hale, who has made extensive observations in regard to church entertainments, gives in the *Forum* an outline of what came under his notice during a single year. He mentions a church in Massachusetts which produced in regular theatrical fashion "Violet in Fairyland" and "A Comedy of Errors up to Date." A number of churches in the same state joined in giving a "laughable performance" entitled "Aunt Jemima's Album." The young people in a church in Iowa gave a "New Woman Social." "The Mystic Midgets" is produced by a church in another quarter. And so his list continues. These are but a few of the semi-theatrical performances that are being given all the time in our churches all over the land. A few paragraphs selected in full from Mr. Hale's trenchant pen will not be out of place here. He says:—

"I have, however, no hesitation in commending—as a successful exhibition of impudent and attractive indecency—the New Woman Social given, according to the New York papers, by the male members of the —— Society of ——. Some of the more engaging toilets worn . . . are described in the despatch: 'W. F. Stimpson, in lilac bloomers with lace trimmings, was irresistible, as was E. H. Taylor in a Mother Hubbard, and with a weeping-willow plume. E. C. Seeley wore shiny black bloomers set off with a gorgeous sash. J. Curtis Martin wore red bloomers and an angelic smile. Olin Henderson, in check bloomerettes, Ward Thompson, in a shirt-waist, and W. H. Dean, with balloon sleeves, were also conspicuous.'

"This is, possibly, funny. But for monumental godlessness made endurable by no saving grace of humor, for simian imbecility, for supreme and inimitable folly unmarred by the slightest suggestion either of common decency or ordinary self-respect, for groveling baseness and depraved vulgarity,— the Trilby Party, otherwise the Foot Social, otherwise the Ankle Auction, stands at the head of the church entertainments for the year. . . . In the Trilby Social . . . the young ladies of the church display their feet—let us say and be polite—from behind a curtain. . . . Men in front of the curtain view what is displayed of one female after another, and then bid for the privilege of taking her to supper.

"The pastor of the —— church of ——, Michigan, having entertained firemen, veterans and blacksmiths, outdid himself in a 'Barbers' Sunday evening.' Scissors, hair dye, cups, soaps, brushes and combs, mirrors and washes, tastefully arranged on the walls and platform, with festoons of towels and rosettes of brilliantine and bay-rum bottles, gave a homelike appearance to the church. Sitting in a barber's chair, the pastor gathered inspiration for his lecture, and then, rising, he pressed home, in the choicest terms of the tonsorial profession, the lesson of the 'razor and the strop.'"

These brief quotations give a picture of what everybody knows to be a condition of the church to-day. In almost every community the churches are vying with each other in producing some form of silly amusement. If we were to go to a show or theater, we should naturally expect to see such performances. But have we actually reached the time when the professed church of Christ is showing herself to be imbecile by the worse than silly shows and counterfeit theatricals that she is giving, to the infinite satisfaction of Satan, while claiming that it is all done in the sacred name of Christ? Who can read of or behold such things without a sense of the deepest sorrow and shame?

If we did not know it to be so, we could hardly give credence to the thought that young ladies supposed to have the moral worth that enables them to connect with our churches, would deliberately make bare their feet, and, sitting behind a curtain, allow a promiscuous drove of men to pass along viewing the scene, and bid for the one he would like to take to supper. How can any one with ordinary respectability, leaving out of the question the refinement of a pure Christian life, think of engaging in such silly, debasing amusements, and presenting the proceeds as an offering to Him who is of "purer eyes than to behold evil," and who can not "look on iniquity"? Can it be that our churches are no longer a haven of safety for our boys and girls, and that when their inexperienced feet are led to the sanctuary dedicated to the Most High, it is only to teach them to be immodest, to say the least, instead of filling their minds and hearts with the purest desires and noblest aspirations? When so many churches thus join hands with the world in seeking amusement, and some of them carry their silly plays even to the very border-land of Sodom, what is there left to hope for?—There is just one bright dawning above the horizon of evil, and that is the sure promise of the coming Saviour. And while we have a few lingering days of probationary time, let us seek to win to the Master as many as we can, so that He can save them from the certain destruction into which this world is so rapidly plunging.

God's power is just as great now as it was on the day of Pentecost, when the people were drawn to hear the preaching of the simple Gospel, not by shows and sensational parade, not by the thought of fun and very questionable amusements, but by the Spirit of the living Saviour. That power is waiting still for all who will receive it. How can we more effectually deny the power of God than by resorting to amusements to draw people to the church? How sad that the church should be so blinded as to be willing to change the experiences and realities of Pentecost for the modern church fair and theatrical display!

There are many who realize the situation, to some extent at least, and are crying out against this terrible condition into which the church of Christ has fallen. Pages of testimony might be given from these, but only a few paragraphs are necessary. The reader has doubtless reflected much on what he knows of this evil existing all about him, for the deplorable condition of the church is not confined to a few localities, but is altogether too universal.

Rev. Walter A. Evans says: "Evangelical Christianity, born anew in the German Reformation, baptized under the hands of the Puritans and the Wesleys, has already so far apostatized that another reformation is needed to fit the church for the work of the greater century soon to dawn. The cold formalism of a utilitarian religiousness, ornate with pomp and ceremony, makes of the church of the present day, to a very large degree, a valley of dry bones greater than that which Ezekiel saw, and as sorely in need of a divine afflatus to give it life. Social discontent, born of pinching poverty on the one hand and riotous riches on the other, gambling, intemperance, commercial dishonor, political corruption, and the whole pestiferous brood of evils which prey upon the nation and threaten its peace if not its perpetuity as a free republic—they *all* find their coveted opportunity, when they do not find their abetment, in the worldly ideals, the grasping covetousness, the denominational pride, the sectarian selfishness, the moral cowardice, and the spiritual apathy of the church. . . .

"Why is it that there are so many lodges to every church, and that so large a part of the humanitarian and reformatory forces that make for human weal in the present life, are centering outside the church? Why is it that, as every minister of the Gospel knows is the case, so large and increasing a body of noble, honorable and high-minded men of every community, men who fear God and revere Jesus Christ, are standing studiously aloof from the church? . . .

"But some one will exclaim: 'Our organizations! Look at our new organizations, millions strong!' To which one might fittingly reply in the words of . . . Mr. B. Fay Mills, 'They are very deceiving.' Or one might, by way of amplification, say that multiplication of organizations within the church, wisely constructed to fit the social instincts of youthful human nature, colossal conventions worked up systematically after the most approved methods of a political canvass for twelve months previous—they may cause a great buzzing of wheels and rattle of machinery that looks very like spiritual vigor. But all this machinery, while it can *use* power, can not generate it. It can neither repair a defective boiler nor replenish a furnace, the real trouble with which is that *the fire is going out*. The adding of another wheel to the machinery does not increase the power. Nay, is not this unprecedented multiplication of organizations itself a striking sign of weakness and spiritual degeneration? May it not be, after all, an attempt to brace a man on his feet by artificial means, when the fact is he is suffering from heart-failure? What is the matter with the old bottle that *it* won't hold wine? The church of the apostles, the Puritans, and the early Methodists turned the world upside down—*not* by organization, for they had practically none; but by the irresistible power of deep moral conviction, unquestioning faith, and a spiritual unction that was the outcropping of a new and divine life. But to-day, instead of one chasing a thousand and two putting ten thousand to flight, it takes a thousand church-members to chase one evil, and then they don't catch it—unless 'there is something in it.' . . .

"The church is made the decoy of the hunters of fortunes; it is utilized as a screen of scoundrels. . . . Yea, it has become a great tree, and respectable sinners—respectability is a *sine qua non*—legal robbers, and pious frauds lodge under the shadow of it. . . . One can not single out any one denomination as being especially guilty of exalting pelf above piety. The same conditions widely prevail, and one is probably as bad as another."—*Walter Allen Evans, in the Arena.*

How pleasing it would be if we could truly say that the statements of Mr. Evans are overdrawn! But every one who thinks, knows that what he says in the foregoing paragraphs is only too literally true. Do we not see that the church is rapidly being filled with all the iniquities mentioned by the apostle, and that it is in reality rapidly reaching the place where it holds only "a form of godliness," while "denying the power thereof"? God has told us what would take place in the last days, and we see it now right before our eyes.

What an opportunity the church is losing! Social discontent, arising from various causes, is looming up on every hand; and instead of the church standing forth amid the gathering storm as a beacon-light and guide in the way of righteousness, we see her shorn of her strength, lying prostrate in the toils of sin.

How appalling the thought! The world is acknowledged by thousands of the most thoughtful men and women of our time to be speeding on to an awful revolution, bidding fair to outdo the French Reign of Terror; and in the face of this crisis, the church, instead of being awake and active in rescuing the perishing and warning the ignorant, is filled with those who are "lovers of pleasures more than lovers of God," having only "a form of godliness," while by indulgence in sin they are "denying the power thereof." With these facts before us, how forcible the prophetic interrogation, "Nevertheless when the Son of Man cometh, shall He find faith on the earth?" And is it any wonder that our Lord, when viewing this time, said, "Because iniquity shall abound, the love of many shall wax cold"?

Any one who is candid with himself must admit, in the moments of his soberest reflection, that the world is indeed in a terrible condition, and that the church, taken as a whole, instead of being awake to the situation, is wasting its time in childish amusement and selfish folly. When the faces of the bravest men are growing pale before the conditions in which our world is floundering, instead of being able to tell them that we have reached the death throes of this reign of sin, and raising the warning note, "Escape for thy life," the pleasure-loving professor is dreamily sounding the sleepy notes of "peace and safety." And how natural that it should be so with one who has only a "form of godliness"! The voice of God, speaking to the very soul, is endeavoring to awaken the conscience to a correct appreciation of the situation. But, being "lovers of pleasure more than lovers of God," they cling to the "form of godliness," and quiet the disturbed conscience by saying, "Peace, peace, when there is no peace." But do not forget that the Lord, when speaking of this time, has said, "When they shall say, Peace and safety; then sudden destruction cometh upon them, as travail upon a woman with child; and they shall not escape." 1 Thess. 5:3.

It is a cheering thought, however, that, notwithstanding all the efforts of Satan to drown the whole church in pleasure and sin in these last days, the Lord still has some in every communion who have not given their hearts to the service of Baal; and by these the voice of warning must be given. Fearful odds, should we take our view from the human standpoint, will have to be met; but, with the voice of a conqueror, our great Leader says, "All power is given unto Me in heaven and in earth;" and, trusting in His omnipotent strength in this time of greatest peril, "we must gather warmth from the coldness of others, courage from their cowardice, and loyalty from their treason."

There are souls everywhere who are crying out for the living God, and they are perplexed by the distressing condition of things that they see around them. Reader, will you not act as a light-bearer for God, and assist in pointing all such to that sure Word that so unmistakably shows all these things to be the tokens by which we may know that "He is near, even at the doors"? Let all the world know of His love, and that He is now earnestly inviting every one to accept the wedding garment, His own perfect righteousness, and thus be made ready to enter into the eternal bliss of the redeemed.

But to do this great work of showing mankind where we are standing, and of telling them the meaning of the portents of this time, it is necessary to be more than mere professors of Christianity. We must be such devoted students of the Word of God that we will know its prophecies and precepts for ourselves, and be able to point with the assurance of definite knowledge to the light that is shining for us from the sacred Book. Any ordinary, dreamy experience that is half of the world and the other half made up of only a profession of the Christianity of the Christ, can never do in such a time as this. There is a work to be done in rescuing the church itself from the stupor into which it has fallen that requires the heroism of faith and Bible power. It will not do to leave it to the minister alone to become the Bible student and the Bible scholar. Every individual must now throw his sectarian differences to the winds, and give himself to the study of the Bible so that he may be sure to stand on the solid rock of divine principle that is born only of a knowledge of divine truth; and then, with the heart made pure and courageous by this heaven-appointed process, we should go forth to do valiant work in arousing as many as can be reached. It is no time for theological speculation in regard to these things. The great facts of this time are staring us in the face, and we should acknowledge the literal truth of what we actually see, and let our labors be according to the pressing needs of the hour. If we see whole platoons of church-members giving themselves to the follies of the world—yes; if, even worse than that, we behold in them the entire train of vices and crimes that characterize this time, we should not surrender to the spirit of critical faultfinding that can do them no good. This faultfinding criticism of the members of the church can not help them, and only breeds infidelity in ourselves as well as in them that hear us. But if we knew from the Word of God what it all means; if we can point to this apostasy in the face of the great light of this age as one of the sure fulfilments of prophecy, the dignity and power of heaven's great truth is allowed to shine out, and the soul may be reached.

God wants men in this time who can see beyond the evils that have taken possession of the church as well as the world. He wants men who can set on high the blazing light of prophecy to show the meaning of this darkness. He wants men who are too intent in the work of reviving the sickly church to find any place for the sneering criticism. The whole world is trembling before its doom, and the church which God has appointed as his agency to rescue the perishing must be warned of the dangerous and traitorous position which it is taking to such an alarming extent.

"LOVERS of PLEASURE"

CHAPTER TWENTY

IN the preceding chapter some attention has been given to the scripture which shows that a love of pleasure under a "form of godliness" is one of the producing causes of peril in the last days. But the subject deserves more particular consideration; for it is the corrupting influences in the world beneath that are used to bring the church down from her proper sphere of holiness. When in any particular age the church becomes corrupt, it is because of her failure to resist the prevailing sins and vices of that time.

So, then, since the love of pleasure among those who have a "form of godliness" will do its part in making times perilous in this age, what a great prevailing passion for the follies of mere fun will be manifested in the world at large! It is true that humanity has ever been given to the pursuit of pleasure. It is natural and God-given for men to wish to enjoy themselves. It has always been the case that a great many will look no higher than the follies of transient and debasing amusements; but in a special sense will the world be given to pleasure at the close of time. Marvelous indeed are the great inventions and the general material progress of this age; and the extent to which the people of to-day are given to fun and pleasure is no less conspicuous.

Speaking of the days that immediately precede His coming, the Master says: "Take heed to yourselves, lest at any time your hearts be overcharged with surfeiting, and drunkenness, and cares of this life, and so that day come upon you unawares. For as a snare shall it come on all them that dwell on the face of the whole earth. Watch ye therefore, and pray always, that ye may be accounted worthy to escape all these things that shall come to pass, and to stand before the Son of Man." Luke 21:34-36.

Words of warning are directed against "surfeiting" (which is another word for overeating) and "drunkenness." The same evil is spoken against in Matthew, as follows:—

"But and if that evil servant shall say in his heart, My lord delayeth his coming; and shall begin to smite his fellow-servants, and to eat and drink with the drunken; the lord of that servant shall come in a day when he looketh not for him, and in an hour that he is not aware of, and shall cut him asunder, and appoint him his portion with the hypocrites; there shall be weeping and gnashing of teeth." Matt. 24:48-51.

Feasting and strong drink are two of the most constant companions of worldly pleasure, and the Lord has taken pains to warn us against these evils. The Father in heaven, who "so loved the world, that He gave His only-begotten Son, that whosoever believeth in Him should not perish, but have everlasting life," seeks to lead men to genuine pleasure and real enjoyment; but among the special snares of the evil one, prepared for the last days, is the intoxication of illusory pleasures and sensual gratifications, so that men may not discern those things that are for their eternal interest.

Intemperance is one of the greatest evils of our day. The city of Chicago alone consumed $80,000,000 worth of beer in twelve months during the last part of 1897 and the first part of 1898; it would be a modest estimate to say that another $20,000,000 was spent for other kinds of spirituous liquors, making a yearly average of nearly $75 for each man, woman, and child in that great city. And Chicago is fairly representative of the rest of the cities of the world.

As soon as it became evident that the United States would have possessions in the Philippines and station an army there, a Milwaukee brewing company despatched three train-loads, aggregating sixty-seven cars, of beer to Manila. This is illustrative of the activity and watchfulness of the traffickers in liquor. They are always on the alert for an opening to push their business, and do not scruple to put plans in operation to create in the rising generation an appetite for drink.

This has been the generation of temperance agitation. A great work has indeed been accomplished. The change in sentiment toward the drink question is truly miraculous. Had it not been for this, it is hard to tell how much more terrible the condition of the world would be at the present time. Yet in the face of this great wave of temperance reform, the liquor traffic has organized its forces so that it is stronger than it ever was; and it is gaining ground every day. Every one knows the control that the saloon has of politics. Elections are influenced, and legislatures and city councils are under the domination of the dealers in strong drink.

Some of our temperance reformers have made most startling exposures respecting the complete control the liquor traffic has gained in many of the oldest and most influential colleges in the land. In this way the liquor dealers are educating the young men and women, who are in turn to be educators in the most influential positions in society, to look upon the use of strong drink as most proper and genteel. What far-sighted cunning is here displayed!

The exposures made by the press generally of the "canteen" business connected with the army, present another illustration of both the activity and the power of the saloon men. They persuaded the army officers that if they would open "canteens" (the army word, by the way, for saloon) in the camp of each regiment, the drink business would be under their official control, and they could "regulate" it. "For," said they, "the soldier is bound to have an occasional glass of beer; and why should he not get it in his own camp, where the danger of going on a regular spree would be wholly cut off? Then if the beer was sold by the direction and consent of the army officers in this way, there would be quite a profit that could be used in supplying comforts and necessities for the camp." Such was the specious reasoning presented, and the "canteen" was allowed to be established.

But it has not worked so nicely as was represented. Most shocking and debasing have been the results of introducing these camp saloons. Drunken brawls that are a disgrace to civilization have been common. And it may not be amiss to ask, If this is an age of real goodness — as it pretends to be; and if the millennium is really dawning, as is supposed by so many — why do not the commanding officers of the army put an end to this "canteen" evil among the soldiers? It is in their power, by a few simple dashes of the pen, to command the ejection of the nuisance from the camp. Some regimental officers have done it, and all could do it if so disposed.

Here, again, is seen the influence of the liquor power. This traffic controls large sums of money. The liquor business in the United States requires a large army, of half a million men; and every one of them is a politician. Whoever expects to be elected to office must reckon with these dispensers of strong drink, and also with the great host of men in the slums and elsewhere that are to so great an extent under their control. The better element of society has been appealed to again and again to rise up against this corruption, and put men in office who were wholly upright; but these upright citizens do not come forward, and the corrupting influences of the saloon are growing stronger every day.

The astounding amount of drunkenness, and the influence of the liquor power in these times, are too well known to require more extended remark in this connection. When we view the situation as it is before our eyes to-day, is it any marvel that the Master should have left us the warning, "Take heed to yourselves, lest at any time your hearts be overcharged with surfeiting, and drunkenness"?

Running after pleasure requires that a great deal of time be spent in idleness; and when people are idling away their time in amusements, there comes the great temptation to drinking and gluttonous feasting. Then along with these evils is that other ruinous and debasing practise of gambling. Men want money to use in pleasure-seeking; and as they do not wish to take the time to work for it honestly, they resort to the races and games of chance. Baseball, the horse-race, and many more of the great train of pleasure-making devices, are used by the gambler to secure money without toil. This is recognized as not only an evil, but a veritable craze. It is by no means confined to men, nor to any one country; for women, and even children, all over the world, are participants in some way in these numerous schemes for securing money by chance. Boards of trade manipulate and gamble in wheat, corn, and other grains; the cotton exchanges make similar speculations in other products of the farm; and the stock exchange places its stakes on the rise and fall of stocks, bonds, etc.

Members of churches, and men of influence and standing in society and in the political field, take their chances on the board of trade or the stock exchange; the professed church itself conducts "fairs," "raffles," and other forms of church lotteries; and with this influence at work in the higher circles, is it any wonder that gambling should have become such a craze in these times?

It is interesting to note how the promoters of these various schemes for pleasure are trying to cover them with a cloak of respectable philanthropy. For instance, here is some worthy charitable institution in need of funds, and the managers of a race-track propose to raise $5,000 or more by giving a day's receipts at the gates. Of course everybody is urged to attend, "because this is in the interest of charity and humanity." An opera company proposes to play for a night in behalf of some worthy object, and every one is again urged to attend, "For," it is persuasively emphasized, "you can have a lot of fun, and then just think that you will be helping the needy at the same time."

It is to the interest of the dispensers of amusements to make their races, games, and plays popular. It will not do to have the more conscientious part of society look upon them questioningly; and they must be credited with long-headed foresight in the course they are pursuing, no matter what opposite attribute is suggested as belonging to those who deliberately walk into such manifest beguilements.

No attempt is being made to present statistics or other facts to bring before the reader the pleasure-loving craze of this age. His mind is doubtless running with lightning speed, in noting the races, the games, the operas, and all the rest of the devices after which the crowds are flocking for fun. It is superfluous to go into detail to present evidence when it is standing in colossal proportions all around us. There are some who find their greatest happiness in the solid business, joys, and work of life; but the great mass want fun, and still more and more fun.

Every day the papers are telling of the suicides that grow out of the disappointments that come in this field of pleasure seeking. Men and women who are given to the glittering sensualities of feasting and drinking, meet with some sudden reverse. They have been in such a hilarious state of pleasure seeking that they can not endure the disappointment, and so their life is taken. It is also a sad fact that many murders are committed so that some further pleasure may be gratified.

The professed church, even, has caught the craze for fun. When it is desired to raise money for church purposes, some entertainment is arranged to draw the people to spend their money for "pleasure" and "charity." When the bulwarks that the church should present against this evil are thus broken down, the world plunges still deeper into its follies; for instead of the church being a barrier against this growing passion for questionable pleasure, it has turned right about face, and has become a positive influence in its favor.

Thus we see that Satan has set the whole world fairly wild in running after pleasures—not the pleasures that build up, and educate, and refine, and ennoble, but pleasures that intoxicate the mind with an insatiable desire for sensuous gratification and exciting sport. Both the world and many in the nominal churches have been dragged into it. The Saviour has warned us against this scheme of the evil one, by which he seeks so completely to charm the world with illusory pleasures that they will not discern the portentous issues of our day and generation. And He has given us the promise: "When He putteth forth His own sheep, He goeth before them, and the sheep follow Him; for they know His voice. And a stranger will they not follow, but will flee from him; for they know not the voice of strangers." John 10:4, 5.

YE HAVE HEAPED TREASURE FOR THE LAST DAYS

CHAPTER
TWENTY-ONE

REFERENCE has already been made to the apostle Paul's statement that "in the last days perilous times shall come. For [or because] men shall be lovers of their own selves, covetous," etc. 2 Tim. 3:1, 2. "Men shall be lovers of their own selves, covetous;" and *because* of these, in connection with other sins, the last days are made "perilous."

Individuals who are completely filled with self-love, caring nothing for others only as a means of gratifying and pleasing themselves, are a very dangerous class. If they fancy that their personal pleasure would be increased by the destruction or violent taking away of the property of others, they do not scruple to do it. If to accomplish their desires it seems advantageous to take the life of a fellow-creature, they wait only to assure themselves that they can accomplish the deed without being caught, and then proceed to the execution of the fearful crime. In short, it makes no difference to those who are wholly given to the worship and gratification of self, how much sorrow and pain they cause another. Neither hunger, cold, nor any or all of the worst forms of suffering, seem to touch them. They are living only for self, and the distress of others is of little moment to them.

The reader is familiar with the Scripture statement, "As it was in the days of Noah, so shall it be also in the days of the Son of Man." Luke 17:26. He also knows that the Bible tells us, in describing the sins of Noah's time, that "God saw that the wickedness of man was great in the earth, and that every imagination of the thoughts of his heart was only evil continually." "And the earth was filled with violence." Gen. 6:5, 11.

Now, just as surely as these scriptures are true, just so surely may we know that in the last days, as in Noah's time, "violence" and great wickedness, — so great that "every imagination" will be devoted to evil, — will be prevalent among mankind. With the picture of this great wickedness of Noah's time before the mind, it must be very evident that the *self-love*, the *covetousness*, that makes the last days "perilous," is the very worst that Satan can produce. Is it any wonder that the apostle, in such emphatic language, tells us that "in the last days perilous times shall come"? For the seeds of "self love" and "covetousness" planted in a heart where "every imagination" is "only evil continually," must produce a fearful harvest.

In the very nature of things, men who are thus "lovers of their own selves, covetous," will grasp for everything they can get hold of. Since "every imagination" is "only evil continually," they will not be at all particular about the honesty of their methods in securing the objects of their covetous hearts. The stronger ones, and those who by some chance are thrown into positions of advantage, will override the weak; and some will thus, through selfish greed and covetousness, amass colossal fortunes to be used in wanton pleasure, while others will be mercilessly ground down by abject poverty.

The apostle James makes this clear beyond a single doubt. He says: "Go to now, ye rich men, weep and howl for your miseries that shall come upon you. Your riches are corrupted, and your garments are moth-eaten. Your gold and silver is cankered; and the rust of them shall be a witness against you, and shall eat your flesh as it were fire. Ye have heaped treasures together for the last days. Behold, the hire of the laborers who have reaped down your fields, which is of you kept back by fraud, crieth; and the cries of them which have reaped are entered into the ears of the Lord of sabaoth. Ye have lived in pleasure on the earth, and been wanton; ye have nourished your hearts, as in a day of slaughter. Ye have condemned and killed the just; and he doth not resist you. Be patient therefore, brethren, unto the coming of the Lord. Behold, the husbandman waiteth for the precious fruit of the earth, and hath long patience for it, until he receive the early and latter rain. Be ye also patient; stablish your hearts; for the coming of the Lord draweth nigh. Grudge not one against another, brethren, lest ye be condemned; behold, the judge standeth before the door." James 5:1-9.

Speaking to the rich men, this text declares, "Ye have heaped treasure together for the last days." This self-loving, "covetous" age is marked by the heaping together of treasure, and none should fail to note that it is "heaped" together "for the last days."

The reader is well aware of the fact that there is no subject to-day more widely discussed than the "relation of capital to labor." And why all this discussion?— It is because colossal fortunes have been grasped, and are in the hands of a few, while a great multitude is suffering from pinching want. Every one knows that this statement is a literal truth; and yet the gnawings of want are not the whole of the cause. The capitalist has taught the world the advantages of combining to crush out competition, and thus make great fortunes in a few years. So the thinking laboring man says: "Why not combine, too, and get our share of this wealth?" "Why not form 'trade unions,' fix a price on our commodity of labor, and compel the capitalist to pay it?" And because of the self-love and covetousness that God has foretold would characterize these last days, there is brought into this struggle between capital and labor a conflict that is becoming more and more intense and perplexing.

Mankind, uninfluenced by the Spirit of the Nazarene, has ever been inclined to amass large fortunes, and hoard them as misers, or spend them in selfish pleasure. From time to time in the history of the past, whole nations have become so corrupted through the wealth that a few could control, that they have gone down amid the strife of their internal revolutions. James Anthony Froude, A. M., says of Rome in the days of Cæsar:—

"The intellect was trained to the highest point which it could reach; and on the great subjects of human interest, on morals and politics, on poetry and art, even on religion itself and the speculative problems of life, men thought as we think, doubted as we doubt, argued as we argue, aspired and struggled after the same objects. It was an age of material progress, material civilization, and intellectual culture; an age of pamphlets and epigrams, of *salons* and dinner parties, of senatorial majorities and electoral corruption. The highest offices in the state were open, in theory, to the meanest citizen; they were confined, in fact, to those who had the longest purses or the most ready use of the tongue on popular platforms. *Distinction of birth had been exchanged for distinction of wealth.* The struggles between plebeians and patricians for equality of privilege were over, and a new division had been formed between the party of property and the party who desired a change in the structure of society. The free cultivators were disappearing from the soil. Italy was being absorbed into vast estates, held by a few favored families, and cultivated by slaves, while the old agricultural population was driven off the land, and was crowded into towns. The rich were extravagant, for life had ceased to have

An alley of poverty, Chicago.

practical interests, except for its material pleasures; *the occupation of the high classes was to obtain money without labor, and to spend it in idle enjoyment."* — *Cæsar, p. 6.*

When Rome was in the condition described by Mr. Froude, there were numerous tribes to the north, who, while considered by the Romans to be more barbarous than they, were nevertheless much more honorable and upright. The corruptions of Rome had not debased them; and these northern tribes conquered her, and, by breaking her territory up into what are practically the nations of Europe to-day, destroyed her large fortunes, and dissipated her corruptions. Thus a new civilization upon a new basis was begun. But the same spirit that was among the Romans, which led certain men, more favored than their fellows, to control all the wealth, continued to work among the new nations founded on the ruins of the old empire; and, during the long course of the centuries, in all the nations of the Old World, a few families have been seeking to hold the wealth and the consequent power that money gives. There have been revolts against the oppressions of this so-called nobility, the most marked being the French Revolution. During the Middle Ages the great mass of the people were kept in such ignorance and superstition that their revolts lacked the intelligent leadership necessary to make them effective.

But when we begin to approach the intelligence of the sixteenth, seventeenth, eighteenth, and nineteenth centuries, a new continent engages the attention of Europe, and so the revolutions that otherwise must have become general long before this time, were held in abeyance by the interest manifested in peopling and developing the New World. America has long been the asylum to which the oppressed and discontented have been welcomed, and freedom and advancement in this country have been a constant object-lesson to the nations of the eastern hemisphere; and who can tell the moulding influence that our free institutions have had in bringing a greater degree of freedom to some of the nations of Europe during the last hundred years? But when America, "the land of the free and the home of the brave," the "asylum for the downtrodden and unfortunate," herself becomes as corrupt as the nations of the Old World, where, on the face of all the earth, is there a "city of refuge"? In the history of all the past, God has borne with nations until they became

Lodging-house for the poor.

wholly given over to evil, and then, as the most merciful, yes, in fact, the only thing He could do, has given them up to destruction. When, in Noah's time, the whole world became "only evil," He destroyed all the evil people by the flood. We have produced abundant testimony to show that in the last days, the same as in the world before the flood, the "earth" will be "filled with violence;" hence the only remedy will be for Christ to come, and take the upright to Himself, and consign the rest to the destruction they have chosen by clinging to their sins.

The wealth of the nobility in the Old World has long held the reins of power, and the reader of history must be impressed with the fact that it has not been without the protest of the anarchist, the communist, the socialist, etc. The sway of the money power in the past has been held in check to some extent by other influences; but it will not continue to be so in these last days of "covetousness," when men are "lovers of their own selves," and "every imagination" is "only evil continually." Hence the grasping hand that would seek to acquire and hold everything for itself will be more and more manifest.

How is it now in America, the great land of equality, where every man is supposed to be on the same footing with every other, and where there is in theory no caste or distinctions of wealth? "In 1833," says Robert N. Reeves, "when Tocqueville visited America, he was struck by the equal distribution of wealth and the absence of capitalists. Half a century later, when James Bryce, author of 'The American Commonwealth,' visited our country, the trusts, monopolies, and concentrated wealth so amazed him that he exclaimed, 'I see the shadows of a new structure of society—an aristocracy of riches.'"

In this country there were no great fortunes fifty or sixty years ago. The people were living contentedly, and the heated discussions of capital and labor that we hear now on every street corner, and read in our papers all over the land, were hardly dreamed of; but it is vastly different to-day. The same writer further says:—

"Never in the history of our country were the people confronted with greater social problems than they are to-day. The strikes, boycotts, and general discontent of late years prove conclusively that there is yet much room for improvement in our social order. . . . Every observant person must admit that *the great concentration of wealth*, whether it be in corporations, trusts, or individuals, has reached a point dangerous to the future prosperity of the nation. . . . The Probate Court records of the various states disclose the fact that millionaires are becoming more numerous, while the smaller property owners are gradually sinking into the multitude of people possessing nothing. . . .

"This power of wealth is the greatest danger that has threatened our country since the Civil War, and against it we must constantly be on our guard."

Mr. Reeves is not quoted to use him as authority in the matter, but simply to give a sample of the articles of which our papers and magazines are full all the time. It is not Mr. Reeves only, but thousands of men and women all over the country, who are speaking after the same order, only many of them express themselves much more strongly. With the facts before them in regard to the vast fortunes on the one hand, and the great destitution and consequent growing indication of turbulence on the other, and without giving attention to the guiding light of the prophecy that shows what all this means, is it any wonder that strong denunciations should be made against these men of vast wealth, and that by so many the future should be looked upon with forebodings of evil?

In the *Forum* of November, 1889, is an article by Thomas G. Shearman, entitled "The owners of the United States."

In this article he mentions two estates valued at $150,000,000 each, five estates worth $100,000,000 each, and more than sixty-three other estates worth from $20,000,000 to $70,000,000 each. Concerning these estates he says:—

"Making the largest allowance for exaggerated reports, there can be no doubt that these seventy names represent an aggregate wealth of $2,700,000,000, or an average of over $37,500,000 each. The writer has not specially sought for information concerning any one worth less than $20,000,000, but has incidentally learned of fifty other persons worth over $10,000,000, of whom thirty are valued in all at $450,000,000, making together one hundred persons worth over $3,000,000,000. Yet this list includes very few names from New England, and none from the south. Evidently it would be easy for any specially well-informed person to make up a list of one hundred names of persons averaging $25,000,000 each, in addition to ten averaging $100,000,000 each. The average annual income of the richest hundred Americans can not be less than $1,200,000, and probably exceeds $1,500,000."

Mr. Shearman also estimates that twenty-five thousand persons own one-half of all the wealth of the United States.

On June 9, 1897, the Hon. Roger Q. Mills, of Texas, made a speech in the United States Senate in which he said, "Mr. Shearman is one of the ablest lawyers in the country;" and concerning his article in the *Forum* he stated that "it was published and republished again in the magazines. It was published in 1889. It has never been questioned. It has been sent broadcast; it has been commented on everywhere; and never have I heard one breath of contradiction or criticism of the article."

Think for a moment what some of the foregoing figures mean. The man with an estate of $150,000,000, if he had to count it one dollar at a time, would need to do quite rapid work if he counted $60,000 in a day of ten hours, and at this rate it would take him seven long years to accomplish his task; if his fortune was in one-dollar bills, and placed end to end, it would reach about two-thirds the way around the earth.

Speaking of the enormous wealth represented by these figures, Mr. Mills, in his speech in the Senate, said: "We have been told that concentrated money is equally as powerful for evil as concentrated swords and bayonets, and that liberty must leave the land where either tyrant rules. We are trampling to-day all these admonitions under our feet. . . . Our ship is driving upon the rocks; and unless we seize the helm, and change its course, the historian will emerge from the darkness to write the melancholy pages of the decline and fall of the great American Republic."

The somber view that Mr. Mills takes of the situation is, as every one knows, shared by thousands of our best and most intelligent men.

The New York *Thrice-a-week World* of June 21, 1897, contained the report of an interview with Mr. Shearman in regard to his figures published in 1889 concerning concentrated wealth. In this interview Mr. Shearman says: "The principles upon which these calculations were made have never been impeached, even by those who object most strongly to the inferences drawn. . . . Taken as a whole, my original figures were much too low."

Among his "original figures" may be classed his article in the *Forum* of January, 1891, under the heading of "The Coming Billionaire." In this article he concludes that if calculation is made on the very lowest basis, some of these vast estates must reach a billion dollars inside of the next forty years. Although this statement of Mr. Shearman was considered very wild at the time it was written, yet only about one-fourth of that forty years are allowed to pass before one holds in his own possession the predicted billion, or about one seventy-fifth of the entire wealth of the United States. It is stated on authority that another man, while he does not possess the whole amount himself, yet he is such a manipulator of finance that he handles, uses and holds within the grasp of his own hands the enormous sum of over five billions in various kinds of properties and securities. The simple millionaire in these days is only a very small fish in the great sea of accumulating fortunes; it takes the billionaire now, or one who has so many millions that he has almost reached the billion mark, to become a real "king of finance." This billionaire does not receive his prodigious fortune as an inheritance, representing the accumulations of many generations of ancestors that have lived before him, but he steps upon the stage of action and finds things so favorable to his covetous designs that in one or two decades of his own brief lifetime he "heaps" up this unprecedented fortune. Who can fail to be impressed by these astounding facts?

In the amassing of wealth there is a combination among the capitalists, so that they can control the sale of the staple commodities of daily life, and by the various means at their command lay the whole country under tribute to them.

In the New York *Thrice-a-week World* of February 10, 1897, was an article with the following head-lines:—

The Profits of the Sugar Trust on Its Refining Business Alone Have Amounted to

$236,240,000 IN TEN YEARS.

This Calculation Is Based on the Sworn Testimony Given by ——————— Its President, and ——— ——————— Secretary and Treasurer, Before the Legislative Committee That Is Now Investigating Trusts

---

This vast sum is made by the trust on just one of the commodities of daily life.

It should be observed in this connection that it took ten years back in the nineties to make that two hundred thirty-six millions. But one of the big trusts that was formed in the first year of the new century made a net profit during the first twelve months of its existence of $140,000,000. Thus that which seemed like an immense thing to the New York *World* in 1897 is wholly swept away in less than half a decade by the much greater accomplishment that comes bearing down upon the world as a veritable avalanche in commercial speculation.

Speaking of a trust controlling another staple commodity, Mr. Henry D. Lloyd says: "A friendly journal, the New York *Sun*, of April 25, 1889, in an editorial paragraph concerning the wealth of one of the trustees, said, 'His regular income is $20,000,000 a year.' Another entirely friendly paper, with sources of information of the very best, put his income two years later at $30,000,000 a year. No denial of the *Sun's* statement was attempted, and the *Sun* never withdrew or modified its figures."—*Wealth against Commonwealth, p. 459.*

A man with a yearly income of twenty or thirty millions of dollars is certainly "heaping together treasures."

But the individual is not satisfied with what he can heap together alone, neither are the powers of the ordinary corporation adequate to his selfish greed. Hence "trusts" have been invented, by means of which the whole business of not merely the entire nation but of the whole world can be monopolized, and compelled to pay a revenue to the covetous worshiper at the shrine of mammon. Among the trusts reported to have been formed in the earlier months of 1898 was the tobacco trust, with a capital of $100,000,000; the electric trust, with a capital of $25,000,000; the silverware trust, with a capital of $30,000,000; the iron trust, with a capital of $200,000,000; the cutlery trust, with a capital of $2,000,000; and so on. The total amount of wealth grasped by the trusts in this country alone for the year 1898 is placed by good authorities at $1,000,-

000,000. In 1898 these figures seemed enormous, and the world was startled by what they might signify. Newspapers fell to discussing the danger; the platform and pulpit took it up, and it was a theme of discussion and agitation everywhere. But soon after this great out-cropping of trusts in 1898 there was the formation of the big steel trust with its capitalization of $1,389,339,956, and other trusts with a capitalization of over $10,000,000 each, making an aggregate of $4,318,005,646. Be particular to note that this enormous figure embraces only the trusts with a capitalization of over $10,000,000 each; it does not take into account the long array of trusts and combines that have a lesser capitalization.

All are familiar with the fact that these large aggregations of capital crush out the small independent dealers, and hold the prices of commodities, and the general interests of business, within their iron grasp.

It would be a wearisome as well as a useless task to try to present anything like a tithe of the great mass of evidence that might be given in regard to the "heaping" together of treasure. Every one knows that the combines of wealth meet us at the very threshold of life, and, following us all the journey through, ask a tribute at every step on the various necessary things of daily use, until finally the portals of the tomb are reached, and even there are we met by the agent of the undertakers' association, who collects his fee before our mortal remains are allowed to be laid to rest.

Meet men everywhere, and their theme is "making money." Money must be had at all hazards. If it can not be obtained honestly, it must be gained in some other way. A. R. Barrett, formerly a government examiner of failed banks, says, in the *Arena:*—

"Statistics show that . . . bank wreckers, embezzlers, and defaulters have robbed the people of this country of . . . an average of over ten millions of dollars per annum; *and this state of things has been growing worse. . . . The cause may be attributed to that desire which seems to pervade all classes to 'get rich quickly' and to live extravagantly.* The means by which the riches are obtained are too little considered. It is unfortunate that political and social power are too often measured by riches, and the temptation to obtain such power is greater than many men can withstand."

According to a statement made by the lord chief justice of England, an average of about $20,000,000 per annum is embezzled in the British Empire. Thus is the Old World outstripping the New in this infamous business.

Such statements of fraud and embezzlement are simply appalling; but when we remember that we are in the time when men full of "self-love and covetousness" are to "heap treasure together," the reverent student of the Word of God will recognize in it the clear fulfilment of prophecy.

Some of the great capitalists invest much of their money in land; and it may be interesting as well as impressive to note the vast estates some of them own. There is one person in the United States who owns four million sixty-eight thousand acres. This is equal to a little more than a ninth of the whole state of Illinois. A syndicate of four men owns an estate of three million acres, or what is equal to more than a twelfth of the state of Illinois. There is another estate of nearly two million acres, and still another of one million acres. There are, besides, several syndicates, each of which owns from five hundred thousand to four million five hundred thousand acres, as well as a long list of individuals, each one of whom owns from fifty thousand to seven hundred thousand acres of land.

Just what use men could ever think of making of such vast amounts of land, it is impossible for any one to suggest. But we are in the "time of the end," and men are engaged in "heaping treasures together for the last days."

We might naturally expect that when there is such an

amassing of wealth on the one hand, there would be a corresponding amount of destitution on the other. And the Scriptures affirm this fact as follows: "Behold, the hire of the laborers who have reaped down your fields, which is of you kept back by fraud, crieth; and the cries of them which have reaped are entered into the ears of the Lord of Sabaoth." James 5:4. Then capital, in these "last days," when men are so "covetous," and such "lovers of their own selves," will oppress the laborer so that he "crieth" out against it, and it is said that the "cries" are heard by the Lord. It is not the purpose of these pages to discuss either the rights or the wrongs of either one of the parties to this capital and labor controversy. The design is to call attention to the prophecy and to invite every one to consider how literally it is being fulfilled in the doings of the day.

Despite the prosperity that may reign in portions of the world at different times, there are whole armies of people in all the large cities that are continually bordering on the verge of destitution, and in many cases the destitution is quite complete. But how cheering is the thought that in spite of this wicked and covetous age, in which Satan is trying to turn every one to evil, there are thousands of kind and sympathizing hearts and hands that are throbbing and working for these unfortunates! These workers in our city missions are constantly finding, amid the destitution there, children six or seven years of age with not a single article of clothing upon them. Families of four or five persons of both sexes are crowded together in one room, sometimes below ground, and this room is used for every purpose. There are tenements in which from one hundred and fifty to two hundred persons, men, women, and children, are herded together like cattle—perhaps it would be more truthful to say hogs—and sleep in heaps upon the landings of the stairs and every other available place. These houses are owned by respectable(?) citizens, who are not satisfied with less than twenty or thirty per cent profit upon their investment.

Within these filthy premises are the "sweat shops" of our cities, where individuals are paid for their work at such starvation rates as forty-five cents a dozen for making "kneepants." The merchant, of course, since he gets his work done so cheaply, and sells his goods at a high price, and perhaps owns the miserable quarters where these "sweated" workers dwell, and gets a good rent for them, has a very handsome profit. The untold misery that exists in these "sweat shops" the day of judgment alone can reveal. Being able only to make a bare existence, these unfortunate creatures are compelled to work every moment of their time from early morn till late at night; they can not stop for sickness or pain so long as they can compel their physical machinery to act; and the quarters they occupy any one would recognize as not conducive to health. One man was asked to repair the roof over his workmen. It was giving them rheumatism, asthma, and consumption. He said, "Men are cheaper than shingles; no sooner does one drop out than a dozen are ready to take his place."

Through the Boston *Herald* Rev. Everett D. Burr gives the result of some of his experiences, as follows:—

"A short time ago I heard of a family in very destitute circumstances. I was told that the father, a steady, hardworking man, had been one of the last discharged from the cordage factory. I went to the house, and found there a family of seven, who hadn't had anything to eat for eight days except beans, and didn't have money to buy even salt.

"The other day when I went to visit a house, a little bit of a girl met me outside the door, and, seeing the basket on my arm, asked me if I had anything to eat in it; 'for, do you know,' she said pathetically, as she laid her hand on a worn little apron, 'I feel awful queer there, kind of sore, you know?'

"Misery . . . exists in these sweat-shops."

"And it is the knowledge fathers have of the suffering of the children at home that makes it harder for them to bear the present state of affairs. Why, men come to us after walking the streets all day, sink into a chair, and almost cry, telling us they can not go home to the children empty-handed."

Childhood, of all times of life, should be relieved from every distressing care and filled up with sunshine and joy. But there is no sunshine in the little hearts in the "sweat shops." Sometimes the father makes the situation worse by giving up to strong drink; but where this is not the case, in these miserable burrowing places (they can not be called by that dearest name, home), not only father and mother have to work all day and until late at night, but little children four and five years of age, in order to assist in supporting the family, are required to work all the weary hours of a long day and evening too. And is it any wonder, under these circumstances, that a gentleman who incidentally remarked in one of these "sweat shops" that he was forty-five years old, was met with the serious and deeply pathetic comment of a little girl, "I should think any one would get so tired of living so long"? How distressing it seems that even in childhood, which is usually buoyant and happy, every spark of joy that makes life worth living is thus snuffed out, and coming years, instead of being filled with bright anticipations, are looked upon with "tired" and gloomy forebodings that are more dismal than the tomb! And how much more distressing is the thought that in this age of self-love and covetousness, hearts are so icy cold that they can press down these poor unfortunates, and make their sad lot harder and harder, instead of trying to send one ray of sunshine across their dreary pathway!

While this distressing poverty is exhibiting itself in all our great cities, we may be met with such head-lines in the papers as those appearing below.

What a striking fulfilment is such an occurrence as this of that verse already quoted from James' prophecy, "Ye have lived in pleasure on the earth, and been *wanton;* ye have nourished your hearts, as in a day of slaughter" (James 5:5)!

Truly, as we read this prophecy, we must acknowledge that in prophetic vision James had presented to his mind a vivid portrayal of these "last-day" scenes; for while the distressing "cries" of the oppressed laborer are still upon the prophet's ears, his attention is

---

LUXURIOUS FEASTS OF ANCIENTS OUTDONE

800 Persons in Attire of Surpassing Magnificence Participate in New York's Greatest Social Function.

HOSTESS DECKED IN PRICELESS JEWELS;

Mrs. ——————— Led the Quadrille, Wearing Gems Valued at a Quarter of a Million Dollars.

GREAT CROWDS SURROUND THE WALDORF.

The most sumptuous, brilliant and costly social function that New York has ever known was the fancy-dress ball given by Mrs. ——————— at the Waldorf last night.

About eight hundred people were there, of whom more than four hundred and fifty were women. The ball placed about $100,000 in circulation.

The ball began at midnight and ended at 5 o'clock this morning. Therefore its pleasures cost at the rate of $100,000 an hour. The cost to the hostess was about $125,000.

It was a superb spectacle. People came thousands of miles to attend it.

suddenly directed to the "wanton" "pleasure" of those who are "nourishing their hearts as in a day of slaughter."

Please read again carefully the first verses of the fifth chapter of James and see how literally they are meeting their fulfilment to-day. Men are most truly and marvelously "heaping together treasure for the last days;" the "cry of the laborer" is waxing louder and louder because of his great destitution, and amid it all is the "wanton" "pleasure" of the rich, individuals among whom, decked in jewels worth a quarter of a million, are dancing at balls which cost a hundred thousand dollars an hour. Truly a more literal fulfilment of the prophecy could not be asked, and as we see these things, can there be any doubt in regard to where we are standing in the history of the world?

Says Bishop Potter: "The *growth of wealth and of luxury, wicked, wasteful, and wanton,* as before God I declare that luxury to be, *has been matched step by step by a deepening and deadening poverty which has left whole neighborhoods of people practically without hope and without aspiration.* At such a time, for the church of God to sit still and be content with theories of its duty outlawed by time, and long ago demonstrated to be grotesquely inadequate to the demands of a living situation, this is to deserve the scorn of men and the curse of God. Take my word for it, men and brethren, unless you and I, and all those who have any gift or stewardship of talents or means, of whatever sort, are willing to get up out of our sloth and ease and selfish dilettanteism of service, and get down among the people who are battling amid their poverty and ignorance — young girls for their chastity, young men for their better ideal of righteousness, old and young alike for one clear ray of the immortal courage and the immortal hope — then verily the church, in its stately splendor, its apostolic orders, its venerable ritual, its decorous and dignified conventions, is revealed as simply a monstrous and insolent impertinence."

The professed churches of Christ certainly have a grave

responsibility in this matter; for many of those who hold such great wealth make a profession of Christianity. And when we consider Him whose whole life was spent going about doing good for others; and of whom it is said He "hath not where to lay His head;" and of whom it is written, "Though He was rich, yet for your sakes He became poor, that ye through His poverty might be rich"—how can we truly be His followers if we are found acting in the contrary manner?

The Word says: "How hardly shall they that have riches enter into the kingdom of God! For it is easier for a camel to go through a needle's eye, than for a rich man to enter into the kingdom of God." Luke 18 : 24, 25. The Lord says further: "Charge them that are rich in this world, that they be not highminded, nor trust in uncertain riches, but in the living God, who giveth us richly all things to enjoy; that they do good, that they be rich in good works, ready to distribute, willing to communicate; laying up in store for themselves a good foundation against the time to come, that they may lay hold on eternal life." 1 Tim. 6 : 17-19.

Comment on the foregoing scripture is unnecessary. Let each one receive it as the direct voice of God, and prepare to make answer to Him in person. The church or the pastor that will bear a carnally-soothing testimony now, seeking to take away the keen edge of God's warning, becomes equally responsible with the man of wealth. The question is that of eternal destiny; and the man who is groping in the dark should not be told that he is all right. He should have his darkness and deception driven away by receiving the clear light of the infallible Word.

The warning given by James should not be overlooked: "Go to now, ye rich men, weep and howl for your miseries that shall come upon you. Your riches are corrupted, and your garments are moth-eaten. Your gold and silver is cankered, and the rust of them shall be a witness against you, and shall eat your flesh as it were fire. Ye have heaped treasure together for the last days." Chapter 5:1-3. Thus does this scripture not only call attention to the "treasure" that shall be "heaped together for the last days," but it also tells of the "miseries" that shall cause these "rich men" to "weep and howl," and of their unused wealth that "shall eat their flesh as it were fire."

The present seizing of the wealth of the world, and its wanton display, by a comparatively few men, form a large part of the seed-sowing for that world-wide reign of terror that is being hastened on. At different times small portions of the world have had to pass through the revolutionary horrors that congested and grinding wealth has produced; but that which confronts us to-day is not local, but universal; and the most distressing poverty that can be found is not more to be pitied than the men of colossal wealth; for smouldering beneath the banquet hall and all the luxuriant, extravagant dissipations and displays of the rich, may be clearly seen and heard the threatening tokens of the social volcano. The position of the rich is not an enviable one. The Word of God places the matter in its true light, and rich and poor alike should give heed to the faithful warnings.

When the Word of God says, "Go to now, ye rich men, weep and howl for your miseries that shall come upon you," it is a warning that is not to be passed by lightly. There is to be not only a "weeping" but a "howling" because of "miseries" that shall come upon the rich. It must be observed that the misery that causes this weeping and howling of the rich is not something that God brings upon them in the form of a judgment or divine punishment, but it is something that "shall come" upon them. In other words, it is the harvest for which they have been sowing. They have aggravated the poor and unfortunate by luxurious vices, and "wanton" extravagance, and now they are simply reaping what they have sown. A more definite truth can not be found than the Bible statement, "Whatsoever a man soweth, that shall he also reap." This is the statement of a divine law that may be observed everywhere. Our reaping must always be the fruit of what we sow.

And in this connection, it should be stated that the man of moderate wealth, the one who has made a good living for himself and family, and built himself a neat and comfortable home, but who can not be ranked among the financial kings, will be struck by the calamities predicted in this prophecy the same as "the great money barons" unless he is put on his guard, and prepares himself against it.

God has permitted little corners of the world at different times to enact some of the scenes that are here foretold as being universal in the "last days." The most notable of these scenes is the one familiarly known to everybody as the "French Revolution and Reign of Terror." Those who are acquainted with the history of that time know that reason was not allowed to act. The virtues of the individual were not investigated. But the popular cry was raised against men and women, and they were marched to the guillotine, in whole platoons, day after day.

Men should be able to read in unmistakable language the signs of these times. The banding together of every trade and laboring occupation of whatever kind, and the popular clamor that is being stirred up against the rich can not be long in reaching a terrible climax. If this scripture prophecy was left entirely out of the calculation, men should learn from the reading of history alone that the conditions of to-day are rushing the world along to a general hurricane of revolution. The situation is such that it can not be averted. Just as surely as effect follows cause, just that surely may we expect to see a world-wide revolution and general reign of terror. In that time the man who lives in a good house will be made the target for the bomb and torch. The fact that he is in comfortable circumstances will be all the evidence required before the "violent" jury that will try his case at the mob's tribunal. Possessing honesty, integrity, and virtue, or lacking these things, will not enter into the count. In times of revolution, reason does not bear rule; it is sentiment and popular impulse that drives the mob along to do their revolting acts of violence.

We have seen in a preceding chapter that these last days are to be characterized by "violence," and this clash between capital and labor is one among the ingredients that will be worked into the stormy conflict. Do not throw this matter aside by saying, "This is such a dark picture." It is perfectly clear from the world's standpoint that the picture is a dark one. It is true, nevertheless, and therefore we should give it our attention; for if we properly consider it, and properly relate ourselves to it, we need not be afflicted with any of the miseries of the time. To close our eyes to the facts that enter into the situation means everlasting ruin.

The truly enlightened Christian will not be found now quarreling with the rich over their possessions; he will not be a party to this controversy between the rich and the poor; he will not espouse either side of it. He will recognize that his work is to point men to the fulfilling prophecy, and thus show them what these threatening dangers mean; for he knows that the time can not be far off when "they shall go into the holes of the rocks, and into the caves of the earth, for fear of the Lord, and for the glory of His majesty, when He ariseth to shake terribly the earth. In that day a man shall cast his idols of silver, and his idols of gold, which they made each one for himself ["lovers of their own selves, covetous"] to worship, to the moles and to the bats; to go into the clefts of the rocks, and into the tops of the ragged rocks, for fear of the Lord, and for the glory of His majesty, when He ariseth to shake terribly the earth." Isa. 2:19-21.

So, then, He of whom it is said, "Justice and judgment are the habitation of Thy throne; mercy and truth shall go before Thy face," will deal in righteousness with all classes,— with those who cling to their riches and wanton pleasure, instead of accepting the "true riches" and the "joys that are forevermore," as well as with the most lowly and poor.

Riches were intended by the Creator to be a blessing to all mankind. What an opportunity the man of wealth has in these times; but soon he will be called to give an account of his stewardship; and if still found at that time to be untrue to his trust, how great will be the confusion and bitter remorse into which he will be thrown! The money now found in the hands of many wealthy men has been gathered by extortion, and the commonest kind of honesty would suggest that it be returned to its rightful owners. But the poor should not take this work of judgment into their own hands by any means; for "behold the Judge standeth before the door," and before that tribunal only righteousness and truth will prevail.

While mercy's door is still held open, let every nerve be thrilled with the one work of pointing all to Him who is the Friend of sinners, and whose coming is only mercifully deferred that all who can possibly be touched by His love may be led to get ready to meet Him, and, amid the unsullied joys of the redeemed, live in His presence forevermore. Reader, will you assist in passing the good news along that Jesus is coming again, and that His coming is near, even at the doors? Men everywhere are unnerved before the thought of the things that they see about them. In the prophetic language of the apostle, their "hearts are failing them for fear, and for looking after those things that are coming on the earth." Help to tell them that this darkness is only the evil that Satan is stirring up in his last desperate effort to destroy mankind. There is a shelter provided for every one, and we should see this, and enter into it before the destruction can overtake us.

CHAPTER TWENTY-TWO

AND the nations were angry, and Thy wrath is come, and the time of the dead, that they should be judged, and that Thou shouldest give reward unto Thy servants the prophets, and to the saints, and them that fear Thy name, small and great; and shouldest destroy them which destroy the earth. And the temple of God was opened in heaven, and there was seen in His temple the ark of His testament; and there were lightnings, and voices, and thunderings, and an earthquake, and great hail." Rev. 11: 18, 19.

This scripture brings us face to face with the "time of the dead, that they should be judged." Observe that the text also says that "the nations were angry." So, then, when the great judgment day is at hand, the nations will not be found at peace.

Another scripture bears the same direct testimony: "And I saw three unclean spirits like frogs come out of the mouth

WERE ANGRY

of the dragon, and out of the mouth of the beast, and out of the mouth of the false prophet. For they are the spirits of devils, working miracles, which go forth unto the kings of the earth and of the whole world, to gather them to the battle of that great day of God Almighty." Rev. 16: 13, 14.

How extensive is the application of this scripture! "The kings of the earth and of the whole world," through the agency of evil spirits, are to be gathered "to the battle of that great day of God Almighty." The Lord has said, "Wo to the inhabiters of the earth and of the sea! for the devil is come down unto you, having great wrath, because he knoweth that he hath but a short time." Rev. 12: 12. It is this evil one who goes to "the kings of the earth" to make them "angry" when he "knoweth" that time is short and the "great day of God Almighty" is almost here. The same evil spirit has sought to keep the people in ignorance of his workings by filling them with the idea that we are approaching a time of universal peace instead of the most awful war that the world has ever seen.

Through the prophet Joel we have a vivid description of the great war preparations near the close of time. He says: "Proclaim ye this among the nations: Prepare war; stir up the mighty men; let all the men of war draw near, let them come up. Beat your plowshares into swords, and your pruning-hooks into spears; let the weak say, I am strong. Assemble yourselves [margin], and come, all ye nations round about, and gather yourselves together; thither cause thy mighty ones to come down, O Lord. Let the nations bestir themselves, and come up to the valley of Jehoshaphat; for there will I sit to judge all the nations round about. Put ye in the sickle, for the harvest is ripe; come, get you down [margin]; for the winepress is full, the fats overflow; for their wickedness is great. Multitudes, multitudes in the valley of decision [margin, Authorized Version, "concision, or threshing"]; for the day of the Lord is near in the valley of decision. The sun and the moon are darkened, and the stars withdraw their shining. And the Lord shall roar from Zion, and utter His voice from Jerusalem; and the heavens and the earth shall shake; but the Lord will be a refuge unto His people, and a stronghold to the children of Israel." Chapter 3: 9–16, R. V.

This scripture also presents the judgment scenes. "For there will I sit to judge all the nations round about." And again: "Multitudes, multitudes in the valley of decision! for the day of the Lord is near in the valley of decision." Now observe that just as clearly as this scripture brings to view the sitting of the Lord "to judge *all* the nations," and the time when the "day of the Lord is near," just so clearly does it say: "Proclaim ye this among the nations: Prepare war; stir up the mighty men; let all the men of war draw near, let them come up. Beat your plowshares into swords, and your pruning-hooks into spears; let the weak say, I am strong."

Thus we find that the Scripture teaching makes it clear that the "last days" will be characterized by the intensity of the

war spirit as well as by the *intensity of wickedness in general*, the marvelous *increase of knowledge*, the *heaping together of treasure*, and the great combining of every masterly deception that the enemy can invent.

The Lord, through His prophets, speaks the truth concerning the nations. There will be a preparation for war; and instead of beating their swords into plowshares, and their spears into pruning-hooks, they will beat their "plowshares into swords, and their pruning-hooks into spears." Observe how different is the language of the Lord from that which many people will be saying in the last days, as has already been shown in chapter 14.

The prophetic declaration is that the war spirit will prevail over the whole world; and what may be seen among the nations to-day? Does the outlook indicate

1. Viking, 700 A. D.
2. Roman or Greek Galley, 300 B. C.
3. Armades, 1098.
4. Venetian, 1300.
5. Spanish, 1492.
6. French, 1600.
7. English, 1700.
8. American, 1814.
9. American, 1835.
10. Monitor, 1862.
11. Merrimac, 1862.
12. First-class battle-ship, 20th century.

Evolution of the battle-ship.

a universal peace? Are not the greatest armies being hastily gathered, and the most marvelous implements of war being forged, that could ever have been conceived in the wildest realm of imaginative fancy?

The following table gives, as nearly as the facts can be obtained from the best statistical authorities, the comparative strength of the principal armies of the world for the years 1869, 1892, 1897 and 1902.

COUNTRIES.	1869.	1892.	1897.	1902.
Germany	977,262	4,500,000	5,225,105	5,561 395
France	825,696	4 350,000	5,014,842	5,076.419
Italy	464,321	1,636,000	2,223,114	3,308,551
Austria	822,472	2,500,000	1,782,400	1,872,178
Russia	1,199,996	4,000,000	5,093,816	5,017,703
Great Britain	251,722	602,000	800,800	1,276,400
Turkey	499,360	1,150,000	1,120,138	1,500,000
Spain	173,785	800,000	1,561,826	937,067
Denmark	50,371	91,000	222,695	93,076
Greece	14,716	180,000	297,964	218,958
Switzerland	350,020	338,000	493,175	554,500
Sweden and Norway	183,561	338,000	276,219	580,000
Bulgaria			226,342	236,270
Servia	25.000	180,000	271,170	350,000
Roumania	38,000	280,000	250,537	241,915
Japan			349,941	632,000
China			631,400	1,000,000
Mexico			165,427	208,984
Brazil			98,142	94,620
Chile			95,714	72,110
Argentine Republic			66,237	73,300
Venezuela			257,764	29,525
Totals	5,876,282	20,945,000	26,524,768	28,934,971

Increase between 1869 and 1892, 15,068,718; increase between 1892 and 1897, 5,579,768; increase between 1897 and 1902, 2,410,203; increase for the whole 33 years, between 1869 and 1902, 23,058,689.

The great Napoleon introduced the idea of putting the whole male population under military conscription. The plan was at first treated as an innovation that should not be carried into practical effect. But, notwithstanding the military genius of Napoleon, and his great ability in gathering and organizing

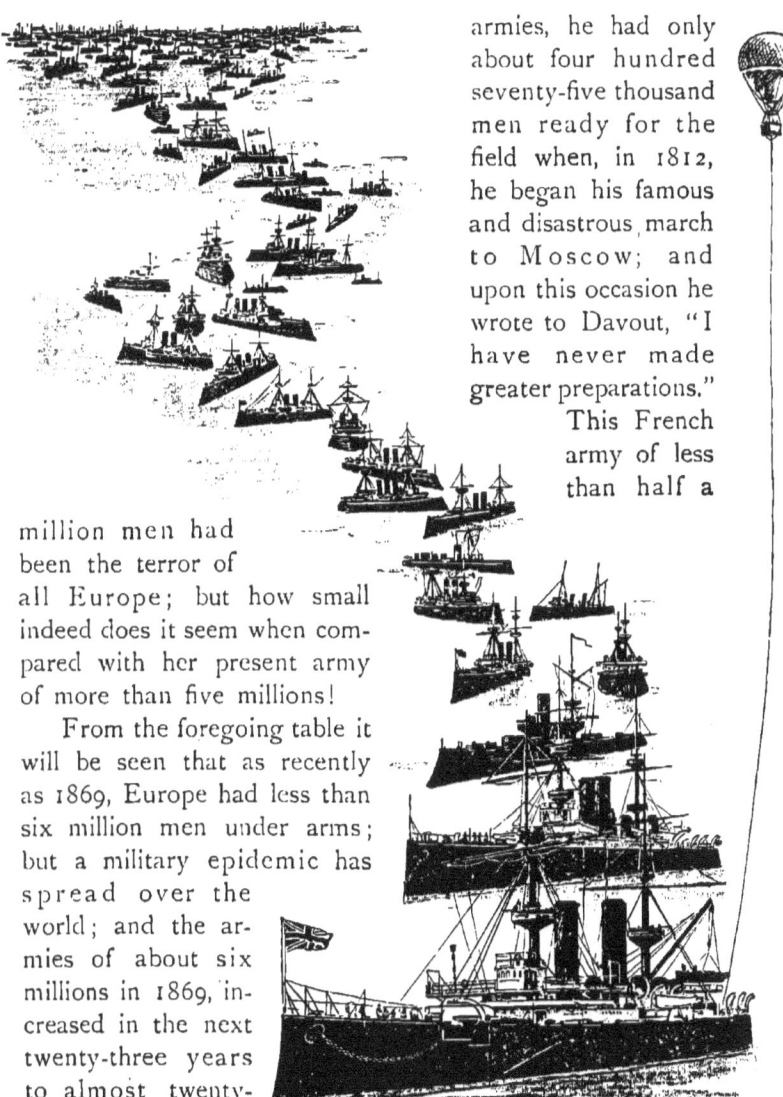

armies, he had only about four hundred seventy-five thousand men ready for the field when, in 1812, he began his famous and disastrous march to Moscow; and upon this occasion he wrote to Davout, "I have never made greater preparations." This French army of less than half a million men had been the terror of all Europe; but how small indeed does it seem when compared with her present army of more than five millions!

From the foregoing table it will be seen that as recently as 1869, Europe had less than six million men under arms; but a military epidemic has spread over the world; and the armies of about six millions in 1869, increased in the next twenty-three years to almost twenty-one millions. And

British navy, 30 miles long. *Revenge* in the foreground.

in the five years between 1892 and 1897, another addition of five and a half millions, and between 1897 and 1902, still 2,410,203 more were added to these unprecedented armies, composed of men who are trained to the highest degree of perfection in the military art. It is a further significant fact that two million four hundred thirty-four thousand ninety-four

The war-ships of the world, one to a mile, would cover a line farther than from New York to Liverpool.

of the number were added to these expanding armies during the one year of 1897. Still more significant than all these other facts is the military fever that broke out so suddenly and so extensively in the United States in the early part of 1898. This country had held herself aloof from the entanglements of Old World politics, and in her majestic isolation felt no need of a great army; but trouble with Spain arises, and with one dashing bound she springs into the very center of the broils of the "angry" nations, and from every human indication she will remain in the turbulent stream of international politics until the final battle of that "great day."

But this marvelous increase in the number of men composing the armies of the world is by no means a full presentation of their vastly-increased power; for the weapons with which Napoleon and the great generals of all former times fought, were mere toys when compared with the weapons that are now being prepared.

Previous to the Rebellion in this country, 1861–1864, breech-loading guns were not in use to any extent. Their introduction placed a weapon in the hands of the infantry that could be fired much more rapidly than the guns they replaced; and immediately other improvements in ammunition, etc., followed, making these breech-loading guns far more effective in range and accuracy. In 1861 Dr. R. J. Gatling invented the gun that bears his name, and the ingenious mechanism of this weapon enables it to fire *from six hundred to twelve hundred shots per minute.* The "Maxim automatic machine gun" is perhaps one of the best known of these modern "lead squirts," as they are popularly called. This gun is fully automatic; that is, when its ammunition is placed in position, the gunner simply keeps his finger pressed on the trigger and directs the aim, and the recoil from each bullet as it is fired ejects the shell, and throws in place and discharges the next bullet, and so on. The operator simply swings the gun to and fro very much as a fireman or a gardener would use his hose, and he pours upon the enemy a literal stream of leaden death. No advancing column can meet such a fire without well-nigh, if not complete, destruction.

Among the illustrations of the awfully destructive work of these machine guns may be cited the fight on the Nile between the British and the Dervishes, in September of 1898. The Dervishes had none of the modern weapons, but showed all the valor of the most warlike armies of former times. They charged upon the British in great numbers, but it was only to be mowed down by thousands beneath the withering fire of the machine guns of the English. The reports stated that less than a hundred of the British were killed and not three hundred were wounded, while the lowest estimates of the Dervishes killed and wounded were fifteen thousand, and some reports said twenty-two thousand. This is but a mere trifle, however, when compared with

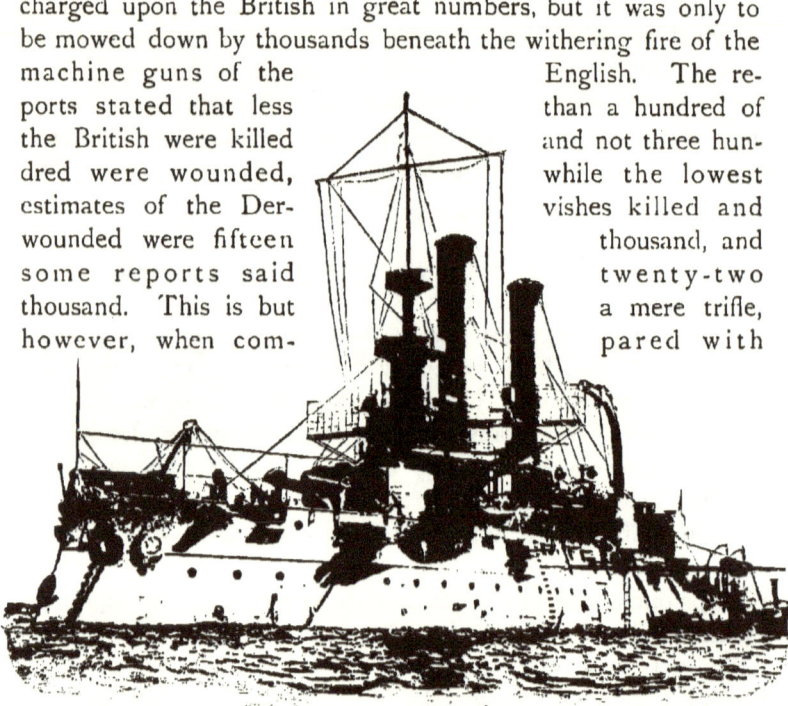

Sea-going battle-ship *Iowa*. She is armored with 14 inches of steel plate, and armed with four 12-inch, eight 8-inch, six 4-inch rapid firers, twenty 6-pounders, four 1-pounders, four Colt guns, two field pieces and four torpedo tubes. Her speed is 17.1 knots; displacement, 11,340 tons.

what will take place when the great conflict shall come between the vast armies of the civilized world, when all are fully armed and equipped with the latest improved and deadliest weapons. But it is not alone in these smaller arms for the infantry that the great improvements have been made. The wars of thirty to forty years ago were fought with old muzzle-loading, cast-iron cannon, and the most of them were smoothbore. While some of these guns had about as large a bore as the guns of to-day, no comparison could be made as to their effectiveness.

All are familiar with the famous battle between the *Merrimac* and *Monitor* in the Civil War of the United States. Mr. John R. Spears thus describes the armament of the *Merrimac:* "The battery of the *Merrimac* contained six of the nine-inch Dahlgrens found in the Norfolk navy-yard, and four rifles designed by Brooke. Two of these rifles were mounted as pivots at bow and stern, and two smaller ones were in the broadside. The pivots were cast-iron muzzle-loading rifles of seven-inch caliber, and they weighed fourteen thousand five hundred pounds each. The reader will appreciate the weight of the gun when it is told that the best gun in the British navy at that time was the sixty-eight-pounder, having a caliber of eight inches and weighing nine thousand five hundred pounds. Moreover, Brooke's heavy casting was reinforced by wrought-iron bands shrunk on. The broadside guns were of the same

Cross-section of revolving turret, showing the men on the inside working the big guns of a battle-ship.

construction, but weighed nine thousand pounds, and were of four-inch caliber. *Brooke's guns were far and away the best then afloat."—History of Our Navy, vol. 4, p. 188.*

John M. Brooke took the lead in the designing and building of the *Merrimac;* hence the references to him in the above quotation. It should also be stated that the *Merrimac* was covered with four inches of iron, laid on a backing of oak timbers.

The *Monitor* had a covering of five one-inch iron plates bolted on, and also backed by heavy oak timbers. Her flat deck was protected by two layers of half-inch iron plates. Her revolving turret was built up of eight thicknesses of one-inch

Washington Gun Factory. Boring and turning heavy guns.

iron plates. She carried in this turret two eleven-inch smoothbore guns, firing solid shot weighing from one hundred seventy to one hundred eighty pounds. Her speed was between four and five knots.

Both of these vessels were built at the same time, the *Merrimac* by the Confederates, and the *Monitor* by the Union forces in the North. The *Merrimac* was completed in time to get in one day's fighting before the *Monitor* could reach the scene of action. There had been much gossip about the building of these two iron-clads, and the rumors descriptive of the *Merrimac* had inspired a good deal of dread among many of the Northern men. But the officers of the Union navy were fully convinced that Lord Howard Douglas "had conclusively demonstrated that an iron-clad would prove more dangerous to her own crew than to the enemy;" so they were full of confidence when they entered the fight against this new engine of war. The *Merrimac* rammed the *Cumberland*, and soon sunk her. She then turned to the *Congress*, and after a little while destroyed this vessel also. She then retired to the Confederate side for the night, thinking to return in the morning and destroy the rest of the Union fleet and the shore batteries as well.

Interior of gun shop, Washington, D. C. Showing mammoth traveling crane.

The *Monitor* steamed into Hampton Roads that night; and when the *Merrimac* came back to resume the fight in the morning, the two vessels engaged in the first battle between iron-clads. They fought each other for six hours. Each vessel tried to ram the other. Shot after shot was fired with the ships almost touching each other. Each side had a new kind of naval equipment, and each fought with the desperate and valorous determination that the novel condition inspired.

The *Merrimac* came into this engagement with a good deal of confidence; for she had been the target the day before for one hundred heavy guns at one time. Some of her parts had been shot away, it is true; but her iron armor was still uninjured; and even after her six hours' fight with the *Monitor*, her armor was nowhere pierced. It is also true that she served her ten guns on the *Monitor* at short range for all of that six-hours contest, and to the best of her ability; still the *Monitor's* armor was also uninjured.

The *Monitor* fired one of her two guns about every seven or eight minutes, thus showing that it took nearly a quarter of an hour to load each gun and get it in position to shoot. The *Merrimac*, having five guns on each broadside, was able to fire one of them on an average about every three minutes while she was doing her best work. One gun crew on the

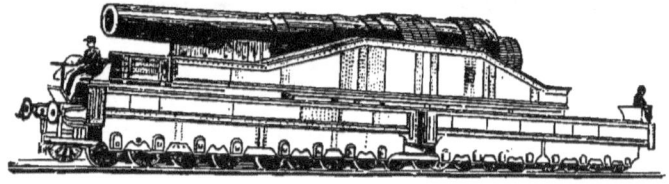

One of the big cannon being transported on a specially-constructed car, made of the best boiler steel, and requiring 32 wheels to support it.

Merrimac became so disheartened with their inability to break through the armor of the *Monitor*, that they ceased firing, saying as they did so, "We can do her about as much damage by snapping our fingers at her every two or three minutes."

This battle between these two iron-clads brought out the very best there was in all the world up to that time in the way of cannon as well as naval vessels. This matter has been presented somewhat in detail, in order to show the contrast between naval warfare then and now. The first battle between iron-clads was fought in the recent past; but both the ships and cannon of that time are very primitive when placed beside those in use to-day.

For instance, if it had been the battle-ship *Oregon* that met the *Merrimac* — or, for that matter, had she met the *Merrimac*

THE BATTLE OF MANILA, MAY 1, 1898.

On the left the Spanish fleet — Spanish sailors using rapid-fire gun. On the right the American fleet in line of battle.

and the *Monitor* combined — on that March morning in 1862, the story would have been very different. It was considered remarkable then that the *Merrimac* and the *Monitor* began firing at each other when they were a mile apart, even though their shots could make no impression on the iron walls at which they were aiming. But the *Oregon* would not consider it a very great feat, in the quiet waters of Hampton Roads, to turn one of her big thirteen-inch guns on a target like the *Merrimac* at a distance of three miles, and expect to hit her with nearly every shot. She has four of these thirteen-inch guns, and one of them can be loaded, aimed, and fired about every three and a half to four minutes. All four of these guns can be swung to either broadside at the same time; hence one of these thirteen-inch shells can be thrown from her four guns combined on an average of one a minute. These shells, weighing eleven hundred pounds, are thrown with five hundred fifty pounds of powder; and instead of one of them bounding from the sides of the *Merrimac*, it would crash through such a vessel from side to side, or from end to end, for that matter, and still have force enough left to drive through two or three more such craft. The striking energy of a thirteen-inch shell as it leaves the muzzle of the gun is thirty-three thousand six hundred twenty-seven foot-tons. That is to say, if its force was gradually applied, it would lift that number of tons one foot high — a sufficient force to lift the cruiser *Vizcaya* (several times heavier than was the *Merrimac*) four feet into the air.

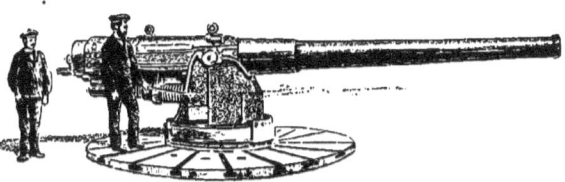
Marine gun on deck of ship.

These facts show that a battle-ship like the *Oregon* could have kept completely out of the range of the *Merrimac's* and the *Monitor's* guns while she easily broke the vessels to pieces with her thirteen-inch shells. But, in addition to thirteen-inch guns, battle-ships of the *Oregon* class carry eight eight-inch guns, four six-inch guns, twenty six-pounders, and six one-pounders, besides several Gatlings or some other type of the machine gun. Eight-inch guns are now built that are fired four times in sixty-two seconds, practically once every fifteen seconds. The projectile weighs two hundred fifty pounds, and will perforate twenty-one inches of iron. It can be imagined how quickly a battery of these guns would have made a pepper-box of the *Merrimac* or *Monitor*. Then following the eight-inch are the six-inch guns, which are now built so that they can be fired six times in a minute. Their projectile weighs a hundred pounds, and will pierce fifteen inches of iron. But if none of these larger guns were used against a craft like the *Merrimac* or *Monitor*, the torrent of steel that could be thrown from the small machine guns would drive through every port-hole, and in a moment of time kill every man aboard.

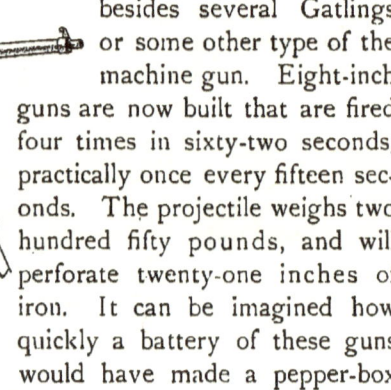

The Maxim automatic machine gun; fires 700 rifle bullets a minute.

Thus we see how completely the last thirty-six years have revolutionized the weapons of war. When we consider the difference between the very best battle-ship of 1862 and one of the best ships of to-day, we see that no comparison can be made; and nothing has been said about the twelve to eighteen-inch steel armor with which the modern man-of-war is covered. The best guns of 1862 might fire indefinitely at such steel walls, and make no impression upon them.

It is next to impossible to keep track of the improvements in the military and naval profession; for what may be truthfully said to-day is likely to be entirely out of date to-morrow. But suppose we take one of the many battle-ships that are now building. The Harveyized steel plates, which a few months ago were considered the best for armor, must be replaced by the "Krupp-gas-process" plates, which are such an improvement over the Harvey plates that armor ten and eleven inches thick has all the power of resistance possessed by the fifteen-inch to eighteen-inch Harvey armor. This allows a vessel to be built with all the strength and resistance of the *Oregon* or the *Massachusetts*, and yet by thus lightening her armor her coal supply may be so increased that she can keep at sea much longer. This very latest battle-ship would have four of the monster thirteen-inch guns already described. She would also have eight eight-inch and six six-inch quick-fire cannon, the effectiveness and the rapidity of action of which have already been mentioned. Then she would have among her smaller guns some four-inch cannon firing fifteen thirty-three-pound shells a minute, and such machine pieces as the Maxim nine-pounder, that fires sixty of such missiles per minute — one every second. She would have some six-pounder automatics, firing one hundred fifty shots per minute; also some

[Courtesy of *Scientific American*.]
The machine gun that fires a nine-pound shell every second.

The French quick-fire field gun.

of the one-pounders firing three hundred shells a minute, and then the military masts and other convenient parts in this most modern battle-ship would have a proper supply of the regulation machine guns, firing from six hundred to twelve hundred of the common infantry rifle-bullets per minute.

Such a modern ship, of course, would have a well fortified base of supplies. These fortifications would be built after the

[Courtesy of *Scientific American*.]
Rafferty Range Finder.—Gun detachment working out range, distance, and direction of the enemy.

most approved plans of modern times; and in addition to the small machine guns, and the rapid-fire cannon already described, some of the eight-inch and thirteen-inch guns would be mounted on disappearing carriages. These carriages enable the gunner to load his piece, take his aim, and fire from behind the embankments, without being exposed to the direct fire of the enemy. In this modern fort would also be several batteries of up-to-date mortars. The harbor that the mortars protect is all diagrammed; and by careful practise and calculation, it is possible to drop a shell in any section where a hostile ship is located. The mortar battery is out of sight behind the impenetrable embankments, and its action is wholly directed by telephone by the commander, who is on some eminence of observation out of danger from the enemy's guns. This fort would also be

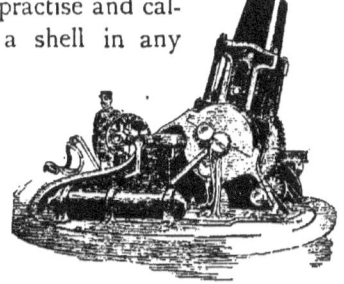
[Courtesy of *Scientific American*.]
Mortar elevated for firing.

supplied with one or more sixteen-inch breech-loading cannon. The latest and biggest gun of this type is a few inches less than fifty feet in length, and weighs one hundred forty tons. The powder chamber is over one and a half feet in diameter and about nine feet long. The shell weighs two thousand three hundred seventy pounds, and the powder charge is one thousand sixty pounds. The shell will leave the muzzle with a velocity of two thousand feet per second and an energy of sixty-four thousand eighty-four foot-tons; or, in other words, the power behind this big shell as it leaves the cannon would lift sixty-four of the biggest freight locomotives ten feet into the air. At a distance of two miles this shell would pass through twenty-seven and one-half inches of steel. See the accompanying

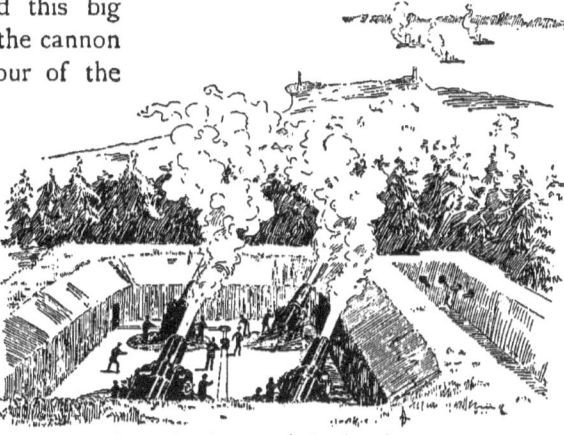
One section of a mortar battery in action.

diagram, which shows the actual penetration of a shot fired from one of these guns.

This modern fort would also have several of the big six-inch, eight-inch, ten-inch, and fifteen-inch pneumatic dynamite guns. The six-inch dynamite gun throws a two hundred forty

Actual penetration of a trial shot from a 16¼-inch, 110-ton gun. The missile passed through 20 inches compound plate, 8 inches wrought iron, 20 feet oak timbers, 5 feet granite, 11 feet concrete, and buried itself 6 feet in a brick wall.

pound shell, charged with fifty pounds of one of the modern high explosives, to a distance of six thousand yards; the eight-inch gun throws a three hundred forty pound shell, charged with one hundred pounds of high explosive, to a distance of five thousand yards; the ten-inch gun throws a five hundred pound shell, charged with two hundred pounds of high explosive, to a distance of four thousand four hundred yards; and the fifteen-inch gun throws a one thousand pound shell, charged with five hundred pounds of high explosive, to a distance of two thousand four hundred yards, while the same gun throws a two hundred forty pound shell six thousand yards. There are three separate fuses attached to these

[Courtesy of *Scientific American*]
A piece of 16-inch armor plate, showing effect of modern cannon.

dynamite shells to accomplish their explosion; one in the head, which acts on immersion; one in the base, which acts when a solid substance is hit; and the third explodes the shell after sinking to the bottom, in case the immersion fuse should happen to fail.

The *Scientific American Supplement* says:—

"In the official test of the three fifteen-inch guns near Fort Winfield Scott, San Francisco, it was required that thirty-four per cent of hits should fall within a rectangle measuring three hundred sixty feet by ninety feet, at a range of five thousand thirty yards. In the actual test seventy-five

(Courtesy of *Scientific American*.)
ALL-STEEL.   NICKEL-STEEL.   COMPOUND.
Results of armor-plate tests.

per cent of the shots fell within this rectangle, and a rectangle of two hundred ten by one hundred fifty-six feet would have contained them all.

"This test was made with shells charged with one hundred pounds of explosive, the composition of which was: Nitroglycerine, eighty-seven per cent; guncotton, seven per cent; camphor, four per cent; carbonate of magnesia, two per cent.

"In the same test, two shells of this size were fired from different guns at a hillside three thousand seven hundred yards distant across the harbor entrance. They struck sixty-one feet apart. The craters formed in the soft red rock by the explosions were bowl-shaped, one being twenty feet in diameter by four feet deep, and the other thirty feet in diameter by six feet deep."

Sighting with the Dudley pneumatic dynamite gun.

The reader understands, of course, that the shell is thrown from these dynamite guns by the force of compressed air, so as not to give such a sudden shock as to explode them in the gun from which they are fired. What would be the effect of the bursting of one of these shells on the deck of a ship or anywhere near it in the water!

Now, it would not be making a wild conjecture at all to say that if all the navies of every nation in all the world, covering every moment of the earth's history down to March 9, 1862, when the *Merrimac* and the *Monitor* fought their duel, could all be resurrected, together with all their great commanders and valiant marines, and all gathered into one place, a single battle-ship, with all the latest and best improvements, would have no fears nor run any great risks in meeting them alone and single-handed.

The modern battle-ship would have her base of supplies protected by all of these great and destructive modern weapons; and she would steam out fearlessly into the wilderness of sails and masts, of schooners, and galleys, and sloops, and frigates. She would not fear their guns; for if she chose, she could keep out of their reach all the time, while she broke the fragile hulls of their vessels to pieces with her ponderous shells. Perhaps she would not use a thirteen-inch gun except when she had from a dozen to forty or fifty of her enemy's vessels in line at short range, and could pierce them all at once. It would be futile to try to mass a great force against her, and board her, overpowering her men and capturing her in that way; for her machine guns would mow down the enemy faster than they could approach her. Then if they should by some chance gather about her in such overwhelming numbers that there would be danger of her being boarded, her powerful engines would drive her through the water so fast that her enemies would soon be left far behind; and any vessels that chanced to be in her track would be cut in two like the foam of

[Courtesy of *Scientific American*.]

The 15-inch pneumatic dynamite gun.

the sea. In a word, let it be said that the wildest and most fanciful nursery tales that the lowest depths of superstition, combined with the highest flights of imagination, have produced, would not be equal to the thrilling facts, if a thoroughly modern battle-ship could enter the conflict with anything and everything that the naval world produced previous to 1862. What does it all mean? Have you ever thought about it?

Perhaps mention should be made of the fact that these modern rapid-fire and machine guns were called out by the necessity of finding something that would destroy the torpedo-boats. One of the earliest attempts to use the torpedo-boat occurred in the Civil War of the United States. All the nations immediately took to experimenting with this form of craft, and soon they had a boat that would run as high as thirty to thirty-three knots an hour. The torpedo was also improved, until it could be sent straight ahead under its own electric power for a thousand yards at the speed of thirty-one knots, and it carries from one hundred to two hundred pounds of guncotton with which to blow up the object at which it is aimed. While these terrible instruments have been in process of development, the rapid-fire and machine guns have been invented and perfected for the purpose of destroying them and the boats that carry them. How successfully this has been accomplished was demonstrated by the inability of any torpedo-boat to get within striking distance of the American fleets in the war with Spain.

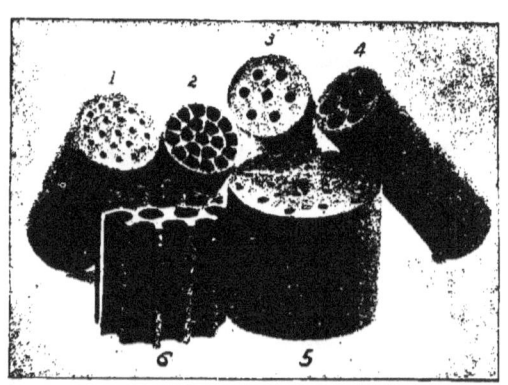

Some grains of slow-burning powder. Nos. 1, 3 and 5 show the powder before it is burnt, and 2, 4 and 6 after.

The slow-burning, smokeless powder has been one of the most important factors in the development of these powerful modern guns. This powder, as shown in the illustration, does not explode all at once, but begins to burn through the holes in the center; and the longer it burns, the greater is the surface that is exposed, thereby increasing the power as the projectile travels through the barrel of the gun. Thus it will be seen that in these newly-devised weapons a mass of powder is not ignited all at once, to make a great bursting force on the gun itself, but the projectile is started with a sort of pushing movement that continues to increase all the time it is traveling from the breech to the mouth of the cannon. With this slow-burning powder it has been possible greatly to increase the length of the gun, while the diameter is not so great by any means as it would have to be with the old-fashioned powder.

But it may be safely said that experiments with slow-burning powder are only in their infancy. There can be no forecasting what may be done with it in the immediate future. Mr. Hudson Maxim, brother to Hiram Maxim, the inventor of the wonderful machine guns that bear his name, has done as much as any one to develop slow-burning powder, together with the various high explosives. He offers a plan of a gun that, by using this kind of powder, will throw a shell charged with half a ton of guncotton about nine miles, and one charged with a ton five miles. This powerful charge will explode where it strikes, no matter whether that be on a ship's deck, in the water, or on the land. Half a ton of guncotton exploded within eighty-five feet of the strongest battle-ship would destroy it, and a ton would be fatal to it if exploded within one hundred sixty-eight feet, while if he is successful in making his gun throw shells charged with a ton of nitrogelatine, he would destroy a battle-ship if the shell struck within two hundred fifty feet of it. Mr. Maxim calls these frightful missiles aerial torpedoes, and his weapon an aerial torpedo-gun. The best scientific men and journals consider his project feasible, and that sooner or later he will be successful in perfecting it.

It has already been stated that one modern battle-ship might successfully combat the combined navies of all time previous to 1862; and it would not be chimerical or an outbreak of fancy to say that were any one of the great nations

Blowing up of the *Maine.*

of to-day equipped with magazine breech-loading rifles, machine guns, small rapid-fire cannon, dynamite guns, etc., and the Pharaohs, and Nebuchadnezzar, and Cyrus, and Alexander, and Hannibal, and the Scipios, and Cæsars, and Cromwell, and Napoleon, and Grant, and Sherman, and Lee, and all the rest of the great military leaders of all time previous to 1862, could bring all their armies into the field, armed as each one fought in his day, they would be mowed down by these modern engines of death before they could possibly get close enough to strike any very telling blows. This sounds like fiction, but how literally it is fact instead! Is it not truly significant? Does it not show a wonderful transformation? What does it mean?

At the siege of Baza, 1325, the Saracens are said to have had some rude cannon in which powder was used. There is evidence that gunpowder was known and used in very much remoter times; but it was not materially improved in its power and effectiveness until within the last quarter of the nineteenth century. During these recent years, however, not only is the powerful "slow-burning" powder devised, but other explosives are invented that are much more terrific than the simple powder. General Nelson A. Miles says truly, "There never was a time in the whole history of the world when so much ingenuity, wealth, and skill were employed in the invention and construction of the appliances of war." Why is this intense activity, and this advancement in the realm of war, all stirred up in one generation?

While God has prepared most marvelous agencies for carrying His Gospel to all the world, Satan will pervert the great railway and steamship facilities into a means of speedily gathering the immense armies of earth to "the battle of that great day."

Battle-ship *Maine* after explosion.

A hundred years ago armies had to be marched from place to place, or carried, when possible, by the old sailboat. How slow do these methods seem when compared with the steamship and railway facilities of to-day for mobilizing large armies! When the time is reached for

God to withdraw His restraint, how quickly can all the armies of the world be gathered to Armageddon!

Some are gathering an unwarranted consolation from the idea that these weapons of modern warfare are becoming so fearful in their destructiveness that men will be afraid to engage each other in battle. Never was there a greater delusion. Soldiers are trained to war, and when ordered to charge the enemy they do it regardless of consequences. They expect

[Courtesy of *Scientific American*.]
Ten-inch breech-loading rifle being fired from a disappearing carriage.
[From an instantaneous photograph.]

to be killed, in all probability, and they face death with determination. This is the history of the soldier during all time, and the wars of to-day serve to demonstrate that the soldier of to-day will face the weapons of to-day as valiantly as men of former centuries faced their enemies who were armed with nothing more formidable than swords and spears. Indeed it will be seen as the conflict deepens in these last days that there will be an intensity and ferocity in battle that is as much greater than anything of former times as the military weapons of these days outstrip those of the ancients. The spirit of violence, which as we have already seen is to characterize these days, will take possession of the soldier, as well as every one else who will yield to it, and he will be driven onto the field of battle with all the furies that can be engendered by the demons of war.

In speaking of "Courage in Modern Warfare," the *Scientific American* says of the war between Spain and the United States:—

"The present conflict has proved that the theorists were altogether wrong—at least so far as they discounted the value of the personal equation. Daring, dogged endurance, indomitable pluck, forehanded aggressiveness, self-possession in the critical moment—all the qualities, indeed, that went to make the ideal soldier in the days of the three-deckers and the muzzle-loading rifle, are as much a decisive factor now as then."

Eight-inch gun mounted on Babbington-Crozier disappearing carriage, lowered and ready for aiming.

England carried into South Africa the most highly perfected weapons of these days, but the Boers faced them with bravery and courage—and, on the other hand, the Boers were armed with modern weapons, and thousands of the homes of Britons give silent evidence to the courage of their troops in the face of high-power cannon and the murderous rain of machine guns. In her war with Russia, whole battalions of the Japanese army, including officers and men, were mown down like grass, but still they charged again and again.

Pride of nationality and the ambition to achieve renown on the field of battle always have been and always will be sufficient incentives to drive men into the face of death, even when it seems almost certain that no one will come out alive. But, notwithstanding this courage that has never yet been wanting in soldiers, there is a feeling of dread in the hearts of men at the contemplation of the fearful slaughter that will be made in the next great wars.

The support and equipment of these great armies and navies are taxing the resources of the nations to the utmost; and this tax must ever become more and more burdensome, until the final crash is reached; for the expensive navies and their equipments that were thoroughly up to date five years ago are now so far behind that they have to be almost built over anew; and the equipments of the soldier that were the very best five years ago have to give place to more modern weapons instead. In this mad military race each country is anxious to keep abreast of the times; but, while they supply the most perfect facilities to-day, there is no assurance that the papers to-morrow will not announce some new weapon that will render useless all the previous great expense incurred for the munitions of war.

A few statements from leading military men and statesmen will be both interesting and instructive in showing how they view the war situation at this time. General Nelson A. Miles, commander of the United States Army, after his inspection of the armies of the Old World, said:—

"I have seen all the great armies of Europe except the Spanish army. *What I have seen does not indicate that the millennium is at hand, when swords will be beaten into plowshares.*" "There are two impressions entertained by many of our people that, in my opinion, are not well founded, even if they can not be regarded as illusions; and they are certainly entitled to full and impartial consideration. One is that we have reached the millennium, that the world has become sufficiently enlightened to abhor war, and to settle all its national and international affairs on intelligent and humane principles. *What facts warrant such a pleasing sentiment, belief, or hope?* The heralds of time that record the passing years and months record also national strife and wars in some part of the world. There never was a time in the whole history of the world when so much ingenuity, wealth, and skill were employed in the invention and construction of appliances of war."

The great German military leader, Von Moltke, in describing the war struggles and preparations of recent years, wrote thus:—

"Generally speaking, it is no longer the ambition of monarchs which endangers peace, but the impulses of a nation, its dissatisfaction with its internal conditions, the strife of parties, and the intrigues of their leaders. The great wars of recent times have been declared against the wish and will of the reigning powers. To-day the question is not so much whether the nation is strong enough to make war as whether its government is powerful enough to prevent war."

At the beginning of 1896 Mr. Franklin Matthews wrote the following, and his statements are striking even to-day:—

"The new year opened with the long roll in the armed camps of Europe. It sounded also through the United States, and its echoes reverberated against the mountains and in the valleys of Venezuela and every other country on the American continent. The clash of arms was heard in Southern Africa, and the eyes of every nation were fixed intently on Great Britain. Armenia and its horrors were forgotten. Would England fight? The great, proud, and boastful England was face to face with as great a crisis as any nation in modern times has ever met. She was alone, and the war-dogs of every other country were almost eager to jump at her throat. Her people had sung, 'Britannia Rules the Waves,' until the nation had almost felt herself invincible.

"The United States early in December challenged this haughty spirit. England's mock heroics and suppressed laughter at the audacity of this country were soon changed to astonishment at the serious situation; and then it was seen that no nation, England especially, could afford to engage in conflict with this country. Then Germany, apparently with no other purpose than to humiliate the greatest commercial nation on the globe, practically threw down the gauge of battle by an announcement that England must give up her protectorate of the Transvaal Republic. *The English people, outraged by what they deemed an insult, and maddened almost to desperation, simply waited for a single hostile move on the part of Germany's emperor to touch a match to her guns, and let the havoc of probably such a war as the world never saw run through Europe.*

"Then it was that the long roll sounded. Russia set her eyes toward Constantinople, France set hers toward Egypt, Germany set hers toward England's colonies, and the sultan trembled again when he realized that the Armenian atrocities had not been forgotten.

"Every war office in Europe went over its plans of strategy. Every plan of mobilization was scrutinized. Every nation took account of its stock, of its munitions of war, and of its financial strength. *The nervous strain of keeping the peace, with millions of soldiers ready to fight at any time, seemed to be exhausted, and the people began to ask if it were possible to prevent the flames of international jealousy and hate from bursting forth into*

On a Chinese war-ship.—Battle of the Yalu.

strife, with practical anarchy and chaos as the price to be paid for it."

Mr. William E. H. Lecky says in regard to the growth of expenditures for war purposes in England, "Between 1835 and 1888 it is said to have increased by no less than one hundred seventy-three per cent." And in regard to the great armies of Europe he further says:— "With the present gigantic armies, wars have, no doubt, become less frequent, though they have become incomparably more terrible; but can any one seriously contend that the unrestrained and reckless military competition of the last few years has given Europe any real security, or that either the animosities or the aspirations that threaten it have gone down? Are its statesmen confident that an ambitious monarch, or a propitious moment, or an alliance, or an invention that materially changes the balance of forces, or some transient outburst of national irritation injudiciously treated, might not at any moment set it once more in a blaze? *To strew gunpowder on all sides may, no doubt, produce caution, but it is not the best way of preventing an explosion."—Democracy and Liberty, vol. 1, pp. 306, 312, 313.*

Japanese sailors working a rapid-fire gun.

As long ago as May, 1894, the *Review of Reviews* said the following concerning Europe's costly armaments: "The European nations are beginning to droop and totter beneath the ever-accumulating burden of military expenditure. There is hardly a country among them that is not at the present time struggling desperately to choke the deficit which is staring it in the face. In England Sir William Harcourt was £5,000,000 short, which must be provided for by new taxation. The

Indian Empire is proposing to tax all imports except cotton five per cent ad valorem to meet its deficit, besides adopting other expedients unpopular but necessary. In France there is a deficit of nearly $30,000,000, about half of which it is proposed to cover by a refunding of loans at a lower rate of interest, and the remaining half is to be obtained by increased taxation on incomes and spirits, with taxes on succession duties. In Italy the new finance minister frankly admits the existence of a deficit of about $50,000,000, to be met, no one knows how. The country can not bear increased taxation, and the chances of any minister who ventured to propose retrenchment and the disbanding of surplus employees would be practically worthless. *Everywhere the statesmen are seeking with feverish anxiety for new sources of revenue, but everywhere the insatiable maw of armaments demands more and more millions.*"

Is it any surprise that such unparalleled preparations for war should have caused the Marquis of Salisbury to state:—

"What would you say is the great change that has passed over Europe since the older of us were young men?—*It is this tremendous increase* in the burdens which the necessity of self-defense has cast upon *every nation of the world. That burden goes on getting higher and higher;* a larger and larger part of the population is devoted to military service; more and more money has to be spent in the provision of mechanical apparatus of war; and as the conquests of science are extended, not only are all previous efforts determined to be obsolete, and have to be thrown away, and something new introduced in their place, but a larger and larger proportion of public wealth has to be devoted to this unremunerative purpose.

"*The burden has become so serious to many nations that many have thought that the day will come when nations will rather rush into war and provoke a decision once for all*, than to continue to groan under the suffering which modern necessity forces upon them."

In a later speech he further said upon this subject:—
"We have had an invitation from his imperial majesty the emperor of Russia, to attend a congress for the disarmament of the nations. I offer a most hearty tribute to the motive by which that invitation has been dictated. I admire the character which can have produced it; and as far as assistance and sympathy from us can help him in the task he has undertaken, that assistance and sympathy are entirely at his disposal. But while we earnestly concur with him in his views and desires, we may be permitted to think that until the happy days have arrived when his aspirations are crowned with success, *we must still have regard to the dangers that surround us, and provide the precautions which are necessary.* [Cheers.] In some respects the era of this great proposition, which I think will be an epoch in the history of men—the era of this great proposition *has been marked by unhappy omens.* It is the first year in which the mighty force of the American Republic has been introduced among the nations, whose dominion is expanding and whose instruments, to a certain extent, are war. I am not implying the slightest blame—far from it—I am not refusing sympathy to the American Republic in the difficulties through which they have passed; but no one can deny that their appearance among the factors of Asiatic, at all events, and possibly of European diplomacy, *is a grave and serious event, which may not conduce to the interests of peace,* though I think that in any event it is likely to conduce to the interests of Great Britain. [Hear! Hear!]

"*But what has been pressed upon us is that the subject matter of war is terribly prevalent on all sides.* You see nations who are decaying, or whose government is so bad that they can neither maintain the power of self-defense nor the affections of their subjects. You see this on all sides, and you also see that when the phenomenon takes place there are always neighbors who are impelled by some motive or other—it may be from the highest philanthropy, it may be from the natural desire of empire—are always inclined and disposed to contest with each other as to who shall be the heir to the nation which is falling away from its old position. And that is the cause of war. *Still more serious is the consideration which recent events have forced upon us that these wars come upon us absolutely unannounced and with terrible rapidity. The war-cloud rises in the horizon with a rapidity that obviates all calculation, and, it may be, a month or two months after the first warning you receive you find you are engaged in or in prospect of a war* ON WHICH YOUR VERY EXISTENCE IS STAKED.

"Let us remember we are a great colonial and maritime power. There have been great colonial and maritime powers, four or five, but they have always fallen, because they had a land frontier by which their enemies could approach, and by which their metropolis could be struck. We have no such land frontier; *but if we ever allow our defenses at sea to fall to such a point of inefficiency that it is as easy, or nearly as easy, to cross the sea as it is to cross a land frontier, our great empire, stretching to the ends of the earth, supported by maritime force in every part of it, will come clattering to the ground when a blow at the metropolis in England is struck.* Our whole existence, not only our whole prosperity, but the whole fabric by which our millions are nourished and sustained—*they all depend on our being able to defend our own shores against attack, and that ability depends on our power at any moment of summoning to our aid a maritime force far larger than any opponent can bring to bear against us.* If you will think out these ideas, you will see why we can not admit that in the present state and temper of the world we can intermit our naval and military precautions. *They must be kept constantly on foot.*"

All the foregoing statements are representative. They are just such statements as the papers and magazines are full of

THE BATTLE OF SANTIAGO, JULY 3, 1898.

On the left the Spanish fleet making for the sea. The American ships lined up on the right, headed by the Brooklyn.

all the time. And this war spirit is ever growing more and more intense.

"Four years ago it was possible to speak of the far eastern question as a problem reserved for our children. Indeed, even at a later date Lord Roseberry's eye detected it only as a shadow lurking 'in the dim vistas of futurity.' To-day, however, the question is already definitely posed, and the most sanguine of statesmen will not refuse to recognize that it has introduced a new peril into the field of international politics."— *Fortnightly Review, February, 1898, p. 321.*

There is no more significant sign of our times than the fact that the recent war with Spain has involved the United States in complications that will from this time on keep her entangled in this "far eastern question." This country is now not only one *of* the great powers, but one *among* the contending nations. Hereafter when European powers are quarreling, the United States can not be an idle looker-on. Thus has the war disease spread until every nation is in the throes of its delirious fever.

The year 1898 revolutionized the sentiment of the United States upon this subject. From being a nation that proposed to remain in its isolation and freedom from the constant broils of the Old World, it suddenly makes a right-about-face. Nearly a quarter of a million men were called to arms to fight Spain, and from the minister in the pulpit to the urchin in the street the war spirit was applauded, and all the country was aflame with the excitement. The school-children proposed to build a battle-ship; the little boys had their clothes trimmed like those of the soldier and marine; and popular orators dwelt upon the expanding destinies of the Great Republic; and the people have been educated to the position where they love to have it so.

The foregoing statements and quotations from leading men of national and international reputation are not designed to be exhaustive, neither has it been the aim of the author to get the most recent or the most striking utterances. The aim has been to get representative statements, and to present existing facts in such a way that it may be clearly seen that the conditions of this time are a striking and literal fulfilment of the predictions of Him who can read the future as we read history.

More need not be said to show that the military spirit is one of the ruling passions of the age. And when we note the terribly destructive implements that have been devised, how vivid and impressive are the words of the prophet as he views these scenes and describes these times! He says: "My bowels, my bowels! I am pained at my very heart; my heart maketh a noise in me; I can not hold my peace, because thou hast heard, O my soul, the sound of the trumpet, the alarm of war. Destruction upon destruction is cried; for the whole land is spoiled; suddenly are my tents spoiled, and my curtains in a moment." Jer. 4: 19, 20.

What burning emotions must have been surging in the mind of Jeremiah when he exclaimed, "I can not hold my peace, because thou hast heard, O my soul, the sound of the trumpet, the alarm of war"! The terrible scenes of the "battle of that great day" were passing before his vision. He hears the "alarm of war;" the awful weapons that, under the insane fury of demons, have been forged against the day of Armageddon, are doing their terrible work; city after city is demolished under the frightful hammering of shot and shell; ship after ship goes down with dead-strewn decks; regiment after regiment is mowed down by the swift scythe of the wargod; the earth is burdened with its dead; the homes of the people are in desolation; and sorrow is on every hand. It is the sight of these things that stirs every emotion of the prophet's soul.

How impressively must the very scenes of war preparation

in which we now dwell, have been caused to pass before the prophet Joel when he wrote: "Proclaim ye this among the nations: Prepare war; stir up the mighty men; let all the men of war draw near, let them come up. Beat your plowshares into swords, and your pruning-hooks into spears; let the weak say, I am strong. Haste ye, and come, all ye nations round about, and gather yourselves together; thither cause Thy mighty ones to come down, O Lord. Let the nations bestir themselves, and come up to the valley of Jehoshaphat; for there will I sit to judge all the nations round about. Put ye in the sickle, for the harvest is ripe; come, tread ye; for the winepress is full, the fats overflow; for their wickedness is great. Multitudes, multitudes in the valley of decision! for the day of the Lord is near in the valley of decision." Joel 3: 9-14, R. V.

Also please read again the following scriptures, and listen to the Spirit of God as He impresses them upon the conscience: "And the nations were angry, and Thy wrath is come, and the time of the dead, that they should be judged, and that Thou shouldest give reward unto Thy servants the prophets, and to the saints, and them that fear Thy name, small and great; and shouldest destroy them which destroy the earth." Rev. 11: 18. "I saw three unclean spirits like frogs come out of the mouth of the dragon, and out of the mouth of the beast, and out of the mouth of the false prophet. For they are the spirits of devils, working miracles, which go forth unto the kings of the earth and of the whole world, to gather them to the battle of that great day of God Almighty." Rev. 16: 13, 14.

Who can read these clear words of God, and not be deeply impressed that they are now having a most literal fulfilment? Listen, I entreat you, to the voice of God speaking to the soul by His Spirit through His Word. Do not heed those who in this time of peril are saying, "Peace and safety," who are asserting that this world is about to join in a universal peace. Even amid the din of these last-day preparations for war, the voice that falsely assures peace will be raised higher and higher. But mark that the Word of God forewarns us in clear and positive language: "When they shall say, Peace and safety; then sudden destruction cometh upon them, as travail upon a woman with child; and they shall not escape. But ye, brethren, are not in darkness, that that day should overtake you as a thief." 1 Thess. 5: 3, 4.

It may be possible, if one sets out to look for them, to find human interpretations and speculations that will apparently set aside these plain words of Jehovah. But you are urgently invited to consider the interpretation that the Spirit of God is impressing upon your conscience as you read the foregoing scriptures and compare them with the things that you see in the world to-day. It is the interpretation that God's Spirit places upon God's own Word that you will have to meet in the judgment.

It is an indisputable fact that as we read the words of the Lord an unseen messenger is continually whispering conviction, away down deep in that inner consciousness that no human mind can penetrate, and where God alone can enter. Under the spell of unbelief you may deny this, yet even while making your denial the voice keeps on with its sweet, and tender, and refined, and quiet entreaties. This very whispering of your Heavenly Father, as He emphasizes and impresses the import of His words upon the very depths of your conscience, is the evidence that He entreats you to consider. We can not turn away from these tender pleadings, these most faithful warnings, without bringing upon ourselves the most terrible consequences.

Note with clearness that this voice must come to you in and through the very words of the Bible. Impressions that come in any other way may be the insinuations of the enemy of truth; but this enemy can not use the Bible in his work. God alone can speak through it. He has arranged it this way so that, even though we stand in the presence of a full realization of all the issues of eternity, yet may we hold the joys of that abiding security that can be found only in resting upon the solid foundations of Omnipotence.

It is because the world is to-day facing the conditions that will drive it in a very little while upon that terrible and final battle-field of Armageddon that it is so earnestly hoped and urged that God's Word may have a chance to do for you the work that He designs it should. There is no question about the clearness of the scripture prophecy. The only uncertainty lies in the matter of the heed that will be given to these plain words.

CHAPTER TWENTY-THREE

NOTWITHSTANDING the war fever that is in the world to stir up the marshaling of these great armies and navies, and cause their equipment with these modern munitions of war, a general crash among the nations has so far been averted. But let no one be calmed by the thought that the war spirit, having been held back from serious outbreaks thus far, the general onslaught therefore may never come. There is a mighty hand holding the forces of evil in check, until "this Gospel of the kingdom shall be preached in all the world." Every one must have the opportunity to hear the message of salvation, and until this work is accomplished the Lord will hold back the demons of war so that they can not precipitate the world-wide strife. In assurance of this we have the following words of the prophet:—

"And after these things I saw four angels standing on the four corners of the earth, holding the four winds [strife, war, commotion] of the earth, that the wind should not blow on the earth, nor on the sea, nor on any tree. And I saw another angel ascending from the east, having the seal of the living God; and he cried with a loud voice to the four angels, to whom it was given to hurt the earth and the sea, saying, Hurt not the earth, neither the sea, nor the trees, till we have sealed the servants of our God in their foreheads." Rev. 7:1–3.

"Wind" and "winds," in these symbolic prophecies, denote war and strife, and this scripture not only gives added evidence of the warlike condition of the world at the close of time, but also informs us that these "winds," or "wars," are held by the mighty angel of God till His work is accomplished of seeking out and "sealing" those who will accept Him.

In doing this work of holding the "winds" of war the Lord makes use of many agencies. He has many men everywhere whose whole being revolts at the atrocities, the cruelties, and the brutalities of war. It is wonderful how they have filled the world with diplomats that have been so successful in bringing about "peace congresses," and creating peace sentiment that often holds rulers by the sheer force of shame from involving their dominions in war. These disciples of peace, whether found among men who have charge of the diplomatic affairs of state or in the realm of the pulpit or the press, must be sustained in their heaven-appointed work.

We must not, however, make the mistake of confusing those who are thus working for the peace of the world with that other class, who, without any reason, are telling us that there is no danger; who are saying that any one is a pessimist who points out with distinctness the facts concerning the war-threat that hangs over our world. The individual who is intelligently working to hold the world in the embraces of peace recognizes what a difficult task it is. He clearly sees the dangers that threaten us; and seeing these dangers, he works with devotion, because of his love of mercy and hatred of brutality, to save his fellow-men from the horrors of war.

When we take a careful view of the occurrences of recent times, it is clearly apparent that some unseen force is holding back the war dogs, that they may not be turned loose upon the world. The news will come to us one day that all Europe is on the verge of war. Statesmen will gravely say that they do not see how it can be averted; but in a little while it is all hushed. Then in a few days or a few weeks there will come the rumors that the Orient is all astir, and affairs in China must be settled on the battle-field. This, too, will be gravely discussed for a brief space, only to subside and amount to nothing serious. In another brief space things in South America, or in some other part of the globe, will create a great commotion, and all the nations will review their resources of army and navy to see what they can do in case of a world's conflict. But here again God has men of strong mind and purpose, and of great skill and power, and the torrents of blood are not allowed to flow. On other occasions war will actually break out, and the great armies and navies will be put under motion, but in a little while all is calm again. Such things as this have not occurred in such a remarkable manner in by-gone ages. Particular note should be made of these things, for they are fulfilling prophecy. God is indeed fulfilling His promise to hold the "winds" of war and strife until, as His prophetic Word expresses it, "we have sealed the servants of our God in their foreheads."

It is necessary to see all these things in their true prophetic light in order not to be deceived by any of the delusions and deceptive voices of this time. While listening to one of those who are saying "peace and safety" in this time when the whole world is on the verge of "sudden destruction," unless we are enlightened by the prophecies, it is easy for us to fall in with his siren words, and look upon the efforts for peace as a sure evidence that we are to have no more war. It is easy for us to be flattered by the thought that we of this day and age are too enlightened and too humane ever to go to war; but theories and facts do not always agree; and what we need to do is to learn to look at the facts. We can not truly and clearly see the facts concerning our own times unless we keep standing beneath the great search-light of prophecy so that the focused rays of this brilliant luminary may cause us to perceive the true character of every shadow of darkness, through beholding the gems of all-pervading foreknowledge. When we see the facts in their true light, and understand their meaning, we know that all these symptoms that are mistaken for an evidence of a millennium of world-wide peace are nothing short of the indisputable evidence that God is fulfilling His prophetic promise to hold back the spirit of war till all can have a chance to hear and accept the "Gospel of the kingdom" that is being preached "in all the world for a witness unto all nations."

Reader, does it not fill you with wonder and gratitude that the Father of all mercies is so mindful of your eternal interests? For, once these mighty engines of destruction are set in motion, where is the power of mind that would enable one to turn away from the terror of the horrible massacre to seek and find salvation? The Lord has promised, and His promises are sure, to keep all who trust Him. By every means that divine and infinite love can suggest, He is inviting all to accept Him; and to as many as will receive Him the promise is: "He shall dwell on high; his place of defense shall be the munitions of rocks; bread shall be given him; his water shall be sure. Thine eyes shall see the King in His beauty; they shall behold the land that is very far off." Isa. 33:16, 17.

"In that day shall this song be sung in the land of Judah: We have a strong city; salvation will God appoint for walls and bulwarks. Open ye the gates, that the righteous nation which keepeth the truth may enter in. Thou wilt keep him in perfect peace, whose mind is stayed on Thee; because he trusteth in Thee. Trust ye in the Lord forever; for in the Lord Jehovah is everlasting strength." Isa. 26:1-4.

The dream of a universal peace can never be realized in this world while it is filled with wicked men; for "the wicked are like the troubled sea, when it can not rest, whose waters cast up mire and dirt. There is no peace, saith my God, to the wicked." Isa. 57:20, 21. But of the Saviour, so soon to come in the clouds of heaven, the same prophet says: "The government shall be upon His shoulder; and His name shall be called Wonderful, Counselor, The mighty God, The everlasting Father, The Prince of Peace. Of the increase of His government and peace there shall be no end, upon the throne of David, and upon his kingdom, to order it, and to establish it with judgment and with justice from henceforth even forever. The zeal of the Lord of hosts will peform this." Chapter 9:6, 7. And of the Prince of Peace the inspired poet says, in Ps. 72:2-7, R. V.:—

"He shall judge Thy people with righteousness,
And Thy poor with judgment.
The mountains shall bring peace to the people,
And the hills, in righteousness.
He shall judge the poor of the people,
He shall save the children of the needy,
And shall break in pieces the oppressor.
They shall fear Thee while the sun endureth,
And so long as the moon, throughout all generations.
He shall come down like rain upon the mown grass:
As showers that water the earth.
In His days shall the righteous flourish;
And abundance of peace, till the moon be no more."

The day that is about to burst upon us will be filled with terrors for him who is unprepared for it; but for him who has been reading and heeding the warnings and admonitions of the Father in heaven, it will be the gladsome day of all the ages. Let each one ask himself, On which side am I standing? If on the wrong side, do not tarry, but hasten to accept the lingering mercy and salvation that are still offered.

Who can say how soon the divine decree will cease to hold this angry strife in check? And when that day of universal and awful war comes, we must be under the protection of the Infinite to avoid being borne down beneath the furious charge

DIVINE RESTRAINT OF THE SPIRIT OF WAR   263

of the angry nations of earth. In these fleeting days of probationary time, each one should hasten to unite with the Saviour, not merely that he may be saved himself, but that he may be instrumental in guiding others to the shelter from the gathering storm. For let it be ever borne in mind that our God is calling for men to be soldiers indeed. While the demons of war are stirring men to become experts in spreading the desolations and sufferings of the battle-field, the Prince of Peace is also exerting His divine power to charm men with the entrancing and substantial joys that center in the eternity of bliss that His coming is about to bring to this world.

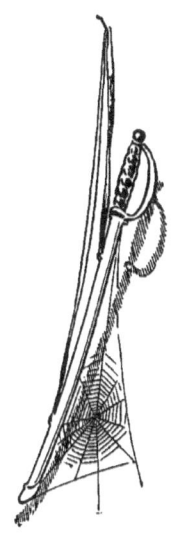

CHAPTER TWENTY-FOUR

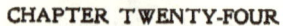

IN the Lord's great prophecy of His second coming, as recorded by Luke, He says: "And there shall be signs in the sun, and in the moon, and in the stars; and upon the earth distress of nations, with perplexity; the sea and the waves roaring; men's hearts failing them for fear, and for looking after those things which are coming on the earth; for the powers of heaven shall be shaken. And then shall they see the Son of man coming in a cloud with power and great glory." Luke 21:25–27.

Mark these further signs that the Lord has given by which we may know of His coming. Not only has He told us, as seen in preceding chapters, what the character of the people

THE ELEMENTS

will be in the last days, and of the anger of the nations, etc., but He proceeds to describe the condition of the very elements at the close of time, with a definiteness that would be impossible without a perfect foreknowledge of these events. He says, "There shall be signs in the sun, and in the moon, and in the stars;" also a "roaring" of the "sea and waves." There has always been a "roaring" to the "sea and waves." Hence when this prophecy is fulfilling, there will be storms by sea that will cause a commotion beyond anything seen before. And this very "roaring" of the elements will carry with it the unmistakable evidence and conviction that the day of judgment is right at hand; for just as surely as God has given these things as signs of the coming day, just so surely will the conviction settle deeply into the heart that

He is telling us by these things that His Son is soon to come. The greatness of these extraordinary signs in the elements is graphically stated in verse 11 of this same chapter in Luke: "And great earthquakes shall be in divers places, and famines, and pestilences; and fearful sights and great signs shall there be from heaven."

Men inspired by Satan may attempt, as did the magicians in Moses' day, to set at naught some of the evidence God has given of the approaching end of time. But here are "signs"

"Fire, and pillars of smoke."

from "heaven," "fearful sights and great signs," so unmistakably clear that all not only *may* see, but *must* see; and, seeing them, they can not escape the conviction of what they mean. The prophet Joel says:—

"And it shall come to pass afterward, that I will pour out My Spirit upon all flesh; and your sons and your daughters shall prophesy, your old men shall dream dreams, your young men shall see visions; and also upon the servants and upon the handmaids in those days will I pour out My Spirit. And I will show wonders in the heavens and in the earth, blood, and fire, and pillars of smoke. The sun shall be turned into darkness, and the moon into blood, before the great and the terrible day of the Lord come. And it shall come to pass, that whosoever shall call on the name of the Lord shall be delivered; for in Mount Zion and in Jerusalem shall be deliverance, as the Lord hath said, and in the remnant whom the Lord shall call." Joel 2 : 28-32.

Observe that the foregoing scripture states that all these great signs in "sun," "moon," and "earth" are to appear *"before the great and the terrible day of the Lord come."* Peter quotes this prophecy of Joel in full in Acts 2 : 16-21. He also makes clear the time when it applies; for he says, "It shall come to pass in the *last days"* that all these things will be seen. So, then, beyond a peradventure, the "last days" are to be specially distinguished by "wonders in the heavens and in the earth, blood, and fire, and pillars of smoke." As these things are seen the conviction deepens in every heart that "the great and the terrible day of the Lord" is right at hand.

"I beheld the mountains, and, lo, they trembled. . . And all the birds of the heavens . . . fled."—*Vide p. 271.*

Isaiah testifies to the condition of the elements in the last days in language quite as forcible and pointed as that of Joel.

He says: "Howl ye; for the day of the Lord is at hand; it shall come as a destruction from the Almighty. Therefore shall all hands be faint, and every man's heart shall melt; and they shall be afraid; pangs and sorrows shall take hold of them; they shall be in pain as a woman that travaileth; they shall be amazed one at another; their faces shall be as flames. Behold, the day of the Lord cometh, cruel both with wrath and fierce anger, to lay the land desolate; and He shall destroy the sinners thereof out of it. For the stars of heaven and the constellations thereof shall not give their light; the sun shall be darkened in his going forth, and the moon shall not cause her light to shine. And I will punish the world for their evil, and the wicked for their iniquity; and I will cause the arrogancy of the proud to cease, and will lay low the haughtiness of the terrible. I will make a man more precious than fine gold; even a man than the golden wedge of Ophir. Therefore I will shake the heavens, and the earth shall remove out of her place, in the wrath of the Lord of hosts, and in the day of His fierce anger." Isa. 13:6-13.

"The foundations of the earth do shake."

This scripture also points to the time when "the day of the Lord is at hand;" and in harmony with scriptures noticed in preceding chapters, it shows that men, because of their iniquity, "arrogancy," "pride," and "haughtiness," make it necessary for the Lord to pronounce the decree, "I will punish the world for their evil," and "destroy the sinners thereof out of it." But do not fail to note that this scripture says, "I will shake the heavens, and the earth shall remove out of her place, in the wrath of the Lord of hosts, and in the day of His fierce anger."

Thus this prophecy, too, forewarns us of a very great commotion in the "heavens" and in the "earth" when that great day is imminent.

But hear Isaiah further: "Behold, the Lord maketh the earth empty, and maketh it waste, and turneth it upside down, and scattereth abroad the inhabitants thereof. And it shall be, as with the people, so with the priest; as with the servant, so with his master; as with the maid, so with her mistress; as with the buyer, so with the seller; as with the lender, so with the borrower; as with the taker of usury, so with the giver of usury to him. The land shall be utterly emptied, and utterly spoiled; for the Lord hath spoken this word. The earth mourneth and fadeth away, the world languisheth and fadeth away, the haughty people of the earth do languish. The earth also is defiled under the inhabitants thereof; because they have transgressed the laws, changed the ordinance, broken the everlasting covenant. Therefore hath the curse devoured the earth, and they that dwell therein are desolate; therefore the inhabitants of the earth are burned, and few men left."

"From the uttermost part of the earth have we heard songs, even glory to the righteous. But I said, My leanness, my leanness, wo unto me! the treacherous dealers have dealt treacherously; yea, the treacherous dealers have dealt very treacherously.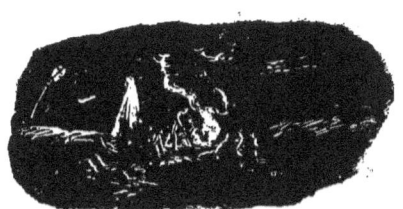

"The land shall be utterly emptied."

Fear, and the pit, and the snare, are upon thee, O inhabitant of the earth. And it shall come to pass, that he who fleeth from the noise of the fear shall fall

17

into the pit; and he that cometh up out of the midst of the pit shall be taken in the snare; for the windows from on high are open, and the foundations of the earth do shake. The earth is utterly broken down, the earth is clean dissolved, the earth is moved exceedingly. THE EARTH SHALL REEL TO AND FRO LIKE A DRUNKARD, AND SHALL BE REMOVED LIKE A COTTAGE; and the transgression thereof shall be heavy upon it, and it shall fall, and not rise again. And it shall come to pass in that day, that the Lord shall punish the host of the high ones that are on high, and the kings of the earth upon the earth. And they shall be gathered together, as prisoners are gathered in the pit, and shall be shut up in the prison, and after many days shall they be visited. Then the moon shall be confounded, and the sun ashamed, when the Lord of hosts shall reign in Mount Zion, and in Jerusalem, and before His ancients gloriously." Isa. 24: 1–6, 16–23.

Again in this scripture is the great sinfulness of earth's closing days presented. "The earth also is defiled under the inhabitants thereof; because they have transgressed the laws, changed the ordinance, broken the everlasting covenant," says the prophet. He states also that "the treacherous dealers have dealt treacherously; yea, the treacherous dealers have dealt very treacherously;" and, speaking of the earth, he says, "The transgression thereof shall be heavy upon it." Note, too, that this scripture adds its testimony to the fact that the elements will be raging at the close of time. Observe its thrillingly-clear statements: "Behold, the Lord maketh the earth empty, and maketh it waste, and turneth it upside down." And again, "The land shall be utterly emptied, and utterly spoiled; for the Lord hath spoken this word." Then follow the startling statements: "Fear, and the pit, and the snare, are upon thee, O inhabitant of the earth. And it shall come to pass, that he who fleeth from the noise of the fear shall fall into the pit; and he that cometh up out of the midst of the pit shall be taken in the snare; for the windows from on high are open, and the foundations of the earth do shake. The earth is utterly broken down, the earth is clean dissolved, the earth is moved exceedingly. The earth shall reel to and fro like a drunkard, and shall be removed like a cottage."

When the Lord is "making the earth empty" and "waste" and "turning it upside down;" when the very "foundations of the earth do shake;" when it "is utterly broken down," and "clean dissolved;" when it is "moved exceedingly"—aye, when *"the earth shall reel to and fro"* like the unsteady movements of the "drunkard," and "shall be removed like a cottage," surely then there will be a raging of the elements that will strike with terror every soul that is not safely anchored to the Rock of Ages. And who has not been impressed, when observing the fury of our modern hurricanes, tidal waves, and cyclones, that these mighty storms, growing as they are so much more violent and frequent, are surely the beginning of the fulfilment of these prophetic utterances?

On this same subject Jeremiah says: "I beheld the earth, and, lo, it was without form, and void; and the heavens, and they had no light. I beheld the mountains, and, lo, they trembled, and all the hills moved lightly. I beheld, and, lo, there was no man, and all the birds of the heavens were fled. I beheld, and, lo, the fruitful place was a wilderness, and all the cities thereof were broken down at the presence of the Lord, and by His fierce anger. For thus hath the Lord said, The whole land shall be desolate; yet will I not make a full end. For this shall the earth mourn, and the heavens above be black; because I have spoken it, I have purposed it, and will not repent, neither will I turn back from it." Jer. 4: 23-28.

Thus the Scriptures proclaim over and over that "at the presence of the Lord," "shall the earth mourn," the "heavens above be black," "the fruitful place" shall be turned into "a wilderness, and all the cities thereof" be "broken down."

With these scriptures in mind, how impressive is the voice of the modern hurricane and the cyclone, whirling with such terrific fury as to defy description, and the frightful and deafening roar of the tidal wave! Most of the people living to-day have not only seen such pictures

"For thus hath the Lord said, The whole land shall be desolate; yet will I not make a full end."

as those on the accompanying pages, but have seen the furious lashing and twisting of the storms they represent. "For thus hath the Lord said, The whole land shall be desolate; yet will I not make a full end." As these things appear, the conviction deepens in every heart that "the great and terrible day of the Lord" is nigh at hand.

The reader is aware of the fact that there is no portion of the world now that is exempt from these terrific storms. During the history of all past time prior to the middle of last century, comparatively few great storms are mentioned. But in the great storms, as in everything else that characterizes this remarkable age, there has been a most marvelous increase, both in the frequency and the terrific fury of the tempestuous hurricanes that carry such destruction all along their track. Not alone the western prairies, but the more densely-populated districts of the east, with the old historic countries of Europe and the Orient, feel the desolating power of the great cyclone. The cyclone cellars, and other places of refuge from these

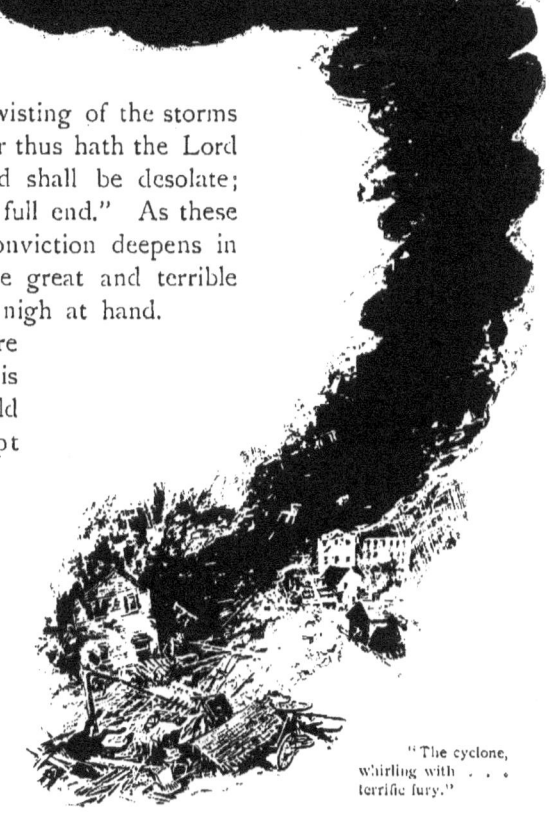

"The cyclone, whirling with . . . terrific fury."

storms (a device, by the way, that our fathers knew nothing about), testify to the fear that has already been created in the minds of men by the desolation of the tornado. But there is a better refuge from raging storms than anything man can devise; and in every "roar" of the elements our ear should catch the call to flee to the strong Tower, the only Saviour.

The reader is well aware of the great tornadoes that have visited destruction upon portions of some of the larger cities, as well as almost wholly to destroy some of the smaller ones, during very recent years. This destruction which has been visited only in part upon the great cities, is yet to sweep over all before the close of time; for we have been forewarned, in the scriptures quoted in this chapter, that "the fruitful place" will become "a wilderness, *and all the cities* thereof" will be

"Storms of hail that leave ruin in their track."

"*broken down at the presence of the Lord, and by His fierce anger.*" Jer. 4:26. The cities, more than any other part of the world, are the great centers of vice and corruption; and because of their gross wickedness, the Lord has given His unfailing word that they shall "all" be "broken down."

This breaking down of the cities because of their wickedness will be done in part, no doubt, through the violent acts of the men who inhabit them; but what their violence fails to do the overwhelming action of the elements of nature will complete. God tells us that Sodom and Gomorrha, those cities of ancient time whose wickedness became so gross as to become a proverb, "are set forth for an example." Jude 7. The destruction of those ancient cities is not any more complete than that which the prophets tell us will be visited upon the debaucheries and sins of the cities of our day.' It should be kept in mind constantly that this is not the statement of some theological theory; it is the presentation of literal facts, that have for their foundation the authority of Him who not only knows the end from the beginning, but who is also the all-powerful One. If there was ever a time when it was proper to theorize and speculate, certainly it is not the case in this time; for we have facts and conditions that are too weighty and all-pervading in their importance for us to allow them to be even obscured, much less set aside, by mere theories.

"And the waters shall overflow."

Not only are tornadoes and storms of that class increasing in violence and frequency, but the earthquake, the tidal wave, and volcanic commotions are becoming much more frequent, and are often felt nowadays in places where the "reeling to and fro" of the earth was never known before. You have observed these great upheavals and demonstrations in nature; the Scriptures tell us what they signify.

Especial attention should be given to the remarkable activity and outbursting of volcanoes in these modern days. Not only have we had the terrific and destructive eruptions of Pelée, but we have had threatenings in many other localities that betoken the forces that are pent up and smoldering beneath.

There are whole sections of the land that are kept in an almost constant tremble, and there is no knowing when or where the next outburst will be.

"Destruction upon destruction is cried."

It will not do to toss these things to one side by saying that such volcanic action has been prevalent over the earth to a greater or less extent during all past time. It is perfectly true that we have had eruptions of volcanoes, and earthquakes in past time that have completely destroyed whole cities and large sections of the country. But these are only samples of the general destruction that has been decreed upon all the cities of this earth in this time when the "violence" of men has become great in the earth, in fulfilment of the scripture predictions that have already been dwelt upon in the pages of this book. The whole world is tottering along the crater's edge, and we are about to witness such desolating destructions as have never been seen. They will not be confined to some small locality; they will be universal. These things are not mentioned to alarm, but to warn

"The Lord . . . turneth it upside down, and scattereth abroad the inhabitants thereof."

and to save. They are facts based upon authority. If you properly consider them, you may not only see the danger but may enter into the shelter that is provided against these times of peril and desolation. The hail-storms of modern times, while not so severe and destructive as they will be, are worthy of note in this connection. The Lord asked Job the question, "Hast thou entered into the treasures of the snow? or hast thou seen the treasures of the hail, which I have reserved against the time of trouble, against the day of battle and war?" Job 38:22, 23.

Then God has "treasures of hail" which He has "reserved against the time of trouble," "the day of battle and war." This "time of trouble," "the day of battle and war," is now right upon us, and we should expect to see a beginning made in the casting out of those "treasures of hail" which God has "reserved" against this time. Concerning these days of exceeding wickedness the Lord says, "Judgment also will I lay to the line, and righteousness to the plummet; and the hail shall sweep away the refuge of lies, and the waters shall overflow the hiding-place." Isa. 28:17.

These "treasures of hail" with which God is about to sweep away the refuge of lies are beginning to be brought out. It is not uncommon to read of storms of hail that leave ruin in their track. And it may not be amiss again to say that the Scriptures have foretold the significance of it. These storms that have already appeared, fearfully destructive though they may have been, are but the beginnings of what will be seen all over the world when God "shall sweep away" the last "refuge of lies," and restore again the purity and truth of Eden.

Not only are these various kinds of storms given as signs of the coming day, but we are told that one of the "seven last plagues" is to be the scorching of men with "great heat" from the sun. "And the fourth angel poured out his vial upon the sun; and power was given unto him to scorch men with fire. And men were scorched with great heat, and blasphemed the name of God, which hath power over these plagues; and they repented not to give Him glory." Rev. 16:8, 9.

Now it is evident that the "seven last plagues" are not as yet being poured out, yet the evidence is conclusive that we are living in the very presence of the time when these plagues must soon begin. In the torrid waves that sweep over the land, the world is having a little foretaste of what that time will be. Particularly during the summer season such head-lines to the news of the day as the following are of constant occurrence: "Elements in a Fury;" "Sun Shows No Mercy;" "Business Paralyzed by Heat;" "Torrid Wave General." Such newspaper headings are very common, and familiar to all. The reader knows these facts too well to require more than the merest mention of them.

How strikingly clear is the evidence God has given us of the approach of that "great day"! Is it not truly marvelous that divine foreknowledge, thousands of years in advance, could present these things so graphically? It is certain that infinite love has exhausted its infinite powers in making clear to us the signs by which we may know that the one event of all the ages is "even at the doors." All this testimony is accumulating, and presenting itself in vivid outlines on every hand. When we hear the "sea and the waves roaring;" when the "fearful sights and great signs" that there shall be from heaven, together with "famines and pestilences," shall be seen in all the land; when we behold "in the earth, blood, and fire, and pillars of smoke;" when the "destruction from the Almighty" is laying "the land desolate;" when "the Lord maketh the earth empty," and "waste," and "turneth it upside down," and it "is utterly broken down," "clean dissolved," "moved exceedingly," and is "reeling to and fro like a drunkard;" when we behold the mountains, and, lo, they tremble, and all the hills move lightly; when we see the "fruitful place a wilderness, and all the cities thereof broken down;" when the "treasures of hail," with which God will "sweep away the refuge of lies," is devastating the land; and when on every hand we see men "scorched with great heat;" aye, when the awful raging of all the elements is in dreadful commotion all about us, and the stoutest of "men's hearts are failing them for fear, and for looking after those things that are coming on the earth"—then it is that our Lord bids us, "Look up, and lift up your heads; for your redemption draweth nigh." These multiplied signs all over the land, terrible in majesty, power, and destruction though they may be, are among the heralds by which God permits the coming of His Son to be proclaimed. The soul is stirred to its deepest and most sublime emotions as the awe-inspiring voice of the elements, in tones of the deepest thunder's roar, entreats the whole world, "Prepare to meet thy God."

Many, in thinking of these things, see only the terror; but our Heavenly Father does not desire that these commotions of the elements, manifested in terrific hurricanes, cyclones, volcanoes, tidal waves, earthquakes, hail-storms, and scorching heat, shall fill the heart with indescribable fear and dismay. These signs are not permitted in order to terrify us, but rather to let us know that this old earth is tossing and "reeling to and fro" amid the shoals and breakers near the farther shore of time, where the reign of sin shall cease. They are evidences that the Son of Man is about to return; and the word of our Father to us is: "Come, My people, enter thou into thy chambers, and shut thy doors about thee; hide thyself as it were for a little moment, until the indignation be overpast. For, behold, the Lord cometh out of His place to punish the inhabitants of the earth for their iniquity; the earth also shall disclose her blood, and shall no more cover her slain." Isa. 26:20, 21.

In this time our Lord assures us: "Thou shalt not be afraid for the terror by night; nor for the arrow that flieth by day; nor for the pestilence that walketh in darkness; nor for the destruction that wasteth at noonday. A thousand shall fall at thy side, and ten thousand at thy right hand; but it shall not come nigh thee. Only with thine eyes shalt thou behold and see the reward of the wicked. Because thou hast made the Lord, which is my refuge, even the Most High, thy habitation; there shall no evil befall thee, neither shall any plague come nigh thy dwelling. For He shall give His angels charge over thee, to keep thee in all thy ways. They shall bear thee up in their hands, lest thou dash thy foot against a stone. Thou shalt tread upon the lion and adder; the young lion and dragon shalt thou trample under feet. Because he hath set his love upon Me, therefore will I deliver him; I will set him on high, because he hath known My name. He shall call upon Me, and I will answer him; I will be with him in trouble; I will deliver him, and honor him. With long life will I satisfy him, and show him My salvation." Ps. 91:5-16.

All these "exceeding great and precious promises" apply at this time. Ponder each one prayerfully. They are all yours. God wants to remove all dismay and terror from the heart of His people in this time when He is preparing to make a complete destruction of all sin. For all who will accept Him as their Saviour, His "perfect love will cast out all fear," and fill the soul with an indescribable joy, and an unutterable confidence, even in the very midst of the most furious of the lashing storms, and while being shaken by the vibrations of the most destructive eruptions that will ever rend the volcanic hills and mountains of our suffering planet. The following treasure of promise should be engraved upon the memory of each one so as to be a constant support and solace in these tempestuous times:—

"God is our refuge and strength,
A very present help in trouble.
Therefore will we not fear, though the earth do change,
And though the mountains be shaken into the heart of the seas;
Though the waters thereof roar and be troubled,
Though the mountains tremble with the swelling thereof,
There is a river, the streams whereof make glad the city of God,
The holy place of the tabernacles of the Most High.
God is in the midst of her; she shall not be moved:
God will help her, and that right early.
The nations raged, the kingdoms were moved:
He uttered His voice, the earth melted.
Jehovah of hosts is with us;
The God of Jacob is our refuge.
Come, behold the works of Jehovah,
What desolations He hath made in the earth.
He maketh wars to cease unto the end of the earth;
He breaketh the bow, and cutteth the spear in sunder;
He burneth the chariots in the fire.
Be still, and know that I am God:
I will be exalted among the nations, I will be exalted in the earth.
Jehovah of hosts is with us;
The God of Jacob is our refuge." Psalm 46, A. R. V.

CHAPTER TWENTY-FIVE

NOT only do the elements overhead testify of the coming day, but the very ground itself is called upon to bear witness to the nearness of the end of time. "And, Thou, Lord, in the beginning hast laid the foundation of the earth; and the heavens are the works of Thine hands; they shall perish; but Thou remainest; and they shall all wax old as doth a garment; and as a vesture shalt Thou fold them up, and they shall be changed; but Thou art the same, and Thy years shall not fail." Heb. 1: 10-12. Here the direct and plain language is used that so truly characterizes the Bible. Speaking of the earth, and of the atmosphere, or heavens, connected with it, the apostle says, "They all shall wax old as doth a garment; and as a vesture shalt Thou fold them up, and they shall be changed." Thus the burden of decay because of the curse occasioned by sin rests heavily on old mother earth, and she "waxes old."

Isaiah bears witness to the decrepitude of the earth, as follows: "Lift up your eyes to the heavens, and look upon the earth beneath; for the heavens shall vanish away like smoke, and the earth shall wax old like a garment, and they that dwell therein shall die in like manner; but My salvation shall be forever, and My righteousness shall not be abolished."

Isa. 51 : 6. Here, again, the statement is made that the "earth shall wax old like a garment." And as the night of sin settles darker and still darker upon it, the curse which sin has caused is more and more deeply felt. Jeremiah, in speaking of the closing days of time, says: "I beheld, and, lo, the fruitful place was a wilderness." Jer. 4 : 26. Then the "waxing old" of the earth involves the changing of places once "fruitful" into a barren "wilderness." The departing of earth's vigor of youth, and the infirmities of age creeping over her, are thus pointed out as among the unmistakable tokens of her approaching dissolution.

There is perhaps no portion of Scripture that sets forth the general decay of the earth as an evidence of the coming end of time more forcibly than the first chapter of Joel's prophecy. The prophet says :—

"Hear this, ye old men, and give ear, all ye inhabitants of the land. Hath this been in your days, or even in the days of your fathers? Tell ye your children of it, and let your children tell their children, and their children another generation. That which the palmer-worm hath left hath the locust eaten ; and that which the locust hath left hath the canker-worm eaten; and that which the canker-worm hath left hath the caterpillar eaten. Awake, ye drunkards, and weep ; and howl, all ye drinkers of wine, because of the new wine; for it is cut off from your mouth. For a nation is come up upon My land, strong, and without number, whose teeth are the teeth of a lion, and he hath the cheek teeth of a great lion. He hath laid My vine waste, and barked My fig tree : he hath made it clean bare, and cast it away; the branches thereof are made white.

"Lament like a virgin girded with sackcloth for the husband of her youth. The meat-offering and the drink-offering is cut off from the house of the Lord ; the priests, the Lord's ministers, mourn. The field is wasted, the land mourneth; for the corn is wasted ; the new wine is dried up, the oil languisheth. Be ye ashamed, O ye husbandmen; howl, O ye vine-dressers, for the wheat and for the barley; because the harvest of the field is perished. The vine is dried up, and the fig tree languisheth; the pomegranate tree, the palm tree also, and the apple tree, even all the trees of the field, are withered; because joy is withered away from the sons of men. Gird yourselves, and lament, ye priests; howl, ye ministers of the altar; come, lie all night in sackcloth, ye ministers of my God; for the meat-offering and the drink-offering is withholden from the house of your God.

"Sanctify ye a fast, call a solemn assembly, gather the elders and all the inhabitants of the land into the house of the Lord your God, and cry unto the Lord, Alas FOR THE DAY! FOR THE DAY OF THE LORD IS AT HAND, AND AS A DESTRUCTION FROM THE ALMIGHTY SHALL IT COME. Is not the meat cut off from our eyes, yea, joy and gladness from the house of our God? The seed is rotten under their clods, the garners are laid desolate, the barns are broken down; for the corn is withered. How do the beasts groan! the herds of cattle are perplexed, because they have no pasture; yea, the flocks of sheep are made desolate. O Lord, to Thee will I cry; for the fire hath devoured the pastures of the wilderness, and the flame hath burned all the trees of the field. The beasts of the field cry also unto Thee; for the rivers of waters are dried up, and the fire hath devoured the pastures of the wilderness. BLOW YE THE TRUMPET IN ZION, AND SOUND AN ALARM IN MY HOLY MOUNTAIN; LET ALL THE INHABITANTS OF THE LAND TREMBLE; FOR THE DAY OF THE LORD COMETH, FOR IT IS NIGH AT HAND." Joel 1: 2-20; 2: 1.

The fifteenth verse of chapter 1 and the first verse of chapter 2 of this prophecy of Joel show that the "day of the Lord" is the time to which the prophet's vision is directed; and his description of what would be seen in the world at that time is most direct and forcible. In the other scripture quoted we have seen that the earth is to "wax old like a garment;" this chapter in Joel goes into particulars, and tells us quite fully what this waxing old means. First, we are told of the insects and worms that would be a destruction to crops. The "palmer-worm," the "locust," the "canker-worm," and the "caterpillar" are mentioned; and then, after calling to the drunkard to "weep and howl" because the wine is "cut off," it is stated, "For a nation is come up upon My land, strong, and without number, whose teeth are the teeth of a lion, and he hath the cheek teeth of a great lion. He hath laid My vine waste, and barked My fig tree; he hath made it clean bare, and cast it away; the branches thereof are made white." Joel 1: 6, 7.

Thus it is seen that not simply the few destructive insects and worms mentioned will be working havoc on vegetation, but a "nation is come up upon My land, strong, and without number," and as the result the vine is laid waste, and the drunkard's wine is cut off; but while his supply of wine is "cut off," the drunkard still has his appetite for strong drink, and so "weeps" and "howls." It is far better to get rid of these perverted desires now, so that in the time so soon to come we will be free in God.

Note the force of other statements in this remarkable scripture: "The field is wasted, the land mourneth; for the corn is wasted; the new wine is dried up, the oil languisheth. Be ye ashamed, O ye husbandmen; howl, O ye vine-dressers, for the wheat and for the barley; because the harvest of the field is perished. The vine is dried up, and the fig tree languisheth; the pomegranate tree, the palm tree also, and the apple tree, *even all the trees of the field, are withered;* because joy is withered away from the sons of men." Joel 1: 10–12.

What a striking expression of the conditions that are to become more and more pronounced and marked in these last days: The field wasted, the land mourning, the harvest of the field perished, the vine dried up, and the apple tree, even all the trees of the field, withered. But this is not all. Read again: "The seed is rotten under their clods, the garners are laid desolate, the barns are broken down; for the corn is withered. How do the beasts groan! the herds of cattle are perplexed, because they have no pasture; yea, the flocks of sheep are made desolate. O Lord, to Thee will I cry; for the fire hath devoured the pastures of the wilderness, and the flame hath burned all the trees of the field. The beasts of the field cry also unto Thee; for the rivers of waters are dried up, and the fire hath devoured the pastures of the wilderness. Blow ye the trumpet in Zion, and sound an alarm in My holy mountain; *let all the inhabitants of the land tremble; for the day of the Lord cometh, for it is nigh at hand.*" Joel 1: 17-20; 2: 1. Who can mistake the import of these thrilling and heart-searching words?

How impressive is this chapter of Joel, telling us how literally and absolutely the earth "shall wax old as doth a garment," and how completely it shall molder to decay! The words of Isaiah make plain the cause of all this: "The earth shall reel to and fro like a drunkard, and shall be removed like a cottage; and the transgression thereof shall be heavy upon it; and it shall fall, and not rise again." Isa. 24: 20.

"The transgression thereof shall be heavy upon it." Then it is the *"transgression"*—the curse occasioned by sin—that results in all this ruin and desolation. The individual who chooses to disregard the laws of nature, has to suffer the consequences of his folly. Instead of the ruddy glow of health, the pallor of the countenance shows that the fires of consuming disease are burning within. And so with our old earth. The curse of "the transgression thereof" is "heavy upon it." Man's gross iniquities have corrupted it, until it, too, is breaking beneath the load, and "waxes old," ready for the consuming fires of the last days. Our kind Heavenly Father would have prevented all this suffering if sinful man had only submitted to the wooing of His divine and amazing love; but this being rejected, the only consistent thing left for the Lord to do is to allow sin to run its course, till the time is reached when every imagination of the thoughts of man's heart is only evil continually. When this time comes, there will be no longer a ray of hope that any one can be made better, but, rather it will be evident that all have become so depraved that the most merciful thing is to bring this reign of sin to an end by the judgments of the last days.

Every tiller of the soil is painfully aware of the fact that it is becoming more and more difficult to raise a crop. Grasshoppers and numerous other pests and crop-destroyers of one kind and another have reached all parts of the land. Under the heading of "The Annual Battle with Insects," Geo. E. Walsh has the following to say in the *Scientific American:*

"For a quarter of a century science has been laboring in the cause of agriculture to reduce the number of garden pests and to hold them in check. The annual battles with the insect foes are carried on energetically from early spring till late autumn; and the farmer or gardener is not quite sure of his crops until they have been actually harvested. In spite of all the protective agencies that science has surrounded the fields and gardens with, disasters of gigantic proportions will break out occasionally through the sudden increase of some obnoxious insect or fungus growth. It is the destruction of the potato crop, one season, by the Colorado beetle; the total failure of the wheat-fields in certain states by the rust or blight, another year; or the wide-spread injury to the cotton plants by the boll-worms. Somewhere within the United States some crop is pretty sure to be seriously damaged by the insects or the fungus growth nearly every season. . . . By the middle of summer, insect foes are swarming all over the garden and on every plant. Plant-lice, or aphides, attack all weak plants, *and they multiply at the rate of from five to twenty millions in a season from one progenitor."*

It is unnecessary·to multiply testimony upon this point. Every one who has anything to do with the raising of fruit or grain, or any kind of plants, knows the truthfulness and universal application of what Mr. Walsh says. Thousands have been impressed by the increasing difficulty of maturing a crop; but have they realized that it is because the earth is "waxing old" and crumbling to decay in consequence of the corrupting transgressions that are polluting it? And this is but another link in the great chain of evidence that shows us so conclusively that "the end of all things is at hand."

A result of this general decay of the earth as we approach the end will be wide-spread famine and pestilence; for has not the Lord said that "great earthquakes shall be in divers places, and *famines,* and *pestilences;* and fearful sights and great signs shall there be from heaven" (Luke 21: 11)?

"Famines" and "pestilences" have been seen in the earth during all the ages, as both history and the Scriptures plainly show, and so in themselves alone could not constitute a sign of the end. But the "famines and pestilences" of past centuries have been as nothing compared with what we may expect in these closing decades of time. The words of the prophet again come vividly to mind: "The earth also is defiled under the inhabitants thereof; because they have transgressed the laws, changed the ordinance, broken the everlasting covenant. Therefore hath the curse devoured the earth, and they that dwell therein are desolate; therefore the inhabitants of the earth are burned, and few men left." Isa. 24:5, 6.

So when the earth becomes "defiled under the inhabitants thereof," then it is that it will be said, "Therefore hath the curse devoured the earth, and they that dwell therein are desolate." And when it can be said that the awful "curse" of sin has "devoured" the earth, any former pestilence or famine will be compared to the experiences of that time but as a shadow. The recent famines in India, the failure of crops in various parts of this country, as well as elsewhere in the world, are but the dim beginnings of what the condition will be when the time so vividly described by the prophets is fully reached.

New forms of disease are constantly breaking out among both men and beasts. These diseases become epidemic, and spread over the land as a destroying plague. Scientific men are studying these growing infirmities and their causes. They have demonstrated that they are all a consequence of the violation of nature's laws and of atmospheric conditions that are growing more and more unfavorable to health. The "surfeiting," the "drunkenness," the licentious vices, against which such faithful warnings have been given in the Word of God, are at the root of all these physical ills of humanity. But pointing out the evil does not cause it to cease. Appetite and passion and a general indifference to nature's inexorable laws, close the minds of men, and the warnings are unheeded.

The knowledge of sanitary and medical science was never so great as it is to-day, never so capable of elevating and purifying the world from its load of corrupting ailments; but men go blindly ahead, in the face of light and of demonstrated facts of physical law, ever plunging deeper and deeper into the degrading and destroying sins against their physical being. It can not be said that it is through necessary ignorance that they are doing this; for it would seem that God is concentrating every ray of light regarding the laws of life and health upon the people of this generation.

Through the applied knowledge of physiological and sanitary law, a wonderful work has been done. The average length of life has been materially advanced; but, as recently pointed out by one of the world's most thoughtful, scholarly, and successful physicians, this lengthening of the average of life is not the hopeful thing that the statistics would indicate. The recent achievements of science enable the doctor to keep those afflicted with the numerous infectious and contagious diseases alive for a much longer time than formerly; but it is only that they may produce their kind, who will be still further weakened by the accumulating tendency to disease. Thus even the lengthening of life is not producing the results that appear on the surface. There can be no disguising the real fact that the race is growing weaker; and it is made clear by both the Word of God and our common every-day observation that all this is because of the "transgressions," the "surfeiting," the "drunkenness," and the prevailing vices of this age.

The very earth itself is groaning because of "the transgression thereof" that is "heavy upon it." The pollutions of mankind, their transgression of physical law, their failure to observe the most thoroughly demonstrated principles of sanitary science, create a soil for the growth of the germs of decay and pestilence; and Satan, who is "come down unto you, having great wrath, because he knoweth that he hath but a short time," exerts his power to increase and intensify the ever-expanding evil. This evil one has been in the school of sin for six thousand years; he has access to the laboratories of nature, and his extended research enables him to know how most successfully to combine the elements of transgression to produce the most malignant seeds with which to scatter the epidemic of decay. Some may be inclined to regard this lightly; but let us look at the striking utterances of the Word of God, listen to the voice of His Spirit impressing these words upon the soul, view the real and startling facts as they stand out around us, and prepare soon to meet this plain and unbroken testimony at the bar of the Eternal.

Our Father in heaven is not the author of such suffering as appears in the world to-day; it sometimes seems hard to understand why He permits it, even. But sin has lifted its hideous and cruel head in this planet of ours, and all the universe of God must have the object-lesson of what Satan, by his reign of hatred and self-serving, would accomplish. He has sought to make it appear that the Father in heaven is a "hard man, reaping where" He had "not ·sown, and gathering where" He had "not strewed." So sin must be allowed to develop. Its consequent miseries, its debasing and polluting corruptions, its cruel torments, must ripen into the harvest of evil. Then all will see for themselves what the terrible fruits of sin are; and the declaration of the rebel chief's proposition that our God is a "hard man" will be forever overthrown by the unanimous testimony of the universe. When the last vestige of sin is destroyed, and with it all the suffering and sorrow that it has produced, with what exultation will "every creature which is in heaven, and on the earth, and under the earth, and such as are in the sea, and all that are in them," join in that swelling anthem, "Blessing, and honor, and glory, and power, be unto Him that sitteth upon the throne, and unto the Lamb forever and ever" (Rev. 5:13)!

This song of deliverance will soon be sung by the redeemed of God, in the presence of all the universe. What a happy day it will be! and how we should rejoice at each fresh evidence of the return of the "Prince of Peace"! The world is now waiting to hear the good news of His coming, and to be entreated to prepare to meet Him. God is calling for each one. He is now saying, "Go out into the highways and hedges, and compel them to come in." The compulsion that He uses is the divine force of His matchless love; and may we be admonished, by all these signs of His coming, to receive the heavenly Guest into our hearts, and so not only be ready to meet Him, but become messengers of righteousness through whom others may be won to the "Lamb of God, which taketh away the sin of the world."

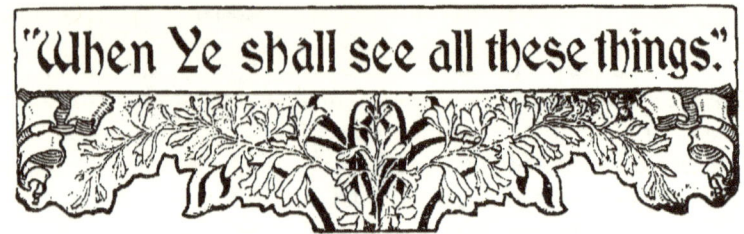

"When Ye shall see all these things."

CHAPTER TWENTY-SIX

SO likewise ye, when ye shall see all these things, know that it [margin, "He"] is near, even at the doors." Matt. 24:33. We are bidden by this word of the Master to "*know*," when we shall see "*all* these things," that He is near, even at the doors. "When these things *begin* to come to pass, then look up, and lift up your heads; for your redemption draweth nigh." Luke 21:28. When we "*begin*" to see the signs that the Saviour has pointed to as the tokens of His soon coming, then are we to "look up, and lift up our heads;" for our redemption "*draweth nigh;*" but when we see "*all*" the signs He has mentioned, then are we to "*know*" that He is "*even at the doors.*"

There have been deceptions of Satan in all the past centuries, but never such deceptions as his millenniums of experience and long schooling in the ways of sin will enable him to present in these last days.

There have been here and there some very remarkable things scattered along through the ages of the past; but nowhere and at no time has there been an age so filled with a bewildering mass of achievements, discoveries, and inventions as the one in which we live.

The Gospel has made miraculous advancement as the centuries have come and gone; but it was reserved to the latter part of the nineteenth century to build the great printing-presses, the railways, and the steamships, and send out the printed Scriptures into the homes of the kindreds and tongues of earth.

Great errors have spread over sections of the earth in bygone days; but nothing has ever more firmly rooted itself in the minds of "many people" than the unscriptural present-day doctrine of a peace millennium.

There have been plague-spots of crime in different ages and localities; but never since the days of Noah has it been so apparent that the greater portion of the human race was sinking into the lowest depths of injustice, violence, and vice.

Formality, superstition, and consequent apostasy have in many different periods planted the seeds of corruption and evil in the church that claimed to represent the Son of God; but never has the church, in the presence of such opportunities, facing such difficulties and dangers, possessing such intellectual possibilities and material facilities for good, and holding such stores of light, seemed to stand in such a lukewarm, careless, and compromising indifference.

The pleasures and follies of idle amusements have always played a part among Satan's devices to lure men to sin; but never as to-day has the world been given up to the fun that debases, debauches, and destroys.

There have been wealthy men in every nation and in every age; but never has there been such a "heaping" together of treasure, connected with the "cries of the laborers," as is seen and heard at the present hour.

There have been "wars and rumors of wars;" but never before have the nations of all the earth been so "angry," and never has it been made manifest that the "spirits of devils" had gone to the "kings of the earth and of the whole world, to gather them to the battle of that great day."

There have been great storms and pestilences here and there all down the ages; but never have the lashing elements filled the inhabitants of earth with such forebodings as now.

There have been failures of crops and consequent famines in different localities and at divers times; but never as now has the evidence made itself seen and felt that the earth is "waxing old like a garment," as beneath its load of "transgression" it begins to crumble to decay. While these things may have been seen to some extent in the past, they have not appeared all together, and over the whole face of the earth. The Master did not tell us that when we should see any one of these things in some isolated locality we were to know that His coming was near, but it is when we see "all these things." They may all be seen to-day, and they will become more and more marked and pronounced as these closing moments of time go by.

When we see these things "begin to come to pass," we are to "look up;" but when we see "all these things," then are we to "*know* that He is near, even at the doors." How do these things impress you? Do you see "all these things"? Let each answer to his own conscience and to God. Controversy and heated discussion are not invited. Professed Christians have already been cursed with too much of that. But the reader is earnestly entreated closely to heed God's Word, and so prepare for that eternity of existence that is given to all who will accept it. And how joyful the thought that the night of sin is almost ended, and that the heralds of the day of endless glory are trumpeting the invitation, "Come; for all things are now ready!"

"When the Son of Man shall come in His glory, and all the holy angels with Him."

CHAPTER TWENTY-SEVEN

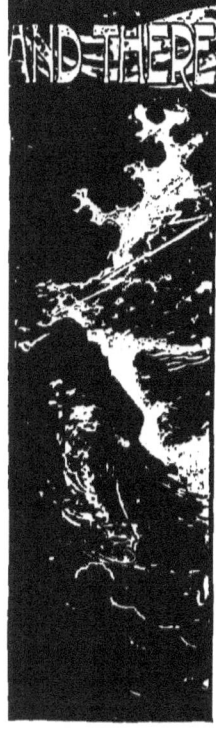

"AND at that time shall Michael stand up, the great Prince which standeth for the children of thy people; and there shall be a time of trouble, such as never was since there was a nation even to that same time; and at that time thy people shall be delivered, every one that shall be found written in the book. And many of them that sleep in the dust of the earth shall awake, some to everlasting life, and some to shame and everlasting contempt." Dan. 12:1, 2. The "great Prince which standeth for the children of thy people" can be none other than Christ, whom this text calls Michael. Christ says of His present position that He is set down with His "Father in His throne." Rev. 3:21. He is seated thus with His Father to act as our intercessor and high priest.

The foregoing text from Daniel tells of the time when He "stands up." His work as intercessor and high priest is finished, and He "stands up" to be robed with the vesture on which is written "King of kings, and Lord of lords." The great day of emancipation is at hand; for "at that time thy people shall be delivered, every one that shall be found written in the book." Dan. 12:1.

Of those whose names were "written in the book" another scripture says: "I saw the dead, small and great, stand before God; and the books were opened; and another book was opened, which is the book of life; and the dead were judged out of those things which were written in the books, according to their works." Rev. 20:12.

Thus do the Scriptures clearly show that to deliver "every one that shall be found written in the book" is the great work of the judgment and the resurrection. This fact is made still clearer and is more fully emphasized by the words of Daniel already quoted: "And many of them that sleep in the dust of the earth shall awake." Dan. 12:2. Thus from every standpoint how clearly may it be seen that this "standing up" of Michael is associated with the judgment scenes and the resurrection at that great day when Christ shall come.

O, the sublime joy of the thought! The church in all the ages has been singing of the glorious day when every sleeping child of God shall be brought from the grave to enjoy the bliss of endless life and to possess the substantial realities of eternity. The church of past ages has had to content itself with the prospect of participating in the blessedness of these resurrection scenes at some distant future time; but now the day is at hand! The hour is almost here! The Lord has caused the guiding stars to be charted by which we may know it.

When this view of deliverance for God's people — even the resurrection day — was presented to the prophet, observe that he saw that there should be "a time of trouble, such as never was since there was a nation even to that same time." Daniel had a wonderful view in minute outline of the rise and fall of nations, beginning with his own day and reaching down to the second coming of Christ. All the bloody scenes of all the bloody wars that would arise during all the conflicts, the struggles and oppressions of the ages, were made to be familiar to Daniel's prophetic eye. Yes, even the French Revolution, with its shocking brutalities, its horrors, and its "Reign of Terror," was viewed by the prophet. And then the vision of the "time of the end" is given him; he sees the difficulties, the evils, and the perplexities; he beholds that which causes Michael to "stand up" as "King of kings and Lord of lords;" and then he pens the prophetic words, "There shall be a time of trouble, such as never was since there was a nation even to that same time."

To those who have read of the terrors in France during her revolution a hundred years ago, and who may be familiar with the history of other national calamities, and the many times of trouble that our world has seen, it may be a startling revelation that none of those scenes in the past furnish a parallel to which this "time of trouble" in the "time of the end" may be likened; yet such is the declaration of the Scriptures. In view of the condition of our world to-day, what else is there to expect? As we enter the time when, as the Word of God foretells, "every imagination of the thoughts" of men's hearts will be "only evil continually," the only result that can follow will be an unprecedented "time of trouble." It will be as much worse than the "time of trouble" resulting from the abandoned wickedness in Noah's time, as the population of evil-doers is greater now, and as Satan's ability to deceive has by long practise become more acute and cunning.

Other scriptures bear testimony that the closing days of earth's history are a "time of trouble." Luke records the Master's words as follows: "There shall be signs in the sun, and in the moon, and in the stars; and upon the earth distress of nations, with perplexity; the sea and the waves roaring; men's hearts failing them for fear, and for looking after those things which are coming on the earth; for the powers of heaven shall be shaken. And then shall they see the Son of Man coming in a cloud with power and great glory." Luke 21:25-27.

Thus has the Lord foretold the "distress of nations, with perplexity," that will exist on the earth at the time of His coming. Not only will the nations be in "distress" and "perplexity," but there will be the "sea and the waves roaring." Men will see these "things which are coming on the earth," and their "hearts will fail them for fear." Such is the Word of God, and such are the literal facts.

The reader is familiar with Paul's statement in 2 Tim. 3:1-5, which tells of the "perilous times" that shall come "in the last days." He knows of the great list of sins there enumerated that shall exist not only in the world, but among those who "have a form of godliness," which sins are the producers of the last-day perils. Selfishness, avarice, and the cruelty of sin have ever been a source of danger in the world; but this danger reaches its climax in the "time of trouble," and occasions "fears," "perplexities," and "perils" in the "last days."

Other scriptures sounding the warning of dangers that will exist in the closing years of earth's reign of sin are doubtless before the mind; but perhaps in none of them is the situation more vividly portrayed than in the words of Zephaniah:—

"And it shall come to pass at that time, that I will search Jerusalem with candles, and punish the men that are settled on their lees: that say in their heart, The Lord will not do good, neither will He do evil. Therefore their goods shall become a booty, and their houses a desolation; they shall also build houses, but not inhabit them; and they shall plant vineyards, but not drink the wine thereof. The great day of the Lord is near, it is near, and hasteth greatly, even the voice of the day of the Lord; the mighty man shall cry there bitterly. That day is a day of wrath, a day of trouble and distress, a day of wasteness and desolation, a day of darkness and gloominess, a day of clouds and thick darkness, a day of the trumpet and alarm against the fenced cities, and against the high towers. And I will bring distress upon men, that they shall walk like blind men, because they have sinned against the Lord; and their blood shall be poured out as dust, and their flesh as the dung. Neither their silver nor their gold shall be able to deliver them in the day of the Lord's wrath; but the whole land shall be devoured by the fire of His jealousy; for He shall make even a speedy riddance of all them that dwell in the land." Zeph. 1:12-18.

The word "Jerusalem" sometimes applies to the professed church of Christ as well as to the literal city of the Jews, and in the foregoing quotation it very clearly denotes the church. Not only do these words of Zephaniah add their harmonious testimony to what other scriptures say concerning our times, but a most solemn warning is given to professed Christians "that are settled on their lees," and who "say in their heart, The Lord will not do good, neither will He do evil." This is the time of the church's greatest responsibility; for "the great day of the Lord is near, it is near, and hasteth greatly." Zephaniah says, "The mighty man shall cry there bitterly;" he says it is "a day of trouble and distress;" it is "a day of wasteness and desolation;" it is "a day of darkness and gloominess, a day of clouds and thick darkness." The prophet also adds that it is "a day of the trumpet and alarm against the fenced cities, and against the high towers," showing, of course, the spirit of war that shall be in the land; and because of these impending perils, the church should be intensely active in her Master's work.

What solemn heed should be given to the warnings sent to this wicked age: "I will bring distress upon men, that they shall walk like blind men, because they have sinned against the Lord." And "neither their silver nor their gold," which, as previously shown, they have heaped "together for the last days," "shall be able to deliver them in the day of the Lord's wrath." Surely this scripture adds a most decided testimony to the fact that there shall be a great "time of trouble" just before the coming of the Just One.

We have already seen that the last days will be full of satanic deceptions. What perils and trouble these deceptions will lead men into, only divine foresight is able to reveal. We have been forewarned that at the "coming of the Son of Man," even as in "the days of Noah," "every imagination of the thoughts" of men's hearts will be "only evil continually;" that "all flesh" will "corrupt his way upon the earth," and the earth will be "filled with violence;" that judgment will be "turned away backward," and the corrupting vices of Sodom will pollute the world; that a "form of godliness" will take the place of the power of the Gospel in the church, and in consequence many professors of Christianity will be "lovers of pleasure more than lovers of God." We have read the scriptures that tell of those who will heap "treasure together for the last days," and also have heard how the cry of the laborers will be raised in consequence of this oppression. The present conflict between capital and labor is indeed most vividly set forth in the inspired Word. Our minds have been impressed by the predictions of the awful work that will be done by the "angry" nations, as they are gathered by the evil spirits to "the battle of that great day." The Lord has told us that the elements in the physical world will break forth in terrific storms and earthquakes, until the earth shall be "utterly broken down," "clean dissolved," "moved exceedingly"—yea, that it "shall reel to and fro like a drunkard, and shall be removed like a cottage," on account of the transgression "that shall be heavy upon it." Then, too, the earth is "waxing old like a garment;" in its decaying condition crops are uncertain, and famine and pestilence will fill the world.

But in the face of all these plain statements of the Lord, and while standing in the time when the facts that fulfil His Word are a present, living reality, men will say: "Do not be disturbed. There is no 'time of trouble' ahead. Rest easy; for the nations will 'learn war no more,' and it is 'peace and safety' ahead of us."

Many have uttered these false assurances of peace ignorantly. It has been taught them, and they have taken it for granted that it is so; but the Lord's Word is plain, and He is seeking by its mighty power to dispel the delusion. There are many who are beginning to see the danger ahead, and are raising the signal of alarm. They do not all understand the meaning of the perils that are on either side of us, and that loom up still darker in front of us; yet, nevertheless, they see them.

Archbishop Ireland says: "The bonds of society are relaxed; traditional principles are losing their sacredness, and perils hitherto unknown are menacing the life of the social organism." — *The Church and Modern Society, p. 4, 1897.*

It is with no indistinctness that the celebrated archbishop says that *"perils hitherto unknown are menacing the life of the social organism."*

Leo XIII. spoke on the subject as follows: "It is not surprising that the spirit of revolutionary change which has so long been dominant in the nations of the world, should have passed beyond politics, and made its influence felt in the cognate field of practical economy. The elements of a conflict are unmistakable: the growth of industry, and the surprising discoveries of science; the changed relations of masters and workmen; the enormous fortunes of individuals, and the poverty of the masses; the increased self-reliance and the closer natural combination of the working population; and, finally, a general moral deterioration. The momentous seriousness of the present state of things just now fills every mind with painful apprehension; wise men discuss it; practical men propose schemes, popular meetings, legislatures, and sovereign princes are all occupied with it; and there is nothing which has a deeper hold on public attention."—*Encyclical Letter on the Condition of Labor.*

Leo very clearly saw the difficulties that are arising. He saw that the "momentous seriousness of the present state of things just now fills every mind with painful apprehension," and "that there is nothing which has a deeper hold on the public attention." He saw the elements coming together that will combine to make the great and final "time of trouble."

Mr. Benjamin Kidd says: "To the thoughtful mind the outlook at the close of the nineteenth century is profoundly interesting. *History can furnish no parallel to it.* The problems which loom across the threshold of the new century *surpass in magnitude any that civilization has hitherto had to encounter.*"—*Social Evolution, p. 1.*

E. Benjamin Andrews, formerly president of Brown University, on returning from a trip to Europe, said: "No well-informed person in Europe seems to believe that peace is destined to endure there very long. On all hands people are preparing for war. Armies and navies are strengthened; fortifications multiplied; immense war treasures of gold piled up; all possible hypothetical plans of campaign, offensive and defensive, studied and discussed; firearms, great and small, ceaselessly experimented upon and improved; civil measures subordinated to military, and statesmen to great army men and navy men. Within a few months I have read several articles on the defense of London in case of an attack from the continent.

"Moreover, where all sorts of maneuvers for alliances are going on, there is wide-spread distrust of treaties and the national friendships that exist. Almost never before, I think, did so many nations of Europe feel themselves hopelessly isolated. Great Britain is in distress on this account; so is

Germany. Family ties between crown-wearing persons amount to nothing. When Nicholas, of Muscovy, visited London a year ago, he sojourned some days in Germany both going and coming. On each occasion William besought his dear cousin, almost with tears, for some word of assurance that the Russians meant peace. 'Cousin,' was the reply, 'if you Germans wish security, make terms with France.' It was a stone instead of bread; insult, not comfort; yet it is said William dare not show resentment, remembering the size of the Muscovite army and its nearness to his eastern borders."

Señor Crispi, Italy's greatest statesman, says: "Europe resembles Spain from a certain point of view. *Anarchy is dominant everywhere.* To speak frankly, there is no Europe. The European concert is only a sinister joke. Nothing can be expected from the concert of the powers. *We are marching towards the unknown.* Who knows what to-morrow has in store for us?"

It is unnecessary to comment on the foregoing quotations. They are but selections from utterances that are heard continually from the platform and the press, and they show that many men are awake to the fact that a great storm is gathering. They see the "distress of nations," and are perplexed; their hearts are "failing them for fear, and for looking after those things which are coming on the earth;" they realize that "perilous times" have come, and see the rapidly-approaching "time of trouble." And yet, if they would only turn to the light of God's Word, and allow it to illuminate, purify, and cheer their hearts, they would know what it all means, and would not be "perplexed" nor "fear." We have already seen that the angels of God are commissioned to "hold" the "winds" of strife in check till all have a chance to flee to the safe shelter so divinely provided. When that restraining influence is withdrawn, the judgments of God will fall upon the persistently impenitent.

In these "perilous times," and while "men's hearts are failing them for fear" because they see the unmistakable approach of that "time of trouble, such as never was since there was a nation," do not give the trumpet the uncertain sound. Do not say, "Peace, peace, when there is no peace;" but hold aloft the light of the blessed Bible, so that men may know its great prophecies and see that "city of refuge," whose bulwarks are laid by the all-powerful hand of Omnipotence; whose foundations are sure to all eternity; and whose inhabitants shall never know sickness or sorrow.

CHAPTER TWENTY-EIGHT

WE have been considering the Bible description of the conditions that will prevail all over the earth at the close of time. We have seen the inspired statements concerning the "time of trouble" and the last-day "perils;" we have read from the Book of God of the "waxing old" of the earth, and that "the sea and the waves" will be roaring; we have learned of the "angry" nations, and of those who oppress the laborer, and "heap treasure together for the last days;" we have found also that God has foretold the vice, the crime, the injustice, and the violence that will fill the land. Looking at this picture only, we see nothing but darkness, distress, and wo; but there is a great light shining through it all, and far above and beyond it.

Will our heavenly Father allow Satan to curse the world with deceptions, and corrupting and distressing sins, and He do nothing to show the blessings and the joys of truth and goodness? Will He allow the evil to lift its hideous though bedecked and gilded head to the most consummate heights of folly, that it may the more surely plunge men to the lowest depths of wickedness and wo, and do nothing to expose the danger, and save the beguiled and deluded objects of His love? The first advent of Christ was heralded by the anthems of angels; the miraculous power and love of the Saviour were manifested in preaching to the poor, healing the sick, and raising the dead; at Pentecost there was a mighty outpouring of the Spirit of God; and will this dispensation, so wondrously begun in the demonstration of divine power, be allowed to close in obscurity and weakness? Will its glorious light be made to flicker dimly, or be buried beneath the rubbish of this sinful time?—No, never, never!

Without doubt the eighteenth chapter of Revelation presents the strongest, the most scathing, and the most heart-searching condemnation of the sins of the last generation, that can be found in the inspired Book. Read the entire chapter, and allow it to quicken your sense of the divine displeasure with wrong; but do not fail to observe closely the opening sentences:—

"And after these things I saw another angel come down from heaven, having great power; and the earth was lightened with his glory. And he cried mightily with a strong voice, saying, Babylon the great is fallen, is fallen, and is become the habitation of devils, and the hold of every foul spirit, and a cage of every unclean and hateful bird." Verses 1, 2.

How sublime is the description of this mighty angel who lifts such a strong voice against the sins of Babylon! This babel of evil that seeks by its corruptions completely to overthrow the last generation of men, must be exposed. Light must be thrown in upon these hidden, iniquitous works of darkness that make the last days "perilous," and cause an unprecedented "time of trouble;" and so the heavenly messenger is sent to "lighten the earth with his glory." Here is a promise that fires every emotion of the soul with the entrancing thought that in the very stronghold of iniquity, and amid its most desperate working, the Master exerts His mighty power, and "the earth is lightened with His glory."

THE EARTH WAS LIGHTENED BY HIS GLORY 309

The Lord left the promise with His church that "these signs shall follow them that believe: In My name shall they cast out devils; they shall speak with new tongues; they shall take up serpents; and if they drink any deadly thing, it shall not hurt them; they shall lay hands on the sick, and they shall recover." Mark 16:17, 18.

The Master inspired one of His apostles to repeat this

"And I saw another angel come down from heaven, having great power; and the earth was lightened with his glory."

promise by saying, "God hath set some in the church, first apostles, secondarily prophets, thirdly teachers, after that miracles, then gifts of healings, helps, governments, diversities of tongues." 1 Cor. 12:28.

It is true that soon after he uttered the foregoing assurances concerning the gifts He had placed in His church, a great apostasy began; it is true that the "mystery of iniquity" found its way into the hearts of those who professed the name of Christ, and what He once delighted to call His church became a wicked and cruel misrepresentation of His righteousness, His mercy, and His love. But after men had gone to the very depths of this apostasy; when they had bound themselves about with all the gloom and superstitions of the Dark Ages, then it was that they began to awaken to a realization of the craving in the soul for something that could not be found in their pilgrimages, their penances, and their exacting forms of creed-bound service. Our God was following them all the time. He yearned over them with love. He kept giving them all the light that their eyes, so used to darkness, could endure. And when the awakening time came, His Word was again sought, and read as never before. The printing-press multiplies copies of it; missionaries put it in other languages, and carry it to all the world; and the new day of Gospel light unfolds as fast as men will turn to God, and become the bearers of His gems of truth.

The outgrowth of this light from God is the breaking of the shackles that have for so long enslaved men's minds. The world is encouraged to think, and the resultant monuments of thought rise to mountain heights in the marvelous material productions of this surpassing age. The Lord is leading; and if mankind would only follow, every one might be saved from the thraldom of sin, and be carried still higher and higher into the unfolding glories of the Eternal.

As men are led to study and believe the Bible, some will be developed through whom God can manifest His "gifts" that He "has set" "in the church." To some will be given the "word of wisdom;" to others, the "word of knowledge;" to others, the "gift of faith;" to others, the "gifts of healings;" to others, the "working of miracles;" to others, the gift of "prophecy;" to others, the "discerning of spirits;" to others, the gift of "tongues;" and to others, the "interpretation of tongues." 1 Cor. 12:8-10.

That was a wonderful manifestation of the power of the Spirit of God, when at Pentecost the "gifts" worked powerfully in the church; but under the outpouring of the Spirit in these last days, these gifts that formality and unbelief have driven out, will return to do a mightier work. Satan sees the unfolding of the Lord's great plan. He becomes enraged that he can not hold men in the superstitious errors of darkness. He plans in his most masterly way to deceive mankind. He can lead many into such gross crimes and vices that nothing short of the dawning judgment day will cause them to look up to God; others can be kept in a sort of genteel infidelity, that looks with pity upon him who believes the Word of the Lord; but there are many others who, while they hold to the Bible, yet do so in a careless, nominal way, and without appropriating its vitalizing truth; and special delusions must be prepared for these. Satan knows that God is educating His true followers, who are now scattered in every clime, and worshiping under so many denominational names, to do a mighty work. "It shall come to pass in the last days, saith God, I will pour out of My Spirit upon all flesh; and your sons and your daughters shall prophesy, and your young men shall see visions, and your old men shall dream dreams; and on My servants and on My handmaidens I will pour out in those days of My Spirit; and they shall prophesy; and I will show wonders in heaven above, and signs in the earth beneath; blood, and fire, and vapor of smoke; the sun shall be turned into darkness, and the moon into blood, before that great and notable day of the Lord come; and it shall come to pass, that whosoever shall call on the name of the Lord shall be saved." Acts 2:17-21.

The evil one knows these prophecies concerning this mighty outpouring of God's Spirit "in the last days." He knows that God has said that a mighty angel has been commissioned to enlighten the earth with his glory; and if you have never before seen the cunning of Satan, witness the counterfeit "healers" and "faith cures" that he is sending out to flood the world with their pernicious and misleading notions. And those persons who hold to the Bible in a careless, indifferent way; the ones who do not dig for themselves into its great mines of truth, so that they may be fortified by a personal knowledge of just what God's own Word says, are the ones who will be most easily beguiled by the sophistries of Satan.

If no other evidence can show you that God is preparing to do a marvelous work in these last days, under the outpouring of mighty pentecostal manifestations of His Spirit, just witness the counterfeits that are being sent out to discredit this oncoming work of the Lord. Men and women are rising up everywhere who talk glibly about the gifts of miracles and healing that God has placed in the church. A superficial knowledge leads one to believe that all their teaching is warranted by Scripture; but a deeper knowledge, a daily study of the Word, a devoted faith in its teaching, and a full surrender of the will to God—through which comes the possession of His "gift" of the "discerning of spirits"—are the only things that enable us to know whether these persons are pretenders, or whether they are sent out by the authority of Heaven and with power from on high.

Of this one thing be sure: when the Master places His "gifts of healing" upon a man, that man will be able to say, as did Peter to the lame man at the gate of the temple, "In the name of Jesus Christ of Nazareth rise up and walk;" and those words will contain the power of God and the malady must go. What God does is perfect, and there will be no doubt about the reality of the healing. The skill of a physician will not be needed to tell the patient that he is well; for the ruddy glow of health will testify that a soul has been breathed upon by omnipotent power. Men of faith may pray for the afflicted, and God's Word says that "the prayer of faith shall save the sick" (James 5:15); but he who has the "gifts of healings" is commissioned of Heaven to *command* disease, and divine power obliges it at once to depart.

But let it be remembered that there will appear what seem from every human standpoint to be miraculous healings, which are nevertheless not done by the power of God. We have already learned that, to enforce his great deceptions in the last days, Satan will work "with all power and signs and lying wonders." You may ask, "Why is he permitted thus to work?" — It is that the malignant virus of sin may be made manifest, and its deceitful workings fully known; but God shows His care for His creatures by unmasking the monster of evil, so that all may know its real character. He also fills His Word with promises that enable every one to shun the charms of sin, and stand at all times in the blazing light and power of truth. Yes, the reader may even be one of those who join with the mighty angel in these closing hours of time in filling the earth with the light and glory of the Lord.

It must be evident to any one who has taken the time to consider the Bible evidence, that the consummating conflict of all the ages is even right now upon the world. The forces of darkness, of crime, of sensuality, of sin, of destruction, are arrayed on the one hand, but rising as a star of hope on the other is the increasing light of Gospel truth and power. This Gospel light is destined to spread till all the world is filled with its splendid glory. There never were such issues in the world before to call out the unreserved heroism of service. Never before have men had the inspiration that comes from standing on the threshold of the resurrection, and of breathing, after only a little further period of waiting, the Eden perfumed zephyrs of the eternal world. Never before have men had every exalted and exulting emotion stirred by the definite knowledge that all the angels of heaven are being marshaled to escort the King of eternity, the world's Redeemer, on His triumphal advent journey to this needy and sinking world. Knowing that He would have men and women who would be possessed with such soul-absorbing themes as these, our heavenly Father could safely foretell the enlightening of the whole earth with His divine glory.

Tell it everywhere; tell it over and over again, "Glorious things are spoken of thee, O city of God!" Let all the world know that God sends His mighty angel from heaven, and the earth will be lightened with His glory. Receive the Word of God. Stand in the fulness of the power of faith; and as our Father pours out His Spirit to accomplish His mighty work, He will use you as His instrument of righteousness, service, and glory.

A REFUGE IN THIS TIME OF DISTRESS

CHAPTER TWENTY-NINE

IN the consideration of these prophecies that are fulfilling in our time, it is clearly noticeable that the cities are all to be broken down because of their crimes and wickedness. Hence there must come a time at no distant day when every one who hears and respects the Word of God will take his family, and retire from the city to a safer and more secluded place. Some, no doubt, will be needed in the cities until near the very last day of time, to give the message of the soon coming of Christ, and to show men that the end of all things is at hand. But there will be many women and children, and some men as well, that it would be useless and distressing to expose to the sufferings and evils that will exist in these congested centers of population. In view of these things it is high time now that every one who has the responsibility of a family should be casting about for some secluded country retreat in which to give them a haven of rest.

In the time of the French Revolution and Reign of Terror the violence of the time was confined almost wholly to Paris and a few of the leading cities adjacent to this capital of the nation. There were large out-lying country districts that hardly knew of the raging of the Revolution, much less felt its dire distress. Happy indeed were the people in that time who stayed by the pleasant and peaceful occupation of tilling the soil. To them there was but little knowledge or fear of the Revolution, and they had none of the miseries that were shaking the empire. The history of that time may offer some suggestions and consolations in regard to these times that are now confronting us.

One of the noticeable facts of recent years is the growing dislike for the farm and agricultural pursuits in general. In consequence of this sentiment there has been a corresponding flocking to the cities. It is a well-known fact that the cities are growing in population altogether out of proportion to the rest of the country. This very tendency to leave the farm will make numerous openings for those who would seek the quietude of peace in the country places.

The farm is the natural place for man. Everything that we have to live upon must come from the husbandman. When God created man in the beginning, He put him in a garden; He did not put him in a city. City life is unnatural, cramped, and also unpleasant to the one who has tasted of the real sweets and substances of the country. But no matter what our sentiments may be in this direction, there are conditions here that we must take into account, and conduct ourselves accordingly. The man who has his eyes open to the things that are coming upon the cities in this our time, and who fails to provide for as much peace and quiet for his family as he can possibly obtain, can not be guiltless.

While we should be getting out of the cities as fast as we can arrange for it, yet we must not allow ourselves to become so alarmed as to flee from duty; for there is work yet to be done in these cities, and the thing for each one to decide is what is his duty for to-day; and then manfully stand by it, even if it is necessary for him to suffer everything that is known in the field of persecuting torture. God wants sensible men and also brave men in these times, and He has promised the wisdom that will enable us each one to know day by day what we should do.

But even while prosecuting any of the work of giving the Gospel message of the soon coming of Christ in the cities, we can be studying the country, and seeking to learn how to care for ourselves and families there when we are at last compelled to flee from the cities altogether. The essential work in country life is to know how to till the soil so as to get a livelihood out of it. Since it is from the soil that all must get their living, it is a splendid idea for every one to be studying to know how to get the greatest possible yield from the ground.

Some will not heed these warnings of the prophetic Word of God until they are driven to sorest straits, and then it will be very difficult for them to drop suddenly out of city life, and make a living in the country. Hence it will be necessary for those who can see, right now, through these prophecies, what is coming on the world, to have also in mind the work of being able to help all who will be thrown into distress.

The thought also may occur to some, if the Lord is coming so soon, why should it be necessary to provide for living in the country for a time, away from the violence and vices of the cities, and away from the dangers as the cities are being broken down under the judgments of God? It will take some time to give the warning message of the Gospel of the kingdom in all the world; and while the forces are gathering that will result in the destruction of the cities, and while the evils in general that the prophecies point out as characteristic of the last days are being spread as a dark cloud over the earth, there is no necessity of exposing the weak unnecessarily to these things; and as these evils that are to make the last days perilous will continue to grow worse all the time, it behooves every one to make the escape, particularly for his family, before things become so bad that it will be next to impossible. We must not content ourselves with the idea that since we can live in the city to-day with comparative safety, therefore we may be able to stay for an indefinitely long time yet. By pursuing such a course we may become callous to our surroundings, and like some of the relatives of Lot of old these very warnings sent by the Lord to save us are made the subject of jesting and mockery until the whirlwind of destruction sweeps us away.

It is a pleasure to note that some are so charmed with country life that the ordinary language of prose is inadequate to express their feelings, and so they are led to adopt the sublimer language of poetry, It is hoped that they, with all others who have a realizing sense of the situation, will continue to use every influence they can command to turn the minds of men and women away from the distresses that await the cities and toward the more natural and more-to-be-enjoyed country life.

"Back to the land, my brothers, one and all!
Watch the wild rains across the forests fall;
  Back to the land with all thy heart and soul,
  Scatter fresh seed where the moist furrows roll,—
Hark how God speaks when the fierce thunders call.

"There's very ecstasy of growth in spring,
Flashing in music to the robin's wing;
  The budding vines race heedlessly along,
  Lured by the sweetness in the bluebird's song,—
And all new moons fresh joys to lovers bring.

"Back to the land! Leave the foul money marts,
Wet with the life-blood of a million hearts.
  Down on your knees, and watch the springing seed
  Unfold and follow as the sunbeams lead.
('I am God's work!'—that is the simple creed.)
Oh, better this than all the world-made arts!

"The great, wide wheat belts sleep through dew and night,
Waiting the rapture of the morning light;

The small, sparse corn fields of the toiling poor
For very joy laugh round the cottage door;
And, over them, the mountains' towering height!

"Back to the hills that the first herdsmen knew;
Watch the young pigeons homing down the blue,
Glad that no cruel shot their days may end;
Glad of the rudest shepherd for a friend.
Ay, watch the changeless stars the still night through.

"O, sick, sad soul! made weary of the waste
Of what adds naught, now, to the outworn taste,
That, passing, leaves its gold-gain—ah, to whom,
Since, dead, thou tak'st but thyself to the tomb?
To the green, cleansing land, poor heart, make haste.

"Back to the land, the good, green, happy land!
Back to the laborers with the hardened hand!
Back to the truth that the old prophets saw;
The land is good, I made it! is God's law.
We see it, though we may not understand."
—*Millie W. Carpenter.*

But the most inspiring utterances in regard to the situation that is before us, and the most assuring expressions concerning the advantages of country life, are the promises of the Lord Himself. Some of these sacred words follow, and it is to be hoped that every sentence will be studied closely, and fully absorbed:—

"Woe to thee that spoilest, and thou wast not spoiled;
And dealest treacherously, and they dealt not treacherously with thee!
When thou shalt cease to spoil, thou shalt be spoiled;
And when thou shalt make an end to deal treacherously, they shall deal
    treacherously with thee.
O Lord, be gracious unto us; we have waited for Thee:
Be thou their arm every morning, our salvation also in the time of trouble.
At the noise of the tumult the people fled;
At the lifting up of Thyself the nations were scattered.
And your spoil shall be gathered like the gathering of the caterpillar!
As the running to and fro of locusts shall he run upon them.

The Lord is exalted; for He dwelleth on high;
He hath filled Zion with judgment and righteousness.
And wisdom and knowledge shall be the stability of thy times, and strength of salvation:
The fear of the Lord is His treasure.
Behold, their valiant ones shall cry without:
The ambassadors of peace shall weep bitterly.
The highways lie waste, the wayfaring man ceaseth:
He hath broken the covenant, he hath despised the cities, he regardeth no man.
The earth mourneth and languisheth: Lebanon is ashamed and hewn down: Sharon is like a wilderness; and Bashan and Carmel shake off their fruits.
Now will I rise, saith the Lord;
Now will I be exalted;
Now will I lift up Myself.
Ye shall conceive chaff, ye shall bring forth stubble:
Your breath, as fire, shall devour you.
And the people shall be as the burnings of lime:
As thorns cut up shall they be burned in the fire.
Hear, ye that are far off, what I have done;
And, ye that are near, acknowledge My might.
The sinners in Zion are afraid; fearfulness hath surprised the hypocrites.
Who among us shall dwell with the devouring fire?
Who among us shall dwell with everlasting burnings?
He that walketh righteously, and speaketh uprightly;
He that despiseth the gain of oppressions, that shaketh his hands from holding of bribes,
That stoppeth his ears from hearing of blood, and shutteth his eyes from seeing evil;
He shall dwell on high: his place of defense shall be the munitions of rocks:
Bread shall be given him; his waters shall be sure.
Thine eyes shall see the King in His beauty:
They shall behold the land that is very far off." Isa. 33: 1-17.

The prophet, in the foregoing scripture, directs our attention to the time of the "devouring fire," and to the "everlasting burnings;" he also tells us that "thine eyes shall see the King in His beauty." It is plain to be seen that these expressions refer to the calamities and difficulties through which the world will pass in the last days, and also to the second coming of Christ, when we shall see the "King in His beauty." But even though the righteous be called upon to dwell in the midst of all these calamities that come in the world in the last days, yet do they have the promise that "he that walketh righteously, and speaketh uprightly," "shall dwell on high: his place of defense shall be the munitions of rocks: bread shall be given him; his waters shall be sure."

THE SEVEN LAST PLAGUES

CHAPTER THIRTY

SOME of the scriptures have been presented that show the working of Satan in the last days. His last struggle to engulf the world in sin and pestilential disease culminates in the seven last plagues. The words of Scripture that foretell what these plagues will be are both literal and plain, and with so many of the facts concerning these closing years of earth's history before us, but little need be said upon the subject aside from quoting the Scripture itself. The Word reads as follows:

"I saw another sign in heaven, great and marvelous, seven angels having the seven last plagues; for in them is filled up the wrath of God. And I saw as it were a sea of glass mingled with fire; and them that had gotten the victory over the beast, and over his image, and over his mark, and over the number of his name, stand on the sea of glass, having the harps of God. And they sing the song of Moses the servant of God, and the song of the Lamb, saying, Great and marvelous are Thy works, Lord God Almighty; just and true are Thy ways, Thou King of saints. Who shall not fear Thee, O Lord, and glorify Thy name? for Thou only art holy; for all nations shall come and worship before Thee; for Thy judgments are made manifest.

"And after that I looked, and, behold, the temple of the tabernacle of the testimony in heaven was opened; and the seven angels came out of the temple, having the seven plagues, clothed in pure and white linen, and having their breasts girded with golden girdles. And one of the four beasts ["living creatures," R. V.], gave unto the seven angels seven golden vials full of the wrath of God, who liveth forever and ever. And the temple was filled with smoke from the glory of God, and from His power; and no man was able to enter into the temple, till the seven plagues of the seven angels were fulfilled.

"And I heard a great voice out of the temple saying to the seven angels, Go your ways, and pour out the vials of the wrath of God upon the earth.

"And the first went, and poured out his vial upon the earth; and there fell a noisome and grievous sore upon the men which had the mark of the beast, and upon them which worshiped his image.

"And the second angel poured out his vial upon the sea; and it became as the blood of a dead man; and every living soul died in the sea.

"And the third angel poured out his vial upon the rivers and fountains of waters; and they became blood. And I heard the angel of the waters say, Thou art righteous, O Lord, which art, and wast, and shalt be, because Thou hast judged thus. For they have shed the blood of saints and prophets, and Thou hast given them blood to drink; for they are worthy. And I heard another out of the altar say, Even so, Lord God Almighty, true and righteous are Thy judgments.

"And the fourth angel poured out his vial upon the sun; and power was given unto him to scorch men with fire. And men were scorched with great heat, and blasphemed the name of God, which hath power over these plagues; and they repented not to give Him glory.

"And the fifth angel poured out his vial upon the seat

of the beast; and his kingdom was full of darkness; and they gnawed their tongues for pain, and blasphemed the God of heaven because of their pains and their sores, and repented not of their deeds.

"And the sixth angel poured out his vial upon the great river Euphrates; and the water thereof was dried up, that the way of the kings of the east might be prepared. And I saw three unclean spirits like frogs come out of the mouth of the dragon, and out of the mouth of the beast, and out of the mouth of the false prophet. For they are the spirits of devils, working miracles, which go forth unto the kings of the earth and of the whole world, to gather them to the battle of that great day of God Almighty. Behold, I come as a thief. Blessed is he that watcheth, and keepeth his garments, lest he walk naked, and they see his shame. And he gathered them together into a place called in the Hebrew tongue Armageddon.

"And the first [angel] went and poured out his vial upon the earth; and there fell a noisome and grevious sore upon the men which had the mark of the beast, and upon them which worshiped his image."

"And the seventh angel poured out his vial into the air; and there came a great voice out of the temple of heaven, from the throne, saying, It is done. And there were voices, and thunders, and lightnings; and there was a great earthquake, such as was not since men were upon the earth, so mighty an earthquake, and so great. And the great city was divided into three parts, and the cities of the nations fell; and great Babylon came in remembrance before God, to give unto her the cup of the wine of the fierceness of His wrath. And every island fled away, and the mountains were not found. And there fell upon men a great hail out of heaven, every stone about the weight of a talent; and men blasphemed God because of the plague of the hail; for the plague thereof was exceeding great."

"And the second angel poured out his vial upon the sea; and . . . every living soul died in the sea."

Thus reads the prophecy of John in Revelation, chapters 15 and 16.

The overwhelming mass of sins in these last days, both among hypocritical professors and in the non-professing world, are committed in defiance of the greatest manifestation of the light of the Gospel that has ever illuminated the minds of men. None will be able to plead ignorance. God has sent His mighty agencies to lighten the earth with His glory. And yet, in spite of all this, men give themselves up to "every imagination" of evil; they fill the earth with violence, vice, and injustice; and because there is no justice in the land, the great Judge Himself takes His throne, and in these "seven last plagues" metes out the just penalties that this wicked generation has hitherto eluded.

In these "seven last plagues," it is said, "is filled up the wrath of God." But do not harbor the thought that the "wrath of God" is in any way akin to the murderous, vindictive wrath of sinful man. Man indulges in wrath the same as in any other sin. Human anger is aroused by some selfish impulse, by a desire for revenge, and to gratify vindictive hate, or possibly to resent something that insults human pride or notions of

"And the third angel poured out his vial upon the rivers and fountains of waters; and they became blood."

manliness. All of this is sin. It is the sin that is the very tap-root of murder. "Whosoever *hateth* his brother is a murderer," says the apostle; "and ye know that no *murderer* hath eternal life abiding in him."

Then it is evident that the wrath which God condemns in men, and which He defines as murder, is another thing altogether from the "wrath of God." Many persons have been greatly troubled because the Bible speaks of God's "wrath;" and no wonder, if they have the conception that God's wrath is the same as the revengeful, furious, sinful anger of fallen man. Cease forever to regard our heavenly Father in the light of doing that which He forbids as murder in one of the great precepts of His decalogue!

No! Look at this matter in its true light. The people of this generation are rushing headlong into the most corrupting evils that satanic influence can suggest—doing it under the blaze of the greatest light that Heaven can throw around them; doing it in defiance of the strongest convictions of right; doing it despite the most tender

"And the fourth angel poured out his vial upon the sun."

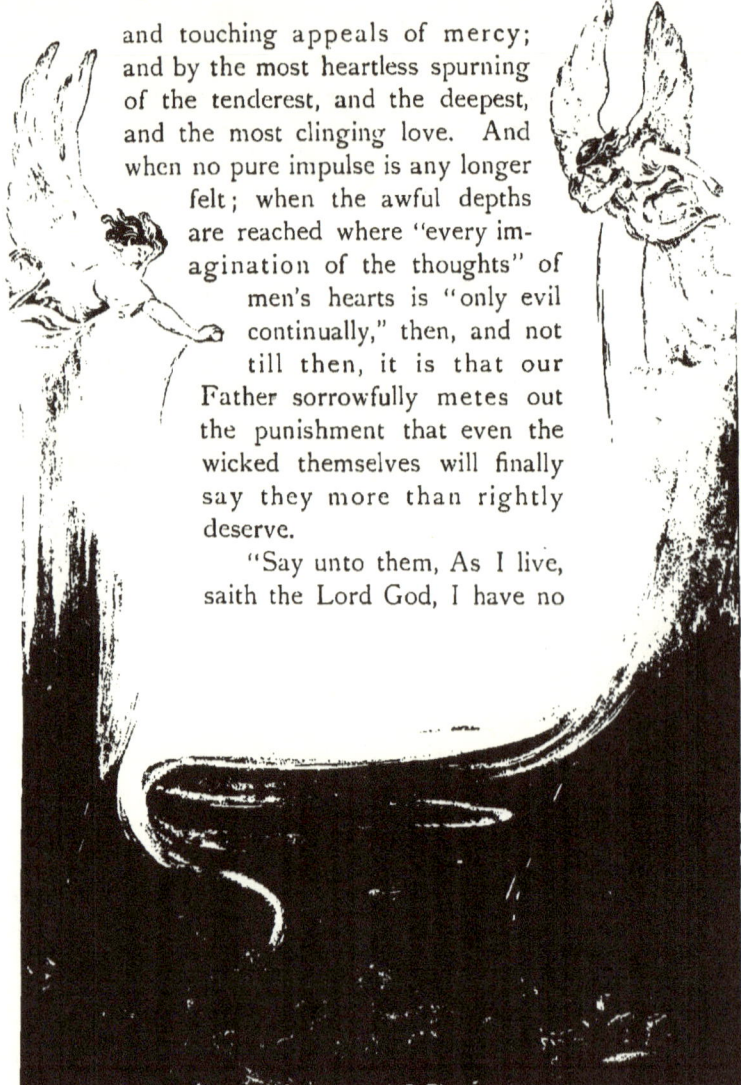

and touching appeals of mercy; and by the most heartless spurning of the tenderest, and the deepest, and the most clinging love. And when no pure impulse is any longer felt; when the awful depths are reached where "every imagination of the thoughts" of men's hearts is "only evil continually," then, and not till then, it is that our Father sorrowfully metes out the punishment that even the wicked themselves will finally say they more than rightly deserve.

"Say unto them, As I live, saith the Lord God, I have no

"And the fifth angel poured out his vial upon the seat of the beast."

"And the sixth angel poured out his vial upon the great river Euphrates."

THE SEVEN LAST PLAGUES

pleasure in the death of the wicked; but that the wicked turn from his way and live; turn ye, turn ye from your evil ways; for why will ye die, O house of Israel?" Eze. 33:11. Hear this entreaty of a Father's love: "Turn ye, turn ye from your evil ways; for why will ye die?"

> "To-day the Saviour calls!
> For refuge fly;
> The storm of vengeance falls;
> Ruin is nigh.
>
> "The Spirit calls to-day!
> Yield to its power;
> Oh, grieve it not away;
> 'Tis mercy's hour."

The Master has sent out His warnings against the evils of this time. They are speaking plainly in the calamities that are multiplying in the earth. He has told the world of the "seven last plagues" that will soon be visited upon the persistent transgressor. He is moving all heaven to touch the sinner by His grace, so that He may save him from this ruin. Oh, who will heed this warning? Is it possible for anyone to spurn so devoted and faithful a Friend?

"And the seventh angel poured out his vial into the air; and there . . . were voices, and thunders, and lightnings; and there was a great earthquake."

CHAPTER THIRTY-ONE

THE "time of trouble, such as never was since there was a nation," is rapidly drawing on. But in the presence of these accumulating perils we have a Refuge. The arm of our omnipotent Father is stretched out to protect and rescue us.

But the reader may be among those who are loaded with corrupting vice and polluting sins, — among those who are unjust, oppressive, and cruel. If so, there is encouragement in the Word even for all such; for it says, "This is a faithful saying, and worthy of all acceptation, that Christ Jesus came into the world to save sinners; of whom I am chief." 1 Tim. 1:15. He saves to the uttermost all "that come unto God by him." Heb. 7:25. Is it possible to get beyond "the uttermost"? Even the "chief" of sinners is called. Indeed, the Lord could call none others in this world but sinners; "for all have sinned, and come short of the glory of God." Rom. 3:23.

"Wash you, make you clean; put away the evil of your doings from before Mine eyes; cease to do evil; learn to do well; seek judgment, relieve the oppressed, judge the fatherless, plead for the widow. Come now, and let us reason together, saith the Lord; though your sins be as scarlet, they shall be as white as snow; though they be red like crimson, they shall be as wool." Isa. 1:16–18.

"Scarlet" and "crimson" are indelible colors; yet the Lord promises that though our sins are like "*scarlet*" He will make them as "snow," and "though they be red like crimson, they shall be as wool." He saves to "the uttermost" even the "chief of sinners." What more could be asked? What more could be given?

We may be at a loss to know *how* He can cleanse such vile sinners, but there is comfort in the thought that God can do many things that we can not understand. We do not know *how* an acorn grows into naught else than the oak, while a grain of wheat planted by its side will just as invariably produce nothing but its own kind. Can you tell how this is? The answer is readily made that "it is nature." But "nature" did not create itself, neither does it generate the power that is so manifest in its workings. It is our heavenly Father who created and sustains all this perfect and beautiful manifestation of life that we (and so often without a thought of what we are saying) call "nature." Nature is matter obeying the voice of God. It is the Father in heaven, all-powerful, ever present, and ever working, who produces all this wonderful life and activity in the natural world.

Know, then, O sinner, that Jesus is infinite in salvation's power! He who commands all the mighty and mysterious forces of nature, says that though your sins be of the deepest dye, they shall be as white as the snow. Then "seek ye the Lord while He may be found, call ye upon Him while He is near; let the wicked forsake his way, and the unrighteous man his thoughts; and let him return unto the Lord, and He will have mercy upon him; and to our God, for He will abundantly pardon. For My thoughts are not your thoughts, neither are your ways My ways, saith the Lord. For as the heavens are higher than the earth, so are My ways higher than your ways, and My thoughts than your thoughts. For as the rain cometh down, and the snow from heaven, and returneth not thither, but watereth the earth, and maketh it bring forth and bud, that it may give seed to the sower, and bread to the eater; so shall My Word be that goeth forth out of My mouth; it shall not return unto Me void, but it shall accomplish that which I please, and it shall prosper in the thing whereto I sent it." Isa. 55:6-11. Read these promises, meditate upon them, believe them, and the Spirit of God will comfort and strengthen the heart through them.

It may be that, though a child of God, your heart is "failing" "for fear, and for looking after those things which are coming on the earth." Perhaps the increasing and awfully destructive storms and earthquakes, and the general commotion in nature, inspire terror. But it should not be so. God promises: "Thou shalt not be afraid for the terror by night; nor for the arrow that flieth by day; nor for the pestilence that walketh in darkness; nor for the destruction that wasteth at noonday. A thousand shall fall at thy side, and ten thousand at thy right hand; but it shall not come nigh thee. Only with thine eyes shalt thou behold and see the reward of the wicked. Because thou hast made the Lord, which is my refuge, even the Most High, thy habitation; there shall no evil befall thee, neither shall any plague come nigh thy dwelling." Ps. 91:5-10.

"Thou shalt not be afraid." How soul-satisfying is this word! The Lord does not merely *admonish* us not to be afraid; He does not say simply that we *ought* not to fear; but He asserts that we "*shall not* be afraid." "For He shall give His angels charge over thee, to keep thee in all thy ways. They shall bear thee up in their hands, lest thou dash thy foot against a stone." Ps. 91:11, 12.

If any are fearful because of the famines that will become more and more prevalent as the earth "waxes old," the Word says: "He that walketh righteously, and speaketh uprightly; he that despiseth the gain of oppressions, that shaketh his hands from holding of bribes, that stoppeth his ears from hearing of blood, and shutteth his eyes from seeing evil; he shall dwell on high; his place of defense shall be the munitions of rocks: BREAD SHALL BE GIVEN HIM; HIS WATERS SHALL BE SURE. Thine eyes shall see the King in his beauty; they shall behold the land that is very far off." Isa. 33 : 15–17. "They shall not be ashamed in the evil time; and in the days of famine they shall be satisfied." Ps. 37 : 19.

Again the Lord says: "When thou passest through the waters, I will be with thee; and through the rivers, they shall not overflow thee; when thou walkest through the fire, thou shalt not be burned; neither shall the flame kindle upon thee. For I am the Lord thy God, the Holy One of Israel, thy Saviour." Isa. 43 : 2, 3. "No weapon that is formed against thee shall prosper; and every tongue that shall rise against thee in judgment thou shalt condemn. This is the heritage of the servants of the Lord, and their righteousness is of Me, saith the Lord." Isa. 54 : 17.

There are no conditions nor difficulties, even in the worst possibilities of the present, or in the portentous days that are just ahead of us, that God does not penetrate with promises that bring hope and comfort and strength.

Satan has summoned all his malignant power in his last and supreme effort to oppress and destroy the people of God; but their danger appeals to the tender mercy and love of their Father;

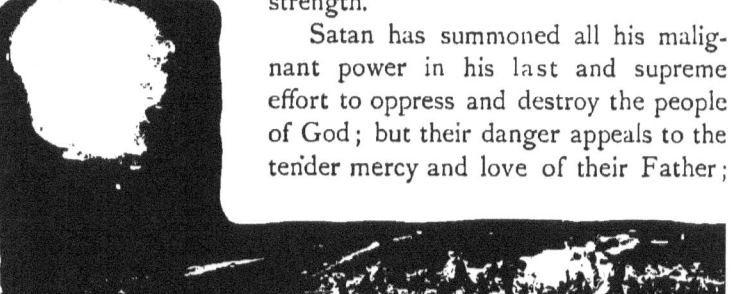

He brought His people out of that dark land, "with a mighty hand, . . . and with signs and with wonders."

and, as expressed in the sublimest of inspired prophecy, there will be heard the shout of the Eternal: "Awake, awake, put on strength, O arm of the Lord; awake, as in the ancient days, in the generations of old. Art Thou not it that hath cut Rahab, and wounded the dragon? Art Thou not it which hath dried the sea, the waters of the great deep; that hath made the depths of the sea a way for the ransomed to pass over?" Isa. 51: 9, 10.

The Lord did wonderful things in the land of Egypt; He brought His people out of the bondage, the gross idolatry and sin of that dark land, "with a mighty hand, and with an outstretched arm, and with great terribleness, and with signs, and with wonders;" but with a mightier and more glorious display of His love and power will He take them out of the accumulating corruptions, the debasing sins and evils of this time. God's exercise of power in that time was abundant in saving His people from Pharaoh's cruel tyranny; but in this time, when Satan is concentrating all his forces of evil, equipped with all the experience and training of the long reign of sin and crime, the occasion demands a corresponding exercise of divine majesty and might. "The Lord also shall roar out of Zion, and utter His voice from Jerusalem; and the heavens and the earth shall shake; but the Lord will be the hope of His people, and the strength of the children of Israel." Joel 3: 16.

How soul-inspiring is the thought that the "last days" are reached, and that in our time the Lord will fulfil His Word that says: "Behold, the days come, saith the Lord, that it shall no more be said, The Lord liveth, that brought up the children of Israel out of the land of Egypt; but, The Lord liveth, that brought up the children of Israel from the land of the north, and from all the lands whither He had driven them; and I will bring them again into their land that I gave unto their fathers." Jer. 16: 14, 15. In that time the Lord took His Israel from Egypt to an earthly Canaan; but in this time He gathers them from every part of the world to lead them into His heavenly and eternal Canaan. How glorious, then, must this final deliverance be, when it so outshines the mighty works of God in Egypt, and is made to stand forth as the one monumental illustration for all eternity of the glorious working of the mighty power of God! "Therefore the redeemed of the Lord shall return, and come with singing unto Zion; and everlasting joy shall be upon their head; they shall obtain gladness and joy; and sorrow and mourning shall flee away." Isa. 51:11.

It is only the poetry of inspiration and the inspiration of poetry that can thus express the "glorious things" that "are spoken of thee, O city of God." Then happy will it be for us if we stand upon the foundation of God's sure Word, so that we may recognize the heralds of that morning that is so soon to break and disclose to every watchful eye and waiting heart the satisfying realities of the eternal day. And as it becomes more and more evident that our Saviour is soon coming, let us pray with the beloved John, "Even so, come, Lord Jesus."

THE TRIUMPHANT VICTORY AND EVERLASTING REWARD

CHAPTER THIRTY-TWO

OUR heavenly Father does not merely point out the dangers of the times in which we live, and tell us what they mean, but He lifts our minds over these difficulties and calamities and destructions, and fastens them upon the completeness of our final victory, and the riches of our eternal reward. The sublime language of the Apocalypse gives a brief description of the song of deliverance and victory that shall be sung in that day. Of that time we read: "And I saw as it were a sea of glass mingled with fire; and them that had gotten the victory over the beast, and over his image, and over his mark, and over the number of his name, stand on the sea of glass, having the harps of God. And they sing the song of Moses the servant of God, and the song of the Lamb, saying, Great and marvelous are Thy works, Lord God Almighty; just and true are Thy ways, Thou King of saints. Who shall not fear Thee, O Lord, and glorify Thy name? for Thou only art holy; for all nations shall come and worship before Thee; for Thy judgments are made manifest." Rev. 15:2-4.

The scripture presented in the preceding paragraph reveals to us a company who have gained a great victory. They are seen standing with the harps of God, and, in a chorus too grand for human words to describe, they make heaven ring with their triumphant song. Oh, the thought of being in that chorus! A single moment of that eternity of joy is worth more than all that earth has to offer. And the Lord has bidden that the glorious news shall be heralded that every one is invited to be there. Every precaution must be taken that no delusion shall overthrow us, and thus rob us of that rich reward.

There can be no question about the fullness and the glory of the sure victory that is but a very short space ahead of every trusting, waiting child of God. It is for each one to decide now whether he will be in that victory, and reap that joy.

Having passed through the victory, we enter upon the reward of which the prophet has chanted:—

"Oh, that Thou wouldest rend the heavens, that Thou wouldest come down,
That the mountains might flow down at Thy presence, as when the melting fire burneth,
The fire causeth the waters to boil, to make Thy name known to Thine adversaries,
That the nations may tremble at Thy presence!
When Thou didst terrible things which we looked not for, Thou camest down,
The mountains flowed down at Thy presence.
For since the beginning of the world men have not heard,
Nor perceived by the ear, neither hath the eye seen,
O God, beside Thee, what He hath prepared for him that waiteth for Him."
        Isa. 64:1-4.

A New Testament comment on the foregoing words of Isaiah reads: "It is written, Eye hath not seen, nor ear heard, neither have entered into the heart of man, the things which God hath prepared for them that love Him. But God hath revealed them unto us by His Spirit; for the Spirit searcheth all things, yea, the deep things of God." 1 Cor. 2:9, 10. Man can not of himself discover what the Lord has in store for him in the future world. "But God hath revealed them unto us by His Spirit."

So great is this reward that men could never gain even the faintest conception of it in this life, did not God reveal its glory through the powerfully-illuminating influences of His Spirit. While it is understood and believed by all Christians that there will be perfect happiness in the world to come, yet all do not know what the Word of God tells us in regard to the realities and literal joys of our eternal abode. We are very particular to have a very definite and positive understanding in regard to the things of this life, but we do not all learn the definite truth that God has revealed in His Word concerning the home in which we are to spend eternity. If men would only take the time to inform themselves in regard to what the Lord, the Creator of heaven and earth, has in store for every one who will stand for truth and righteousness, every dismal cloud would be swept away, and all the dark and painful recesses of the soul would be flooded with light and joy.

We need only to give respectful and thoughtful attention to the plain words of the Lord in order to see the very definite plan that He has for our future and eternal home. Notice the import of these following words from Isaiah:—

> "Israel shall be saved in the Lord with an everlasting salvation;
> Ye shall not be ashamed nor confounded world without end.
> For thus saith the Lord that created the heavens,
> God Himself that formed the earth, and made it;
> He hath established it, He created it not in vain,
> He formed it to be inhabited:
> I am the Lord; and there is none else.
> I have not spoken in secret, in a dark place of the earth;
> I said not unto the seed of Jacob, Seek ye Me in vain;
> I the Lord speak righteousness, I declare things that are right."
>   Isa. 45:17–19.

The Lord tells us in the foregoing words that He formed

the earth to be inhabited, and that He did not create it in vain. Every one knows that the righteous God did not create this earth to be inhabited by a race of sinners. Such a course would not be right, but God says, "I declare things that are right." Then we are to conclude that the Lord formed this earth to be inhabited by a race of right-doing people. He formed it to be a place of happiness and not a place of sorrow, as it has been for so many centuries. But man sinned, and for the time being it might seem to those who have not taken the time to study God's plan, that the Lord has been thwarted in His design. But such is not the case. All sin and every unrepentant sinner will be destroyed out of this earth, and it will be refashioned in all the perfection that clothed it in the beginning, and thus become the eternal abode of the redeemed. If the thought of this earth being cleansed from all sorrow and evil, and then becoming the eternal habitation of the redeemed, seems strange or fanciful to you, do not dismiss the subject too speedily, but study it further. You may be able to see that it is neither strange nor fanciful, and above all may find that it is decidedly scriptural.

When God created this earth, He had a very definite object in view. But it seems that the problem of evil had to be worked out somewhere, and for causes that we may not be able to understand now the conflict came to this earth. However, before the dark head of wickedness had been lifted here, just at the close of the Creator's work of making this world and placing man upon it, He said, "And God saw everything that He had made, and behold it was very good." A little after this statement was made we have the record of the fall of man. After man had descended to sin, the Lord told him: "Cursed is the ground for thy sake; in sorrow shalt thou eat of it all the days of thy life; thorns also and thistles shall it bring forth to thee; and thou shalt eat the herb of the field;

in the sweat of thy face shalt thou eat bread, till thou return unto the ground; for out of it wast thou taken; for dust thou art, and unto dust shalt thou return." Gen. 3:17-19.

The record does not say that the Lord cursed *man* because he had sinned, but He cursed the *ground* for man's sake. It is to help man—or possibly it would be more proper to say that it is for the purpose of keeping man from falling so low that he could never be reached—that this curse is put upon the ground. For after the ground is cursed, mankind must contend against the thorn and thistle and all the rest of the tribe of weeds that they represent. He must now toil till his face sweats, in order to sustain his life. In this ceaseless round of toil he does not have the opportunity to sink into the vices and crimes that come with idleness. There is a dignity and power in labor that tends upward all the time. But it is only the perfectly right and pure man who can trust himself with the unlimited leisure that would be found if there was no curse.

Anywhere we go on the face of this earth we find the crop of weeds in any soil that is not closely and carefully cultivated. Many have wondered why it is that weeds will grow anywhere and everywhere spontaneously. Some have suggested the idea that the little birds carry the seed. But the simple, plain facts in the case are that God has said, "Cursed is the ground for thy sake," and, "Thorns also and thistles shall it bring forth to thee." Hence, everywhere man goes on the face of the earth he must contend against the curse that a wise heavenly Father has placed upon the ground for his sake. That word that God spoke in the beginning is the scientific reason for the weeds springing up everywhere. It will continue so to be until the curse is finally removed.

The perfectly complete way in which this curse will at last be removed is told in the following New Testament prophecy and promise:—

"There shall come in the last days scoffers, walking after their own lusts, and saying, Where is the promise of His coming? for since the fathers fell asleep, all things continue as they were from the beginning of the creation. For this they willingly are ignorant of, that by the word of God the heavens were of old, and the earth standing out of the water and in the water; whereby the world that then was, being overflowed with water, perished; but the heavens and the earth, which are now, by the same word are kept in store, reserved unto fire against the day of judgment and perdition of ungodly men. But, beloved, be not ignorant of this one thing, that one day is with the Lord as a thousand years, and a thousand years as one day. The Lord is not slack concerning His promise, as some men count slackness; but is long-suffering to usward, not willing that any should perish, but that all should come to repentance. But the day of the Lord will come as a thief in the night; in the which the heavens shall pass away with a great noise, and the elements shall melt with fervent heat, the earth also and the works that are therein shall be burned up. Seeing then that all these things shall be dissolved, what manner of persons ought ye to be in all holy conversation and godliness, looking for and hasting unto the coming of the day of God, wherein the heavens being on fire shall be dissolved, and the elements shall melt with fervent heat? Nevertheless we, according to His promise, look for new heavens and a new earth, wherein dwelleth righteousness. Wherefore, beloved, seeing that ye look for such things, be diligent that ye may be found of Him in peace, without spot, and blameless." 2 Peter 3: 3–14.

The foregoing scripture tells us that God's plan is to melt over this old earth, reeking beneath its curse, in the judgment fires of the last day. It also tells us that ungodly men will go into perdition at the same time. The elements of the earth are to "melt with fervent heat;" they are to be "dissolved."

While the earth is thus to be "dissolved" back into its original gaseous elements, it is said that the "works that are therein shall be burned up".

But notwithstanding this melting, burning process, "Nevertheless we, according to His promise, look for new heavens and a new earth, wherein dwelleth righteousness." Fire is one of the greatest purifying agents known; and it is this agency that the Lord will use in purging away from the earth the curse of every vestige of "thorn and thistle," and then out of this molten material there arises a new creation. God does creation's work so far as this world is concerned all over again; and one of the grandest thoughts in connection with it all is that all the redeemed sons and daughters of Adam will be eye-witnesses of the great creative scene. We will have passed through every trial, have come victorious out of every difficulty, and at last will stand with our Creator while He puts our planet through its baptism of fire and fashions it again into the abode of eternal righteousness. This is a theme that is calculated to call forth the liveliest and the highest forms of the imagination. Yet, while this is so, the theme is not an imaginative one. It is not the presentation of a fanciful theory. It is the simple setting forth of literal fact in the plain, direct language of God's own promises. To attempt to argue the case would not only be useless, but it might result in dragging a shade of obscurity over the face of one of the clearest as well as one of the most beautiful truths.

Another one of the scriptures that present these new earth scenes, and give these promises of joy and glory in our redeemed Eden home, is the following:—

"And I saw a new heaven and a new earth; for the first heaven and the first earth were passed away; and there was no more sea. And I John saw the holy city, New Jerusalem, coming down from God out of heaven, prepared as a bride adorned for her husband. And I heard a great voice out of heaven saying, Behold, the tabernacle of God is with men, and He will dwell with them, and they shall be His people, and God Himself shall be with them, and be their God. And God shall wipe away all tears from their eyes; and there shall be no more death, neither sorrow, nor crying, neither shall there be any more pain; for the former things are passed away. And He that sat upon the throne said, Behold, I make all things new. And He said unto me, Write; for these words are true and faithful." Rev. 21:1-5. Thus do the Scriptures in multiplied passages bring before us the new heavens and the new earth. And thus do they show that "the restitution of all things, which God hath spoken by the mouth of all His holy prophets since the world began," will include the renewing of the earth, its cleansing from sin, and its presentation to the redeemed as their eternal home. The beautiful Eden that was lost through sin will also be restored through the redemption work of our Saviour Jesus Christ. Then will come the glorious realization of that other scene viewed by the apostle John on Patmos, and thus described by him: "And I saw, and I heard a voice of many angels round about the throne and the living creatures and the elders; and the number of them was ten thousand times ten thousand, and thousands of thousands; saying with a great voice, Worthy is the Lamb that hath been slain to receive the power, and riches, and wisdom, and might, and honor, and glory, and blessing. And every created thing which is in the heaven, and on the earth, and under the earth, and on the sea, and all things that are in them, heard I saying, Unto Him that sitteth on the throne, and unto the Lamb, be the blessing, and the honor, and the glory, and the dominion, forever and ever." Rev. 5:11-13, R. V. It is said of those who join in this indescribable anthem of victory that "they reign on the earth." This triumphant chorus of praise to the Majesty of heaven takes place at a time when there is not a discordant note of sin in all the great universe of God. "*Every created thing*" engages in the song with heart and soul and mind.

What a thrill of joy is awakened at the thought of being there! No soul on earth can afford to miss such an opportunity. Who can afford to slight the invitation that the Lord has so graciously extended to "every creature"? When this old earth shall be dissolved, and when every particle of sin is burned out of it, and when the new heaven and the new earth shall come forth out of the molten and purified elements, and when all the immortal beauty of this new creation shall be unfolded in the presence of the redeemed, and under the unobstructed gaze of their immortal eyes, if we are not there to join in the shouts of joy and triumph, how terrible will be our everlasting mistake and our everlasting loss!

The substantial reward that is before the truly loyal followers of Christ can be but feebly described by any human instrumentality. The Spirit that searcheth the deep things of God must be sought for our illuminating guide.

The most beautiful spot on the whole face of this earth has some of the tracings of the curse upon it to mar its present beauty so that the mind may be directed to the faultless splendor of Eden redeemed. Our God would not have us fix our affections on the passing things of this life or of this world, but would have us see and lay hold on that which will endure forever. With these clear promises of the redeeming of the earth before us, let us turn to that wonderful prophetic description of what its redeemed conditions will be; and, as we read it, let us ask that God's Spirit may make a living picture of its every expression upon the sensitized films of our souls. The description of the earth in its redeemed condition is in the language of Isaiah, and reads:—

"The wilderness and the solitary place shall be glad for them; and the desert shall rejoice, and blossom as the rose.
It shall blossom abundantly, and rejoice even with joy and singing:

THE TRIUMPHANT VICTORY AND EVERLASTING REWARD 345

The glory of Lebanon shall be given unto it, the excellency of Carmel
 and Sharon,
They shall see the glory of the Lord, and the excellency of our God.
Strengthen ye the weak hands, and confirm the feeble knees.
Say to them that are of a fearful heart, Be strong, fear not:
Behold, your God will come with vengeance, even God with a recompense;
 He will come and save you.
Then the eyes of the blind shall be opened, and the ears of the deaf shall
 be unstopped.
Then shall the lame man leap as an hart, and the tongue of the dumb
 sing:
For in the wilderness shall waters break out, and streams in the desert.
And the parched ground shall become a pool, and the thirsty land springs
 of water:
In the habitation of dragons, where each lay, shall be grass with reeds
 and rushes.
And an highway shall be there, and a way, and it shall be called the
 way of holiness;
The unclean shall not pass over it; but it shall be for those:
The wayfaring men, though fools, shall not err therein.
No lion shall be there, nor any ravenous beast shall go up thereon, it
 shall not be found there;
But the redeemed shall walk there: and the ransomed of the Lord shall
 return,
And come to Zion with songs and everlasting joy upon their heads:
They shall obtain joy and gladness, and sorrow and sighing shall flee away."
 Isaiah, Chapter 35.

The foregoing is a description of the new earth when the "ransomed of the Lord" have entered it with "everlasting joy upon their heads." And when that time comes, all the glory of the far-famed forests of Lebanon shall be given to it, and all the blossoming and fragrant splendor of Carmel and Sharon shall be drawn down to transform every desert and miasmic bog into the pictured realities of the fields and gardens of eternity. And then every blind eye is opened so that it may catch the indescribable beauty, and every deaf ear is made to hear, so that it may revel in the exultant harmonies and melodies, as choir and soloist shall rise to the exalted heights of expressing in the eloquence of sound the impulses that are too sublime for words. Amid these scenes of the rejoicings of the immortal and redeemed, there can be found no speechless tongue; and no defective limb will offer obstruction to the poetic expression of bodily motion when every nerve is vibrating its symphonies at the thought of actually being in the New Jerusalem, the metropolis of the earth made new.

Before these eternal realities that our heavenly Father offers us, all the wealth that this present world can give is transformed into the most beggarly poverty; and the highest temporal attainments that the strongest ambition can paint upon the canvas of the imagination are broken into the immaterial elements of nothingness.

As we look upon the earth we see nothing but distress, perplexity, and unsatisfying prospects. We see, in the prophecy of what the Master told us would take place in these days, "men's hearts failing them for fear, and for looking after those things that are coming on the earth." This distressed condition is all that earth has to offer; but if we take the telescope of prophecy and divinely inspired promise, and look beyond these scenes of the closing days of time over into the fair domains of our heavenly Father, we see the "New Jerusalem, coming down from God out of heaven;" we see the hand of Omnipotence giving our earth its purifying ablution of fire. Out of this curse-destroying crucible we see the work of creation bringing back to mankind its perfect new earth in the vernal freshness and matchless beauty of the blossoming and perfumed splendors of Eden; and finally we see our redeemed and re-created planet swinging anew into her trackless highway of space, peopled by the happy creatures who are settling themselves into the undimmed pleasures and occupations of their eternal existence.

"We having the same spirit of faith, according as it is written, I believed, and therefore have I spoken; we also believe, and therefore speak; knowing that He which raised up the Lord Jesus shall raise up us also by Jesus, and shall present us with you. For all things are for your sakes, that the abundant grace might through the thanksgiving of many redound to the glory of God. For which cause we faint not; but though our outward man perish, yet the inward man is renewed day by day. For our light affliction, which is but for a moment, worketh for us a far more exceeding and eternal weight of glory; while we look not at the things which are seen, but at the things which are not seen: for the things which are seen are temporal; but the things which are not seen are eternal."

"The desert shall rejoice, and blossom as the rose."

CHAPTER THIRTY-THREE

THIS generation is living in the presence of a wonderful array of fulfilling prophecy. The facts are before us, and the evidence is so clear as to leave no occasion for the faintest shadow of doubt.

This generation should be thrilled by the knowledge that all these fulfilling prophecies are to culminate in the one supreme event of the second coming of our Lord and Saviour Jesus Christ.

This generation should grasp its proffered opportunity of proclaiming the glorious Gospel of the kingdom to the ends of the earth.

The events that focus upon this generation are immeasurably sublime. The prophecies that show us that the second coming of Christ is at hand, point also to the great judgment day and the resurrection from the dead. Every son and daughter of Adam who shall be found worthy to have a part in the resurrection of the righteous will soon be called from the death-locked chambers of the tomb. The evergreen crown, woven by the divine Father from the laurels of faithfulness, integrity, purity, and truth, will soon be placed by the Redeemer's own hand on the brow of each one that He rescues by His grace.

Our fathers, through all the generations of the centuries that have come and gone, have loved to talk of the coming time when the dead should be raised at the second advent of the Lord. In order for them to behold that day of consummating triumphs and joy, they had to lift to their eyes the telescope of faith, and cast their look over the struggles and griefs and turmoils of the ages yet unborn. The sure prospects and infallible evidences of that yet distant resurrection day was a theme to constantly fill the soul with joy, even amid the distresses of the most cruel persecutions.

But now we can say, by the same words of faith, that the time is just at hand. Now we can say that these centuries of waiting have all rolled into the past, and that the day is impending when the great reunion of the heavenly family will be taken from the visions of faith, and be bestowed upon us in the literal realities of actual possession. That father, that mother, that sister, that brother, that husband, that wife, that son, that daughter, that bosom friend, that we have been compelled sorrowfully to yield to the relentless grasp of death, is about to be called to life again. Our "Elder Brother," the Man of Nazareth and of Calvary, is about to spread the great banquet of His marriage supper, and give us a personal introduction amid the actualities of immortal life, to Enoch and Abraham and Isaac and Jacob, to Joseph and Moses and Daniel, to David and Jeremiah and Isaiah, to Matthew and John and Paul, and to all the rest of that innumerable company of the redeemed. These things are facts. There can be no mistake about them.

Can you sense it? We have reached the generation that is witnessing the fulfilment of prophecy that makes these sublime events a certainty in this our day. And how should these things call out the very best energies of our lives in proclaiming the message of the soon coming of Christ. The message is to be given in this generation. The time is ripe for it. God is calling for it. Every one who has learned to revere His name, and respect His Word, should answer to the thrilling summons.

The eternal existence of human souls is at stake. If there should be delay in answering to the call, thousands may be eternally lost as the result. When the country stands in peril of a foreign foe, the call to arms is made, and hundreds of thousands respond with the enthusiasm and zeal of patriots. But in such calls only matters of temporary and fleeting interest are at stake, and the call is made by only a temporary ruler.

In this supreme and culminating conflict against the forces of sin our divine Father, the King who inhabiteth eternity, is calling us to a battle-field from which every volunteer (there will be no drafted soldiers) will return wearing the diadem of immortality.

When freedom's cause is at stake, the call to the dangers and hazards of the battle-field loosen in the breast of the patriot the swelling and unconquerable and uncontrollable emotions that rise on the solid foundation of a sense of duty and the undying love for the "home-land." But these emotions, grand as they may be, are confined to the narrow boundaries of this temporal existence in this temporal world. The conflict that is brought within the

"The exact location of a vessel at sea may be determined."—*P. 353.*

field of our vision, and in which we are urged, by the strong voice of these rapidly-fulfilling prophecies, to take an active part, breaks asunder the restricting bands that would confine us to time upon this earth. The issues that are before this generation are widened into

"The exact movements of the heavenly bodies may be measured"—*Page 353.*

the limitless æons of eternity, and the eye is fixed upon that unnumbered throng of redeemed immortals who are rising from the bed-chamber of the tomb in response to the melodious command of our "Elder Brother," our Redeemer, and our chosen King.

We are not wandering in the field of fancy or imagination as we talk of these things. We are dealing with sober facts that stand upon the firm foundation of the never-failing words of the Eternal.

He, at whose commands the worlds sprang into existence, and took up their sweeping and infinitely accurate journeyings in space, is the One who has spoken. His word has never failed, and the more blessed truth is that it can not fail. These prophecies which show us where we are in the night of this world's wanderings in sin can not possibly lead us astray. They are the fixed words of the Infinite, the All-powerful, and the Immortal, and for them to fail is thrust beyond the realm of even the twilight shadows of possibility. Then, with what assurance can we repeat the words that the apostle Peter was inspired to write upon this all-absorbing theme. They read thus:—

"For we have not followed cunningly devised fables, when we made known unto you the power and coming of our Lord Jesus Christ, but were eye-witnesses of His majesty. For He received from God the Father honor and glory, when there came such a voice to Him from the excellent glory, This is My beloved Son, in whom I am well pleased. And this voice which came from heaven we heard, when we were with Him in the holy mount. We have also a more sure word of prophecy; whereunto ye do well that ye take heed, as unto a light that shineth in a dark place, until the day dawn, and the day star arise in your hearts: knowing this first, that no prophecy of the Scripture is of any private interpretation. For the prophecy came not in old time by the will of man; but holy men of God spake as they were moved by the Holy Ghost." 2 Peter 1:16-21.

Our heavenly Father is the Author of all the tender and loving emotions that have ever swelled the breast of the most perfect mother or father. And with all the intensity of His own still higher and more constant love, He is urgently inviting every one of us to-day to be among the joyful participants in the glorious realities of the resurrection day. He is inviting us to be the living witnesses of His saving grace and truth amid all the perilous times of these last days, and to be the ones who will stand upon the earth, and, without tasting death, welcome Him at His coming. He is inviting us to prepare the way for that event in fulfilling that part of the prophecy which says "this Gospel of the kingdom shall be preached in all the world for a witness." What a wonderful invitation! What a great opportunity! And how do these things eclipse the greatest enterprises and the greatest opportunities that the affairs of this world can offer!

Every one may know the positive truth of the immediate second coming of Christ and the impending judgment day and resurrection of the dead as definitely and as clearly as he knows the first rudiments of his arithmetic. The one is just as clear cut and as susceptible of definite knowledge as the other. We learn to know and fully to rely upon figures by the study of arithmetic and the other branches of the science of mathematics. Having studied figures until we understand them, we have no fears that the conclusions derived from them can have any possibility of error. With figures, the exact movements of the heavenly bodies may be measured so that an eclipse of the sun or the moon or the transit of another planet may be determined to the hundredth part of a second; with figures, the exact location of a vessel at sea may be determined; with figures, the civil engineer may survey a tunnel through a vast mountain, and set men to digging from either side, and have them meet accurately; and so in all the field of science, or anywhere else that calculations are made, we rely upon figures to give us correct results.

"I John saw the holy city, New Jerusalem." Rev. 21 : 2.

He who gave to man the science of mathematics and endowed him with the ability to calculate with figures, is the same One who has also given mankind the book of prophecy, and bidden him to "know" when the coming of Christ is "near, even at the doors." And just as the mariner can tell definitely, from the calculations he is able to make, when he is nearing port, so may the student of prophecy tell with even greater definiteness that the inhabitants of earth are riding in the swelling tides that wash the shores of the haven of eternity.

God is now bidding us to enter the school of prophecy, and study under the accurate instruction of the inspired prophets. He asks us to pursue this study until we can approach our fellow men who have not yet entered this school, and tell them, with no uncertain tones in our voices, that the end of all things is at hand; that the judgment day is impending; that the trump of God is about to sound; that the gates of death are about to swing outward, and release the captives of the tomb; that Jesus is soon to be seen coming in the clouds of heaven, and all the holy angels with Him; that the kingdoms of this world are about to become "the kingdom of our Lord and of His Christ;" that the royal cities of earth will give place to the eternally glorious city of our God.

Such is the inspiring, and soul-absorbing opportunity of to-day. Such is the call to every one to join in the battles of the armies of the Lord to proclaim "this Gospel of the kingdom in all the world for a witness unto all nations," so that the end may come.

This call is imperative. It must be accepted now. In a brief time it will be forever too late, and the eternity of joy that our Father is now proffering will have passed beyond our reach.

www.ingramcontent.com/pod-product-compliance
Lightning Source LLC
Chambersburg PA
CBHW030258240426
43673CB00040B/996